THE
SCOTTISH
RUGBY
YEAR
BOOK '95

EDITED BY
DEREK DOUGLAS

SCOTTISH
RUGBY UNION

The Royal Bank
of Scotland

THE
HERALD
Don't miss an issue

MAINSTREAM
PUBLISHING

EDINBURGH AND LONDON

First published in Great Britain in 1994 by
MAINSTREAM PUBLISHING COMPANY (EDINBURGH) LTD
7 Albany Street
Edinburgh EH1 3UG

ISBN 1 85158 629 6

A catalogue record for this book is available from the British Library

Typeset in Bembo by Litho Link Ltd, Welshpool, Powys, Wales
Printed in Great Britain by Scotprint Ltd, Musselburgh

THE SCOTTISH RUGBY YEARBOOK '95

Contents

Foreword

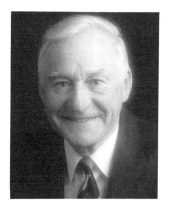

THIS publication is now in its third year and details the activities of the Union and Scottish rugby.

A good Committee will continually examine its structure in order to improve and update the organisation – the Scottish Rugby Union is no exception. To accelerate this change Jim Telfer was appointed Director of Rugby in December 1993, an appointment that is seen as co-ordinating all rugby resources in order to channel them towards one goal, that of keeping Scotland in the top six rugby nations of the world. To achieve this goal Scotland must have a sound Club and District structure, consequently at the Annual General Meeting 1994, the Clubs passed the following motion:

> To restructure the Championship with effect from Season 1995–96 to comprise a Premier League of four divisions of eight clubs each playing on a 'home and away' basis; and a National League with seven divisions of ten clubs each playing on a 'home and away' basis.

In order to create more competition at a higher level, games for the Districts will be played against Irish Provinces. It was felt by some administrators that these games should be developed into a Championship – let us walk before we run! If there is a place for an Inter-District Championship with Irish Provinces I am sure that it will evolve sooner rather than later.

Season 1994–95 promises to be one of excitement with the official opening of the new Murrayfield Stadium with a game against South Africa on 19 November 1994. This new Murrayfield is the culmination of much hard work and foresight by many people who have been involved in the building programme over the last three years. It would be wrong of me to single out any particular body for special mention. However, on behalf of the Scottish Rugby Union, I must thank the Debenture Holders who supported the appeal so quickly and so magnificently, coupled with our bankers, The Royal Bank of Scotland, who have stood by us in the development of the stadium, which will be the best of its size in Britain if not in Europe.

As we put behind us the disappointments of season 1993–94 I know that our players will rise to the challenges of 1994–95 culminating in the Rugby World Cup in South Africa.

G.K. Smith
President
Scottish Rugby Union

The Royal Bank
of Scotland

Preface

THE Murrayfield International victory against Fiji in September 1982 was a milestone for Scottish rugby. It was the first sponsorship of an international rugby match and began a relationship between The Royal Bank of Scotland and the Scottish Rugby Union which has gone from strength to strength through the 12 seasons since then.

During that time there have been 36 Royal Bank of Scotland Internationals at Murrayfield. With 22 Scottish victories, 2 draws and 12 defeats, this has probably been the most successful period in Scotland's rugby history. Both sides have delighted in the partnership and we recently announced its renewal.

We are particularly pleased that the new stadium at Murrayfield is now complete, with a capacity of 67,500 for the 1994–95 season. At last, through the efforts of our friends at the SRU, Scotland has the world-class facilities to match the achievement of its players and the enthusiasm of its supporters. I look forward to a season of great matches, starting with the game against South Africa in November.

We are proud to be associated with *The Scottish Rugby Yearbook* for the third year and I am confident that the great army of Scottish rugby supporters will see this as an essential addition to their bookshelves.

Dr George Mathewson
Chief Executive
The Royal Bank of Scotland

The Royal Bank
of Scotland

Soaring Elegance and Sweeping Grace

A MURRAYFIELD FOR THE MILLENNIUM

By Derek Douglas

THE gentlemen of the Edinburgh Polo Club certainly wouldn't recognise the old paddock now.

The £44m concrete and steel edifice which will take Scottish rugby into the 21st century stands as a spectacular testament to the skills of the architects and builders who by their expertise – almost like alchemists of old – are able to transform such seemingly base materials into a structure of soaring elegance and sweeping grace.

Scottish rugby's new home, with seating accommodation for 67,500, hospitality suites catering for nearly 2,000, and new offices and museum facilities for the SRU, transform Murrayfield into one of the biggest and most modern sporting facilities in Europe.

This latest transfiguration of Murrayfield Stadium may be the most radical yet but, in reality, it is just the latest stage in a process of evolution which has been underway for almost seven decades.

It is a process of development and improvement which stretches back to the 1920s, when the SRU reacted to the growing popularity of the game and abandoned its first permanent home at Inverleith for the Polo Club's wide-open spaces beside the Water of Leith.

The new Murrayfield will be officially opened by the SRU Patron, HRH The Princess Royal, on Saturday, 19 November 1994. South Africa which has just recently re-emerged from its international exile, will be Scotland's guests; the Springboks making only their sixth appearance at Murrayfield with the series standing at three wins to two in the 'Boks' favour. In the overall standings, too, the South Africans are ahead. Since 1906, when Scotland

A smoggy Auld Reekie surrounds Murrayfield stadium in this 1946 aerial shot of the Calcutta Cup match in progress (The Herald)

played the Springboks for the first time, at Hampden Park, the two rugby nations have met eight times, Scotland tasting victory thrice with five wins going to the South Africans.

One of those wins represents the blackest days in Scottish rugby history. The occasion was the 44–0 Murrayfield drubbing which the Scots received at the hands of the South Africans in 1951. Calculated by modern scoring values, the defeat eclipses even that suffered by Gavin Hastings's men against the All Blacks in 1994. Legions of Scots fans will be praying that the new Murrayfield can be 'hanselled' in a manner appropriate to the occasion.

Scottish rugby's long association with Murrayfield began in the early Twenties as the game outgrew Inverleith. And although the land was actually purchased from the Polo Club in 1922 it was not until three years later that the then state-of-the-art stadium rose from the riverside meadows. The new stadium's introduction to the rugby public could not have taken place under more auspicious circumstances. The date was 25 March 1925 and G.P.S. Macpherson's Scotsmen secured the first Grand Slam in Scottish rugby history. They did so with an epic 14–11 win over England. Murrayfield's 70th anniversary falls due in 1995. But, sadly for those with an eye on historical symmetry, that year's Calcutta Cup encounter is to take place a week earlier at Twickenham. There is, though, a certain historical charm in the fact that the septuagenary Murrayfield hits such a milestone in newborn guise, spic and span and more than ready to meet the needs of whatever the 21st century game demands.

But we get ahead of ourselves. The tale of Scottish rugby's quest for a home to call its own begins not at Murrayfield and not in the 20th century at all. It begins in the year 1871 and across the city, five miles to the north-east of Murrayfield.

Raeburn Place, in the Edinburgh suburb of Stockbridge, was where it all began. Here, in the former village which even by 1871 was becoming very much a part of the city, a Scottish XX played an English XX in the world's first rugby union international. Scotland won by a goal and a try to a solitary try from England. In the previous year a match involving Scotland and England, but played under Association rules, had taken place at the Oval cricket ground in London. The Football Association was keen to repeat the exercise in 1871 and issued a challenge through the Scottish press.

The Scots, however, favoured the handling code then, as now, much in favour among the country's public schools and, through the columns of *Bell's Magazine* and *The Scotsman* newspaper, five leading Scottish exponents of the Rugby Rules game proposed a XX-a-side match in Glasgow or Edinburgh on a date to be mutually agreed. The Football Association declined the invitation but it was taken up by English advocates of the handling, XX-a-side code and the Edinburgh Academical ground, Raeburn Place, on Monday, 27 March

Ground staff clear snow from the pitch in preparation for the 1937 Calcutta Cup match (The Herald)

Roseburn Street, 1939. The crowd gathers for the last pre-war Murrayfield match. Scotland lost to England 9-6. (The Herald)

Ten days before the 1959 match against Wales, which Scotland won 6–5, marquees containing braziers were erected on the frost-bound pitch in a successful bid to beat the freeze (The Herald)

1871 was agreed as the time and the place.

The Glasgow Herald of Tuesday, 28 March 1871 reported that that game had been played 'with a most gratifying result for Scotland' and before a 'very large turn-out of spectators', each of whom had paid a shilling for the privilege of being 'in' at the start of something big.

The Edinburgh Academical Cricket Club committee had by no means been unanimous in its decision to allow the match to go ahead. Presumably, they feared for the disruption that the game would cause to the everyday life of the playing fields, utilised as they were not only by the cricket club but by the Academy schoolboys as well. After expenses had been deducted the cricket club received the sum of £13 for the let of their ground but it was clear, even from the outset, that the relationship between the rugby men and the Academical cricketers was not one forged in Heaven and destined to last forever.

The venue of Scotland's next home game in 1873 was the West of Scotland Cricket Club ground at Hamilton Crescent; the fact that Glasgow, or more properly Partick, was considered a suitable venue indicating that the handling code, even then, had influential devotees in the west of Scotland. Immediately following the game, which was played to a draw in atrocious weather conditions, a meeting of all interested parties was held in the Glasgow Academy building at Elmbank Street and it was agreed to form a Scottish Football Union. The Union, which later became the SRU, held its first, official meeting in Edinburgh on 9 October of that year and thereafter the SFU (it changed its name to the SRU in 1924) was the official organiser of all future international matches.

For the next 22 years, with the exception of three further visits to Hamilton Crescent, the Edinburgh Academical cricket ground continued to find favour as the first-choice international venue. However, as indicated by the fact that the very first game had gone there only after a split-vote on the cricket club committee, it became apparent that the SFU would have to find a venue of its own on which to stage its international matches. With a splendid disregard for the international events which were taking place on its doorstep, the Academy refused to be overawed and continued to insist on its pupils making use of the playing field on the morning of international matches.

The SFU decided that the situation could not continue and stepped up its quest to find a permanent location for its international matches. An unsuccessful approach was made to Fettes College, whose governors declined to lease a plot of land where Broughton HS and the Lothian and Borders Police HQ now stand.

By 1895 the relationship between the Union and the Academical Cricket Club had come to an end, the cricketers declaring that, regretfully, Raeburn Place would not be available for lease in future. For the next four years, while the Union continued its efforts to secure a playing field of its own, international matches maintained a nomadic existence with Old Hampden Park and Powderhall in Edinburgh being pressed into emergency service.

But in the meantime, the Union had secured land at Inverleith just a mile or so north of Raeburn Place and, for the princely sum of £3,800 (to be paid for then, as now, with debentures) the SFU became the world's first rugby union authority to enjoy the benefits of its own ground. The moving force behind

Two days before the 1970 Scotland v France game and Murrayfield is under six inches of snow. The terracing can be seen in the background. The electric blanket cleared the snow and Scotland lost!
(The Herald)

the purchase was the SFU's legendary honorary secretary and treasurer J. Aikman Smith. A stickler for the laws and an arch-opponent of professionalism (or anything which smacked of it) Aikman Smith exerted a stern yet benign influence over Scottish rugby for the next three decades and more. In 1926, when asked by King George V why the Scots playing in the England v Scotland match carried no numbers on their shirts, Aikman Smith snorted in reply: 'This, sir, is a game of rugby football, not a cattle market!'

The Inverleith ground, now the home of Stewart's-Melville FP, and incorporating the Daniel Stewart's and Melville College playing fields, was made ready for international use by the construction of an impressive stand. The ground was ready in time for the Welsh match of January 1899 but the wintry weather was responsible for postponement and the official opening did not take place until the game against Ireland a month later.

Sadly for the Scots, the Irish – no doubt apologetic in the extreme! – managed to spoil the party by recording a 9–3 win. However, honour was restored a fortnight later in the rescheduled game against Wales when Mark Morrison's Scottish XV scored an emphatic 21–10 victory over the Welshmen and the SFU's new home, which from the outset was attracting huge crowds, was proving to be a major success with players and viewing public alike.

Inverleith continued in service for a quarter of a century until, by 1925, its restricted size had been overtaken by events. The SFU had attempted to purchase an additional plot of land to the east of the ground on which it had been intended to construct a second stand but negotiations fell through and the decision was taken to begin looking, once again, for a suitable plot of real estate.

And, once again, the man doing the looking was J. Aikman Smith. By 1922 he was reporting to the SFU committee that the ideal site might have been found. The area in question was the 19 acres owned by the Edinburgh Polo Club at Murrayfield. The go-ahead was given and, with yet another issue of debentures, the ground was purchased and work began on building the stand and raising the three embankments which for the next six decades would be such a feature of the Old Murrayfield.

But why *Murray*field? Who was the Murray who has given his name to a sporting stadium known the world over? The answer appears in a housing transaction concluded over 250 years ago when one Archibald Murray, second son of Archibald Murray of Cringletie, near Peebles, built himself a mansion on the policies of Nisbet Park, which at the time was open countryside. The house, completed in 1735, still stands today at the head of Murrayfield Avenue and, much added to, is now a residential home for the elderly.

However, by 1925 the SRU's new Murrayfield stadium was ready for use. The final game at Inverleith was played against the French in January of that year (a 25–4 win) and with subsequent victories over Wales (24–14) and Ireland (14–8), the stage was set for a fairytale, Grand Slam baptism of fire for the new stadium.

Workmen toiled until the last moment putting the finishing touches to the stadium which was to host the biggest rugby union crowd the world had ever seen. As the late Doug Davies, the rugged Hawick forward and a member of the victorious Scotland pack, observed: 'They were still working on the place when we got there. The smell of freshness was everywhere and there were still

A policeman with loud-hailer calls for order at the 1975 Welsh match. Over 104,000, with many more locked out, saw Scotland win 12–10. Murrayfield games were all-ticket thereafter (The Herald)

bits and pieces to be finished off.'

At Inveleith the maximum attendance had been 30,000 but on 21 March 1925 over 70,000 spectators thronged the wonderful new ground for the Grand Slam showdown with England. They were expecting something special and were not to be disappointed.

Fortunes ebbed this way and that as the lead changed hands three times and the participants played themselves almost to a standstill in the bright spring sunshine. Scotland trailed 5–8 at the interval, England having taken the lead with a Luddington penalty goal. Scotland snatched it back with a try by Nelson converted by Drysdale, and then England moved back into the driving seat with a Hamilton-Wickes try, converted by Luddington.

After half-time, England forged further ahead with a try by Wakefield but Scotland fought back with a Wallace try converted by Gillies. Then, with just five minutes left, Herbert Waddell ('showing commendable coolness in a nerve-trying situation,' said the *Glasgow Herald* match report) dropped a goal from the 25-yard line. The ball sailed between the uprights and the partisan crowd cheered with delight. England threw everything but the kitchen sink at the Scots in the closing five minutes and at one point it seemed as though L.J. Corbett was certain to score and deny the Scots their first Grand Slam. The Bristol centre-threequarter was in the clear with the line at his mercy but, again in the words of the *Herald* scribe, he 'fell through sheer exhaustion when another yard would have carried him over'. Scotland continued to defend as if their very lives depended upon it and, with virtually the final kick of the game, England played their last shot when T.E. Holliday, the Aspatria fullback, sent an attempted drop-kick wide of the uprights. That was it. The new Murrayfield had been the setting for one of the most exciting games of rugby ever seen and Scotland had won the historic first Grand Slam.

The massive crowd was ecstatic and the *Glasgow Herald*'s man in the press box wrote in understated prose: 'There was a wonderful scene at the finish, many of the crowd swarming on to the field so that the players had to make their way to the dressing-rooms through a delighted and cheering crowd.'

In the ensuing years the face of Murrayfield continued to change in an effort to keep pace with the demands of the game and the exigencies of the time. Then, as now, the demand for stand tickets was insatiable. In 1936 two wing extensions were added to the already cavernous stand and seating capacity was raised to 15,228. The clock tower, for so many years a feature of the south terracing but now relocated behind the East stand, was presented to the Union in 1929 and in the following year J. Aikman Smith presented the first score-box.

Another innovation took place in 1959 when Dr C.A. Hepburn provided funds to pay for the installation of undersoil heating. Thereafter, the Murrayfield pitch became immune to the vagaries of the often disruptive weather.

With the SRU offices transferred from Coates Crescent to Murrayfield in 1964, the stadium was now, more than ever, the proper HQ of the game in Scotland and still Murrayfield continued to develop and attempt to keep pace with the rapidly expanding popularity of the game.

The Union had been considering covered enclosures or a new stand to replace the East terracing but, at the time, these concepts were laid aside on the

*It is 1982 and the
East stand begins to
take shape*
(The Herald)

*Murrayfield hosts
Grand Slam 1984.
Skipper Jim Aitken
with arm raised in
jubilation*
(The Herald)

grounds of cost. Like most sporting venues, Murrayfield continued to operate a 'come one, come all' policy of admission at the turnstiles. But in 1975, when a then world-record crowd of 104,000 (with many thousands more turned away) jammed in to see Scotland defeat Wales 12–10, the decision was taken on safety grounds to introduce a ticket-only policy with an upper limit of 70,000.

In the early Eighties, with safety considerations on the massive East terracing in mind, and with the continuously rising demand for seated accommodation, the radical decision was taken to demolish the East terraces and to construct a new stand. The £3.15m plan was financed in large measure by a Scottish Sports Council grant and the issuing of 5,000 interest-free, 20-year loans of £400, for which the lender was awarded the right to purchase one ticket for each home international. The stand was in use for the games against Ireland and Wales in 1983 but officially opened by the SRU's enthusiastic Patron, The Princess Royal, or as she then was HRH The Princess Anne, at a special Barbarians fixture in March of that year.

Grand Slam 1990, Murrayfield's third since the opening day Slam achieved with victory in the 1925 Calcutta Cup match. David Sole is chaired aloft (The Herald)

The timing was a year out. Just 12 months later and the East stand would have stood silent witness to a Grand Slam, just as the new stadium had done 59 years before.

This time it was Jim Aitken's men who played out the final act of their Grand Slam drama before the Murrayfield faithful. The visitors this time were the French. The final scoreline of 21–12 does not tell the entire story. The Scots were sorely harried by Jean-Pierre Rives's Frenchmen whose discipline finally deserted them after the Scots, showing great character and courage, had

weathered the French storm and through the boot of Peter Dods had reaped the whirlwind of penalties which the Welsh referee Winston Jones awarded against the Tricolors.

For the Scots the turning point came with Jim Calder's try from a lineout on the French line. It was immortalised as *The Turning Point* in the Royal Bank-commissioned painting by Ronnie Browne. Scotland had won her second Grand Slam and, once again, Murrayfield had provided the backdrop to the action.

It was always intended that the new East stand would be just the starting point for a comprehensive facelift. Initial proposals were for a 65,000 capacity stadium with two-tier stands on the end terracings, the upper deck providing seating accommodation while the lower tiers would provide covered terracings for those who still preferred to watch their rugby from a standing position.

But the Hillsborough soccer stadium disaster meant that the plan had to be re-evaluated. Lord Justice Taylor's inquiry and subsequent report decreed in 1990 that all stadia which came within the remit of the Safety of Sports Ground Act 1975 should be all seated by the start of the 1995 season. As the Act made no distinction between football and rugby, the SRU was left with no alternative but to comply. Murrayfield would have to become an all-seater super stadium.

The design team began work in 1990 but not before Murrayfield had hosted its third Grand Slam. From the moment David Sole led his side out with that slow, almost menacing, gladiatorial march until the final seconds when the

End of an era. March 1992 and the North terracing crush barriers come down in preparation for the new-look Murrayfield (The Herald)

It is June 1992 and the South stand begins to rise from the old terracing (The Herald)

Scots defended like lions to maintain their 13–7 lead, it had become obvious to all 55,000 present that here was a game in a million.

It was a day of high passion, courageous commitment and almost unbearable excitement. It was a day when 'The Flower of Scotland' came of age as the Murrayfield anthem and it was a day, too, when all of the great prizes were on offer to the side which could best hold its nerve. The Grand Slam, the Championship, the Triple Crown and the Calcutta Cup: they were all there for the taking, and they would go to the side which wanted them most. They went to Scotland. It was Murrayfield's third Grand Slam and, surely, it had been the most compelling.

Behind the scenes, though, the redevelopment plans were at an advanced stage. A three-phase plan was approved in 1991. The first phase called for the redevelopment of the terraces to provide continuity with the East stand and the provision of two-tiered seated accommodation for 26,000 spectators along with hospitality provision for around 1,000.

Work began on the new North and South stands at the conclusion of the 1992 Championship season and was completed at the end of December in the same year. The stands, to the marvel of many, were in use by the start of the 1993 season and for the World Sevens tournament in late spring of the same year.

And the Sevens circus had hardly vacated the premises before the builders

The old West stand is gone and, by January 1993, its replacement begins to soar skyward
(The Herald)

moved in again and demolition work began on the grand old West stand. Originally, it had been intended to retain the structure but with the addition of a second tier. However, due mainly to the success of the new Murrayfield debenture scheme, the Union decided to broaden the scope of the plan by opting for complete demolition which would mean 2,500 extra seats and a total ground capacity of 67,500.

As the wreckers moved in it was, for many, like watching the departure of a dear, old friend. From the dust, though, rose the final piece in the new Murrayfield jigsaw. The arena was complete and, just as in 1925 when workmen laboured through the night to make ready the Old Murrayfield, the new stadium was made ready for public inspection on the day of the 1994 Calcutta Cup match only after much burning of midnight oil by a small army of dedicated workers.

The game itself (if not the result) was a more than fitting introduction to the new Murrayfield. Sixty-nine years beforehand 70,000 spectators had marvelled at the new home of Scottish rugby. On 5 February 1994 some 49,500 of their latter-day counterparts did the same. At that game only the central section of the new West stand was in operation. Throughout the summer, work continued on the wing sections and with the project complete in time for the Springboks match the New Murrayfield will be seen in all its majestic glory.

Which is where we came in. Scottish rugby has a stadium more than fit for the 21st century but the pukka, pony-riding gents of the Edinburgh Polo Club still wouldn't recognise the old paddock now.

Melrose Boys Who Make You Wonder

THE McEWAN'S 70/- LEAGUE

By Alasdair Reid

I'M not one to pass the buck, but it really was Neil Drysdale's fault. It was the weekend of the Ireland–Scotland international and we were standing in the bar of the Lansdowne Hotel in Dublin having one of our many discussions on the role of irony in the Gothic novel when the *Scotland on Sunday* writer volunteered the opinion that Boroughmuir v Kelso might be a better bet than Currie v Melrose as the game to watch the following Sunday. The Meggetland match, he said, was a four-pointer, a vital relegation battle between two desperate sides, while Malleny Park would offer nothing more exciting than another easy win for Melrose with a trophy presentation at the end. Me, I wasn't so sure, but on the basis that you can't foul up if the Other Lot are doing the same thing, I came round to Neil's way of thinking.

So there we were at Meggetland, Saturday 12 March, watching this vital, crucial, nail-biting game between Boroughmuir and Kelso and, true enough, it had all the ingredients of a tense and even dramatic occasion. Boroughmuir had clearly realised that the penultimate Saturday of the league season would be a good day to rediscover some form and although Kelso put up brave resistance in the early stages of the game they were overwhelmed by the power of the home pack in the second half. Boroughmuir won 22–3 to keep their place in Division One and consign Kelso to a season in the second. We did, indeed, have a game worth writing about. Or so we thought.

Straight after the final whistle, I put in a call to the clubhouse at Malleny Park. That game had kicked off early and I expected to hear that Melrose had earned their narrow win, picked up their trophy and gone home. Instead, the news was that they had secured their title with their finest performance of the

Jim Telfer, the Melrose director of coaching and now the SRU's new director of rugby, is surrounded by his young charges as a 74–10 win over Currie secures yet another Scottish Championship (The Herald)

season, beating Currie by 74 points to 10. There was no getting away from the fact that the afternoon had been a carnival for Melrose, a free-flowing, high-scoring riot of running rugby and not the dutiful slog we had expected. They had scored a mountain of points. As I realised I had missed one of the highlights of the season, a game that should not have been missed, the sky over Meggetland took on a grey cast, while curious word associations, like *Drysdale* and *homicide*, took shape in my mind.

But perhaps this is too harsh. For in many ways covering the 1993–94 McEwan's 70 Shilling League had become an exercise in Melrose-avoidance long before that game. Everyone in the media faced the same problem; the responsibility to cover the biggest/most important game on the card so often translated itself into an obligation to watch Melrose. This might not seem like much of a problem if you happen to live in the shadow of the Eildon Hills and you view the world through yellow-and-black-tinted spectacles, but in a national newspaper your sense of balance begins to look affected when your match reports giving stirring accounts of the exploits of the Greenyards mob for six weeks in a row. We had to devise strategies to miss watching Melrose, to give reasonable coverage to the 13 other clubs in Division One.

By God, it was hard sometimes. From first to last Melrose was *the* story. On the opening day, when we expected them to sprint off into the distance with a win against Gala at the Greenyards, they astonished us all as they caught their bootlaces in the starting blocks and fell flat on their faces to a 13–14 defeat. Over the next few weeks they wobbled again at Raeburn Place, where they faced a 16–3 deficit before edging a narrow win, 17–16, over Edinburgh Accies, and then at Hawick, where they won 12–10 only after David Gordon's failed conversion of a Brian Renwick try had snatched defeat from the jaws of a well-earned draw for Hawick. From then on, Melrose just kept on winning while the threat from Gala – and later Stirling County – fell away. By the turn of the year Melrose were back at the top of the table, with Heriot's in second place on points difference. The first game of 1994 involved a mouth-watering meeting between the two at Goldenacre.

Now that was a game, an occasion that had everything. It was the biggest club match of the season and as the crowds flocked to the ground you could have driven all the way along the Ferry Road and halfway to Musselburgh before a parking space could be found. The rugby was something, too. Although they conceded a try to Gary Parker straight from the kick-off, Heriot's threatened to do themselves justice for much of the first half. Later, though, they were surpassed, and eventually overwhelmed, by a relentless Melrose performance that was laced throughout by the silver thread of mesmerising brilliance that was Craig Chalmers. The stand-off had endured a shaky start to his season, and was to suffer more in the months ahead, but in scoring one try and creating four more he delivered a thumping reminder of just how good a player he can be. Chalmers was untouchable that day – just as Melrose were to be as they continued their smooth cruise to the title in the weeks and months ahead.

So it was boring watching Melrose? Well yes, in a sense it was. When you

Jed's Grant Farquharson goes for the gap in the Selkirk ranks (The Herald)

No escape: Carl Hogg has no intention of letting Gregor Townsend out of his grasp. Melrose recovered from their league début defeat by Gala to win the Championship again (The Herald)

West of Scotland seem to have the pitch to themselves in this shot from their encounter with Kelso (The Herald)

watch a side display a visible commitment to excellence and an iron-willed determination to win there is a real danger that the spectacle can become just a shade repetitive. Perhaps it is possible to become immune to the tingling moment that arrives when the fulcrum of self-belief tilts in favour of a quality side and they begin to play with the confidence of their status and the determination to savour their moments of greatness. When you watch them do it week in, week out, year after year, you might become bored by it all. It is more likely, though, that you will become an addict.

Last season, in fact, Melrose's solidity, their predictability if you like, was actually important. Their reassuring rock was about the only safe anchorage to be found in an otherwise storm-tossed sea of Scottish rugby. The season's fixture schedule had always meant a strange journey was in store, particularly for the club championship, which kicked off early and was interrupted frequently. As the months went by we saw some bizarre games and recorded some bizarre results. The All Blacks visit and the Inter-District and Five Nations championships passed in a flurry of strange scorelines and some shocking lapses in form. But while other clubs endured white-knuckled rides on their own precipitous roller-coaster of fluctuating form, Melrose soon found a winning groove and stuck with it. Their consistency was a small mercy, something to be grateful for.

And if others resented their success, it is worth remembering that Melrose's consistent quality – on and off the field – was sometimes the only standard that club rugby could fly with pride. At the end of that awesome ten-day period in November when the All Blacks brought the South and then Scotland to their knees with record defeats, the knives were out, ready to carve up the domestic game. The failures were at a higher level, but club rugby became the whipping boy because, we were told, it no longer served the purposes of the representative structure. Melrose became important then because they showed that quality could be found at club level. Frankly, the argument that clubs should politely move aside to allow enhanced district competitions to take place was never credible when you considered how Melrose had already achieved all the things – the facilities for players, spectators and sponsors, the commitment of the club members, the almost tangible sense of community and purpose – that the district set-ups lacked.

Last year, everyone had their pet theories about how the structure of the game could be changed to shape players for the challenges of international rugby. Most involved the construction of a careful hierarchy of district competitions and about 99 per cent of them were utterly wrong. Half of them were wrong because they were just too damned complicated but a good many were also wrong because they ignored completely the need to retain the commitment of those individuals who still graft for the good name, and in the true sense, of amateurism in clubs throughout the country. The danger, it sometimes seemed, was that the architecture of rugby in the next century would begin to look like the architecture of new town planning in the Sixties: fine in theory, except that nobody would want to live there.

Yes, it can be a strange trip, this rugby-writing lark, full of dark and unfathomable mysteries. Every year the rugby press corps meets up at the Selkirk Sevens on the last Saturday in August – like a band of new-age travellers, minus the Alsatians and the personal hygiene – and wonder where

Gavin Hastings in a spot of bother in this Bridgehaugh tussle with Stirling County (The Herald)

the season will take them. Last season, however, we got to the Gala Sevens the following April and we were still trying to figure out where the heck we'd been. Somehow, the whole thing lacked sense or shape. It was a season of incidents, not theme.

A season for head-scratching. Why, for instance, was the ex-Liverpool footballer Emlyn Hughes to be found in the bar of a Cardiff hotel on the night of the Wales–Scotland international, delivering his analysis of what was wrong with Scottish rugby to anyone who could be persuaded to listen? Why, for that matter, was the Grinning One's post-mortem so painfully right? Damned if I knew, and neither would I hazard an interpretation of the moment when, as I drove away from Murrayfield after an international selection announcement one day, the car radio began to play Brian Eno's 'Back in Judy's Jungle':

> *Fifteen was chosen because he was dumb,*
> *Eleven because he was blind.*

Although I must admit it was tempting.

The straight road kept taking us back to the Greenyards. Scotland plummeted down the international order with their 51–15 defeat by the All Blacks at Murrayfield, then bumped along the bottom in the most turgid Five Nations Championship in years; the South won the McEwan's Inter-District Championship, but it was a triumph of monumental insignificance alongside their 84–5 demolition by the New Zealanders a couple of weeks later;

Gala's Tom Weir did make a successful touchdown despite the strenuous efforts of Edinburgh Accies' Dave McIvor and Derek Patterson (The Herald)

Special delivery: Kelso's Phil Dunkley sends back some prime maul ball (The Herald)

Edinburgh redeemed themselves after a forgettable showing in the domestic competition with a couple of fine wins against Irish Provinces in early December . . . And Melrose just kept on winning.

It might not have been the line that Jim Telfer was taking at the time, but that opening-day defeat by Gala might have been the best thing that could have happened to Melrose. On the day, there had been no way back for them after Gregor Townsend had dropped the 72nd-minute goal that put Gala in front, but Melrose had the rest of the season to make amends. I still remember the conversation I had with Stuart Henderson, Melrose's astonishingly hard-working secretary, after the game. He could not bring himself to agree with those who said the season might be more open, perhaps a shade more interesting even, in the light of Gala's win, but he did say this: 'We know what we have to do now. We just have to win every game.' Over the next seven months Stuart's words came back to me time and again as Melrose ploughed on to end the season with a record of 12 wins from 13 games.

So what makes them tick? Why is it that a town with a population that could easily be accommodated in half a dozen Glasgow tower blocks has managed to produce a team that has dominated Scottish rugby for almost half a decade? How is it that they have managed to cram such astonishing riches of talent into a team with an average age of 23 that threatens to dominate the scene for many more years to come? Why, dammit, are they so good? The structure of the club offers no clues, for they have never had the advantage of feeder sides passing on their best players as Hawick and Gala had during their periods of ascendancy. And if you can't credit the structure then you can only credit the individuals concerned.

Ouch! Craig Chalmers suffers the full weight of a Jamie Joseph tackle during Scotland's 51–15 defeat by the All Blacks (The Herald)

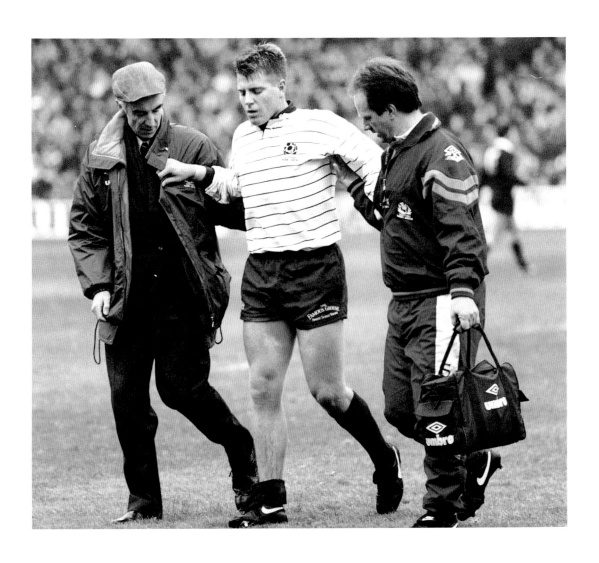

Moment of despair: Chalmers, suffering a recurrence of a calf-muscle strain, requires assistance as he exits from the All Blacks defeat (The Herald)

The Golden Boy: Jeff Wilson scores the second of his three tries despite the close attention of Scott Hastings (The Herald)

The body language says it all: McIvor, Weir and Watt trudge wearily from the pitch after the All Blacks' record 51–15 win (The Herald)

Gavin Hastings is the meat in a Welsh sandwich (The Herald)

Rob Wainwright, a revelation until injury cut short his season, bursts through the Cardiff gloom (The Herald)

Help is at hand for Cardiff casualty Iain Morrison (The Herald)

*Piling on the agony: Andy Nicol sustains rib damage in Wales but his great misfortune
opens the door for Gary Armstrong's return* (The Herald)

England's Kyran Bracken and Neil Back receive a close-up view of Gary Armstrong's Calcutta Cup return (The Herald)

Gary Armstrong's strength through the tackle is one of his major assets (The Herald)

A Calcutta Cup try for Rob Wainwright. Sadly for the Scots, it was not to be enough
(The Herald)

*Tony Stanger brushes aside Brian Moore. Burnell, Sharp, Munro and Hastings are in close
support* (The Herald)

Ken Logan gives Tony Underwood a tongue-lashing! (The Herald)

Every prop has his day: Paul Burnell and Alan Sharp employ the old Scottish tactic of Feet, Scotland, Feet! (The Herald)

Sounds simple, but the problem with rolling the credits at the Greenyards is remembering when to stop. The name-check would tax the larynx of even the most long-winded BAFTA award winner because it just goes on and on. There are the obvious candidates, such as Jim Telfer, and Stuart Henderson and Craig Chalmers and Doddie Weir and the various Redpaths and about half a dozen Browns and then there's the boy-wonder, Craig Joiner, and the makes-you-wonder, Gary Parker, and . . . See what I mean? Too many obvious candidates.

Try to pick out the areas of excellence at Melrose and all you will reveal are the gaps in your thinking. Like any successful club, there are focal points – players, officials, coaches – whose talents are way beyond the ordinary, but it would be missing the most important point to single them out. For even if Jim Telfer is one of the world's top five coaches and Stuart Henderson is in danger of having his council tax assessed on the basis that the Greenyards is his usual residence and even if they have players whose talents are the envy of half the clubs in England, the abiding impression is of seamless quality – in everything they do. They work hard, play hard, entertain superbly and enjoy their rewards – and if anyone knows of another club which offers a child-minding service for the inquisitive offspring of passing hacks equal to that provided by Melrose ex-president Mac Brown then I'd be interested to know about it.

So Melrose were outstanding again, but there were at least some occasions last season when it seemed that the gap between them and the rest might be closing. Those first few weeks of the season opened up the prospect of a

Emergency Ward 10: Watsonians' wounded sit out the Myreside club's clash with city rivals Stewart's-Melville
(The Herald)

Dundee's international scrumhalf Andy Nicol is off and running. GHK's Shade Munro appears a mite concerned!
(The Herald)

League competition that could go to the wire with tense, competitive games all the way, as Gala, Edinburgh Accies and Stirling County fired impressive opening broadsides. Even later, when Melrose had, indeed, disappeared over the horizon as far as winning the thing was concerned and Gala and Heriot's had tailed off badly, there were still some noteworthy salvoes from Watsonians and Boroughmuir and from Stewart's-Melville, fielding a backline of callow talent that had expert orchestration from a rejuvenated Douglas Wyllie.

As a spectacle, and as entertainment, the strike rate in the club championship last year was higher than at any other level and it was a recurring joy to watch the likes of Wyllie weave magic into a game. I had interviewed him early in the season, when he spoke of the importance of enjoying rugby at club level. At the time, he did not consider himself a serious contender for more caps, so it was one of the highlights of the season when he reappeared in the Five Nations Championship only a few months later.

The performance of Watsonians was truly astonishing. In early December they had looked like relegation candidates, second from bottom of the first division with only two wins from eight outings. Throughout winter and spring, however, they rocketed up the table and ended the season in fifth place, level on points with Heriot's who had never really recovered from that defeat at home to Melrose at the turn of the year. The other great leap-frogging act was performed by Jed-Forest, who were heaved out of the danger zone towards mid-table respectability by the powers of persuasion they applied in

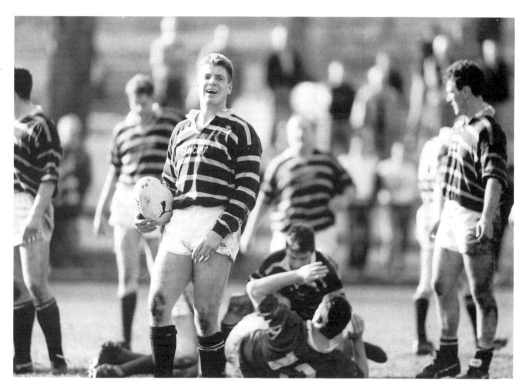

reminding Gary Armstrong that he was, after all, a scrum-half.

Jed-Forest finished eighth, a significant slot given next year's reorganisation of the top divisions into four eight-team leagues, with games played on a home and away basis. Their position represented what will become the cut-off point between the best and the rest of Scottish rugby in the years to come. If there has sometimes seemed too great a gap in standards between the first and second divisions in the past, the imminent arrival of a yawning chasm is something that should focus minds to a remarkable degree. The nerve-fraying lessons of England's Courage Leagues are about to be learned in Scotland, too.

A new template has been created, but it would be insufficient and simplistic to think that the structural changes that are about to take place represent nothing more than a redefinition of a few boundaries within the game. The real lesson from England in recent years is that the tighter format will suit some clubs better than others. Attitude matters when the heat in the kitchen increases and there is no reason to believe that the forces in England that have propelled the likes of Bath and Orrell to the fore while Headingley and Roundhay have plummeted down the pecking order will not have parallels in Scotland.

Scottish rugby scrapes by with a painfully small constituency of players. When the map was redrawn for the first time with the introduction of leagues in 1973, there was a subtle alteration of the very geography of the game, presenting opportunities that were taken, most spectacularly, by Stirling County and Currie. The next batch of changes will alter that map again and

The Happy Smile Club: Craig Chalmers in upbeat mood for Melrose against Jed-Forest (The Herald)

new possibilities will emerge. Fine as the traditions of the Borders and a handful of FP clubs in the central belt may be, there is little doubt that those power-bases are now too narrow for the well-being of Scottish rugby as a whole.

Like the passing of soul music and the great British breakfast, the demise of Borders rugby has been announced with tedious regularity down the years. Somehow, however, they still hang in there, for since those reorganisations in the early Seventies, the Scottish club championship has only actually left the area twice. Yet Melrose's title, Jed-Forest's rally and the re-emergence of Hawick, who finished seventh, could not disguise the fact that this was anything but a vintage season for Borders rugby. The haunted expression that John Rutherford wore on that bleak, black day in November when the New Zealanders came to Netherdale never really left him, for he was humming 'The Flowers of the Forest' all the way through to March, when Selkirk were relegated, having gained only one point from one draw in their 13-match campaign. Kelso's demotion was less clear-cut for they actually won four league games, but it was no less painful for a side that had already endured one spell in Division Two since their heady title-winning times in 1988 and 1989.

The up escalator, meanwhile, was bringing those happy souls from Glasgow High/Kelvinside and Dundee High. It had always seemed something of a fluke that both had been relegated the year before – both had played some superb rugby in 1992–93 – so it was no surprise to see them come back up. GH/K, in particular, performed splendidly under the coaching of Brian Gilbert and Hugh Hamilton, their pack was driven along by Alan Watt, Shade Munro and the Wallace brothers, Fergus and Murray, while Harry Bassi and Cameron Little scored a barrel load of points among the backs. Dundee suffered only one defeat – at the hands of GH/K, strangely enough – while the unbeaten Glasgow boys were duly named Scotland's Team of the Year in the *Herald* Awards at the season's end.

In the lower divisions, there were some impressive results from some outposts of the game, some familiar, some not so. Gordonians' Third Division title suggested that welcome strength might be returning to rugby in the north-east, while divisions four to six were cleaned up by Trinity Accies, Duns and Allan Glens respectively. Annan's storming passage through Division Seven included a 107–0 win over Stirling University that would have been a record in the McEwan's League had not the University failed to fulfil a later fixture. As a consequence, the University were excluded from the remainder of their league programme and had all their results wiped off the books. Mind you, with results like those, perhaps they knew what they were doing.

Even without that giant scoreline, the 501 points Annan scored in their 12 remaining games made them the highest-scoring side in Scottish rugby. Clearly, Division Seven was the place to be for huge scores, for at the other end of the table no side in any division absorbed more than the 516 points conceded by Montrose and District in the played 12, lost 12 campaign that removed them from the national-league structure.

Sic Transit Gloria Montrose, as they often say in the outer reaches of Angus. From the base camp of the seventh division to the summit of the first, there were 89 clubs filling slots between Montrose and Melrose and from the bottom it must truly have seemed like a mountain. If rugby can take credit for anything, though, it is for the way it so often shrinks that mountain, with its essential democracy and its essential goodness. Time and again, I have watched players of international calibre talking on equal terms with players of far less ability, yet not once have I seen one who demonstrated the slightest trace of arrogance when doing so.

It is a spirit that runs through the game in Scotland and beyond, founded on traditions of which rugby is, and should be, fiercely proud. Thinking back over the season just ended, I can think of any number of incidents, large and small, where the spirit was demonstrated again and again in acts of sportsmanship, kindness, warmth and concern. Rugby, and club rugby in particular, has a fundamental decency about it – and on the evidence of last season it is an enduring decency as well.

Greenyards decider: Glasgow's Alan Watt and South's Robbie Brown compete for lineout ball in the South v Glasgow Championship decider (The Herald)

Kiwi Visitors Spoil the Party

THE DISTRICT SCENE

By John Beattie

THE South had become the Scottish District Champions quite nicely, it appeared anyway, without ever stepping out of second gear. An outrageous try against Glasgow at the Greenyards, started by Melrose winger Gary Parker's quick throw, continued by Craig Chalmers with Tony Stanger, and finished off by Hawick flanker Derek Turnbull, sealed it for the Borderers at the start of what had seemed, up until that point, just like any other season. The South, as usual our best district side, were doing well again.

And then it all went horribly, disastrously, embarrassingly wrong. Much of our Scottish pride was snatched from us like a dying breath, as those hulking great brutes from the Antipodes, the All Blacks, came marching North of the Border. The spoil-sports.

Wednesday, 10 November was a sunny day in Gala (perhaps we should have smelled a rat). And amid a cheery border throng, schoolboys chattering like lively little starlings as well as old folk from the 'toon' jostled by nosy parkers from the cities, they had gathered in force to watch their beloved Borderers take on the New Zealanders.

Surely the South, providing the first Scottish opposition to the tourists, could give the All Blacks a sharp reminder that the easy days of England, their first stop on tour, were behind them?

History will recall a day when Scottish rugby took a good long look at itself to wonder whether it was still one of the elite rugby nations that deserved a seat close to that of the best. To heck with sitting at God's right hand, were we still up there beside the Aussies, and, forgive us Lord, the English too?

How could it have happened? Was there really such a gulf? The score, just to

Glasgow drive over for a try despite Bryan Redpath's best efforts
(The Herald)

remind you as you lift this book gingerly from the shelf in the year 2000, was 84–5 to the New Zealanders. Yep, a point a minute, in the days of five points for a try, two for a conversion, and three for a penalty.

And, to be frank, it could have been so much more, as the All Blacks sat on their lead for some 20 minutes of the second half without expending too many calories. Shocking it was. So shocking that many people who stumbled across the scores as they progressed through the day on snippets from the radio imagined a game already finished when it was barely 15 minutes old.

John Rutherford, a magnificent player in his day and a man who had tasted success at every level before 10 November 1993, was the South coach that sunny Gala afternoon. Like the crowd he struggles for an explanation. 'We gave it our best shot I suppose,' he says, 'and you have to go into every game thinking you can win. There's no point doing otherwise. To be truthful, it stunned Scottish rugby.'

Rutherford says that the effects of that game will live for a long time. 'I think that there are some players who will never recover, and I know others whose performances and confidence suffered all season because of it,' he says. 'I personally have never been so depressed in my life. We were absolutely routed. I actually didn't leave the house for two days I was so embarrassed at what had happened. I just could not go out and face people I know in our small community.'

Gala's Hamish Hunter, whose game at loose-head prop lasted barely eight minutes before a damaged hamstring forced early retirement, and who thereby avoided the cataclysmic embarrassment of his colleagues, says that there were two major differences between his side and the All Blacks that day. 'First of all, they didn't try to do anything complicated at all, they were just fired up, skilful, and did the simple things without making mistakes. But the most striking thing was their physical strength. These people were a different breed to us, obviously having spent much more time than we had on the weights. We were overwhelmed, and they were 40 points up before we knew it. It was an experience, but one I wouldn't want to repeat.'

Rutherford says that there are always lessons to be learned. 'Out of all of these appalling things there comes some good. We now know that we don't have district sides that can take on the likes of New Zealand or South Africa. We have to pick district selects, as we will do when South Africa visit later this year.

'The whole structure of Scottish rugby is being examined now, and quite rightly. We have, undoubtedly, fallen behind other countries again,' says Rutherford.

But the district set-up, and here is the real irony of the humiliation of the South by their All Black guests, is, in fact, the perceived route to success, promoted by the rugby administration, as it strives to improve and protect the game in our country. More players, playing more high-level games – that is the message. Imagine, therefore, having one of the emblems of the relevance of your future policy – the champions of the competition – comprehensively defeated in one devastating 80-minute spell.

Synchronised running from the South threequarters in this shot from the District champions' outing against North and Midlands (The Herald)

Arms and legs are everywhere as the South secure lineout ball during their match against North and Midlands (The Herald)

The whole argument assumes, of course, that you can draw a line of correlation between the standard of the domestic competition that's on offer for the best players, and the success of the national team. Some would argue that a pool of good players, coached properly, will always beat poor players taking part in a competition of breathtaking severity. Glasgow Accies playing against the All Blacks every week would never beat Llanelli, even if Llanelli had to play against inhabitants of the Royal Infirmary's orthopaedic ward. Some might say that the physical and tactical difficulty of the games is crucial to the tuition of a budding internationalist. No one has yet been proved correct.

Season 1993–94 was indeed a strange one, because not only did the New Zealanders wreak their havoc, but we also had our friends from over the Irish Sea join us for that peculiar slot in the season occupied by the worst month of the year . . . December. December, and it was always so, tries its best to destroy the hearts of Scottish rugby players. John Jeffrey, the great Scottish forward of the Eighties, has always put forward a sound argument for summer rugby. And most of the articles on the subject seem to see the light of day in December.

Join us the Irish did, but there were no prizes on offer, no league, no cup, and little spectator interest. The press posse watched one game – it was between Glasgow and Munster at New Anniesland – where the combined pencil-holders, the players, and their inevitable entourage outnumbered any spectators.

That was despite having two British Lions on view – Mickey Galwey and Richard Wallace – and this, remember, the symbol of all that is good and progressive in Scottish rugby.

Many people had been sceptical at the start of the season. Would we ever learn anything from the Irish? Wouldn't we just rattle up points against them?

In the end, it was the Irish who expressed doubts. 'To start with we all looked forward to it,' said Neil Francis, the giant lock from Leinster, 'but there are now too many games, and although the competition has been interesting, it has not been as testing as we would have imagined.'

John Rutherford says more basic change is still needed. 'We're doing partly the right thing in playing the Provinces, and I would also like to see us playing English clubs, but most of us now know that it won't happen,' he says.

'But what's important, too, is that we generate some interest, and we make it into a worthwhile competition. Plus – and this is important – we must play the games on a Friday night or on a Sunday. We have to make it so that people can come and watch, and that means other players who would have been taking part in games themselves on Saturdays. We must move away from Saturday games for the Inter-Districts.'

It's hard to disagree with that point. As Glasgow took on the might of Munster that day, the Academical 3rd XV was playing Bute on an adjacent pitch, and a healthy old crowd they had there too. Double figures for sure. In the end, the season took on this fractured appearance:

Before the day of reckoning, the South beat the North and Midlands at

Edinburgh's Derek Patterson whips away ruck ball. The capital side's opponents on this occasion are North and Midlands (The Herald)

Inter-city tussle: Watt, Richardson, Macdonald, Wright and Munro are at the heart of this lineout action from the Glasgow v Edinburgh match (The Herald)

Rugged rucking from the Edinburgh pack in this shot from the inter-city clash (The Herald)

Jedforest, and Glasgow beat Edinburgh at Hughenden, both on 23 October. That set up a play-off at Melrose on 30 October, when the losers played each other for third and fourth place, and the winners for first and second.

As we know, the South were champions, and Edinburgh won over the North and Midlands by 28 points to 26 to snatch third place despite a stonker of a try from Rob Wainwright.

Then, and a minute's silence please, the All Blacks came to town.

After the All Blacks, the four Irish and Scottish Districts went into competition, with the Exiles missing due to club commitments in England. Glasgow and the North and Midlands paired up with Connacht and Munster, while the South and Edinburgh took up alongside Ulster and Leinster.

Border rugby sank even deeper into despair as their men were beaten in both their games, while Edinburgh won their matches.

Bruce Hay, the Edinburgh coach, has now had time to reflect. And he knows that there is to be more of the same next year, whether he wants it or not.

'To be honest, I can't really see the competition going anywhere. It's obvious that we're not going to get the teams we want to play us, and the Irish boys say that they would rather play their club competition.'

These are harsh words from the British Lion, and Hay has been through rugby's hoops more than most. In fact, it's his old friend and sparring partner, the SRU's Director of Rugby Jim Telfer, who is at the helm in the rough sea of changes. 'I can see what Jim is after,' says Hay, 'but he's also saying that the club competition will change to eight teams in the top leagues playing home and away. When that happens then I can see the club competition taking precedence, because concentrating all of the talent in eight clubs will mean that these clubs will almost be district sides in their own right.'

It's a valid point, and one that has been echoed by many. But Telfer's 'Grand Design', with the Districts as the focus, was arrived at after lengthy and widespread consultation.

While the public expect the District Championship to provide better-quality play from better-quality players, it has its anomalies. 'One of the downfalls of the District set-up,' explains Hay, 'is that you somehow never get the best side out on to the field and you always struggle for training facilities, hardly ever getting even a decent set of lights and a hot shower.' People may find it staggering, but it's true.

'And then,' he continues, 'a team like the North and Midlands seems to pull players in from everywhere, so much so that you start to wonder what the point of it is. At one time, it seemed like half the Edinburgh Accies team was playing for North and Midlands.'

But will the District Championship survive in its present format to make Scottish rugby successful in years to come? Bruce Hay thinks not. 'If you look at any of the countries we compete with, such as Wales and England and France, what you notice is that they all put the emphasis on club rugby. In England it's Bath, Leicester and the like, whereas in Wales the Cardiffs and Llanellis still hold power. I think that we will end up abandoning the District Championship quite soon, with the clubs providing the focus of attention.'

Bruce Hay has articulated what many people have been saying over the season. We have examined, and re-examined, our domestic set-up to such an

Despair: Craig Chalmers looks on in disbelief as New Zealand set about piling on 85 points (The Herald)

extent that it has been with fear and trepidation that I open the pages of certain broadsheets, lest I have to read yet one more scribe's view of the way ahead.

Should you have read this far in the year 2000, then can I just make it plain to you that this season, season 1993–94, has been one of the most influential in the history of Scottish rugby. The shock waves have been felt throughout the land. We are like little boys who have suddenly found out that we are no longer the Big Boys in the playground, entitled to respect and admiration throughout Britain.

The days of David Sole, Finlay Calder, John Jeffrey rampaging around the international field, have gone. The disappearance of that once-common success, or at least parity, on the international pitch has meant that the Scottish team right now lacks the pulling power that it might have had in the Grand Slam years to kick-start the kind of District Championship that Jim Telfer has in mind.

But let's not get too depressed. The road to the international side still needs a stop along the District path for now. The likes of Kevin McKenzie and Ian Jardine from Glasgow only proved their international worth on the District field, and so will many others.

The District Championship was not without controversy, and had a significant impact on our rugby lives. That was clear. What is not so clear, is whether it will actually survive in its present form, or indeed survive at all. The argument, as they say, is set to run . . . and run.

Black day at Netherdale for Scotland's District champions as the Kiwis show no mercy (The Herald)

The Royal Bank
of Scotland

The Best and Worst of Times

SCOTLAND'S 1994 SEASON

By Derek Douglas

IT was the best of times. It was the worst of times. It was the season when the new Murrayfield began to take soaring, spectacular shape. It was the season when Gary Armstrong roared back into the Five Nations arena and it was the season when Jim Telfer became the SRU's first Director of Rugby.

A wooden-spoon season. There haven't been many of these in recent years. Throughout the Eighties and into the Nineties, the expectations of the Scottish rugby public have been quite dramatically – often unrealistically – heightened. During those golden years, with the Jim Aitken-led Grand Slam in 1984 and that achieved by David Sole's men in 1990, Scottish rugby followers had come to expect success. Perhaps, having supped regularly from the heady brew of victory, we had all forgotten that, over the historical piece, this was not the norm. During the glory years, and by dint of some cosmic synchronicity, Scotland had been blessed with more than its fair share of once-in-a-generation, world-class performers: the Calders, Rutherford, Sole, Jeffrey, Deans, Milne, Beattie, Paxton, White, Leslie, Hastings, Laidlaw, Armstrong, et al. The coaches during this golden era – Telfer, McGeechan and Grant – made the most of the rugby geniuses who became their charges and, with an astuteness seldom seen in the game, forged the honest journeymen who played alongside this rare elite into perfectly honed, well-drilled outfits who began to look upon victory almost as a birthright and (the mark of genuine winners) to prove victorious in games that they should have lost.

Last season, and perhaps even two or three seasons ago, there were hints that for the time being these days were well and truly over. With a flood of international retirements and the departures, too, of the coaching triumvirate which had seen Scotland through the Eighties, what was bound to follow was a period of hard pounding; a period of consolidation. It was hard not to feel some sympathy for Dougie Morgan and Richie Dixon who had inherited the coaching mantle just as the golden era – epitomised as much as anything by selectorial stability (only 16 players wore the thistle during the 1990 Grand Slam season) – faded into the past.

During the 1993–94 season no fewer than 31 players, at one time or another, turned out for Scotland. This astonishing figure underlines the unprecedented string of injuries with which the team had to contend but also, albeit to a lesser degree, the selectorial uncertainty which resulted from the unnerving nature of the early results.

Shakespeare might have had Scotland's international season in mind when he determined that when sorrows come, they come not as single spies but in battalions. Too true, Will. Put it another way. For Scotland the 1994 international season was just one damned thing after another. And the first of that battalion of sorrows swooped on Murrayfield on an overcast Saturday in November.

Less than a fortnight beforehand Sean Fitzpatrick's men in black had inflicted an 84–5 humiliation on the South of Scotland. There were widespread fears that if Scotland's District champions could be disposed of in such perfunctory fashion then the writing was on the wall, too, for the national side. Those fears were not misplaced. The writing was, indeed, on the wall and the message was clear. Scotland succumbed in desultory fashion to a record 51–15 defeat. Just over two years before, in the World Cup bronze-medal play-off – and even in defeat – Scotland had retained national pride with a 13–6 performance which underlined that the gap between the two sides was of manageable proportions. Now, that gulf was a yawning chasm. It was not just that Scotland had conceded 50 points for the first time in nearly one and a quarter centuries of international competition. It wasn't just that the 51–15 scoreline overshadowed the 44–0 drubbing suffered by the Scots at the hands of the South Africans in 1951. And it wasn't even the fact that this all-time low-point in Scottish rugby fortunes had occurred as the selectors had at last overcome the rugby nation's traditional physical deficiencies by fielding the biggest and heaviest pack ever to wear the thistle. No, the most disheartening aspect of a thoroughly disheartening afternoon was the manner in which the Scots had been laid low. There had been no fire. No pride. And long before the end the entirely fickle nature of public support had shown itself as substantial sections of the Murrayfield crowd had begun to vote with its feet and were making disconsolately for the exits. On this occasion those sent hameward tae think again didn't have far to travel!

The All Blacks had stamped their psychological superiority on the proceedings even before a ball had been kicked. They declined to follow the programme and perform their *haka* before the rendition of 'Flower of Scotland'. Thus, as was to be the case throughout an afternoon of unrelenting Kiwi intensity, they had the final word.

But it was not all doom and gloom. For genuine lovers of the game there was quite a bit to savour. Sadly, though, the most succulent offerings came almost exclusively from New Zealand. And for one New Zealander in particular, Saturday 20 November will long be remembered.

Jeff Wilson's Test debut was the stuff of comic-book heroics. The right-winger's hat-trick of tries gave new meaning to the description 'blond bombshell'. When the Kiwis embarked upon their Northern Hemisphere expedition Wilson was still a callow teenager. He celebrated his 20th birthday on the first weekend of the tour and, despite his tender years, the Invercargill youngster was already an international sportsman, having represented New Zealand at cricket against Australia. On 20 November 1993 at Murrayfield Wilson signalled in quite emphatic fashion that a new star had arrived upon the international scene. Not content with his three tries Wilson also added the conversion which took the New Zealanders over the 50-points mark. Young Wilson will never forget his spectacular international debut and it is unlikely that one Scot in particular will ever forget it either.

Scott Hastings was winning his 47th cap but doing so for the first time on the left wing. He had played as a wing-threequarter in non-Test games for the Lions and for Edinburgh but his selection on the left flank for the first time in a full-blown international was a piece of inspired selection which went horribly wrong. Such was the relentlessly inspired nature of New Zealand's play that afternoon, and so 'hot' was young Wilson, that it is likely that even a seasoned winger would have experienced difficulties. Rugby is a game featuring more angles than Pythagoras ever dreamed of, and despite the fact that he has more than mastered the defensive and offensive angles required in the centre, Hastings too often found himself stranded in an unfamiliar no-man's land.

However, Scotland's most important deficiencies were to be found up front where a pack comprising Watt, Milne, Burnell, Cronin, Macdonald, McIvor, Weir and Wainwright never got to grips with their All Black counterparts. The Scottish forwards lacked the intensity displayed by their rivals and, at times, seemed almost in awe of them. Finlay Calder used to say that to be truly successful an international pack had to contain more 'do-ers' than 'lookers'. On the day this Scotland eight had few 'do-ers' and, in particular, had no one to match the likes of New Zealand's rampaging prop Olo Brown who continuously took the ball on in a manner reminiscent of a top-of-his-form David Sole or the aforementioned Calder.

Behind the scrum, the Scotland line-up was Gavin Hastings, Stanger, Jardine, Shiel and Scott Hastings, Chalmers and Nicol. Dundee's Andy Nicol found himself back on international duty due to the unavailability of Gary Armstrong. Craig Chalmers made the side despite a calf-muscle strain. However, from the outset he did not appear to be his old self and after 56 minutes he retired hurt with a recurrence of the calf complaint. The incident was to have unparalleled repercussions later in the season.

New Zealand led 9–22 at half-time from, respectively, a Matthew Cooper penalty goal, a Marc Ellis try, Wilson's first try converted by Cooper, and a Zinzan Brooke try also converted by Cooper. Scotland's first-half points came from penalty goals by Hastings (2) and Chalmers who took over the goal-kicking duties while the Scotland captain had four stitches inserted in a hand wound.

In the second half, which the partisan crowd viewed with mounting apprehension, New Zealand played without quarter. Frank Bunce ran in for the Kiwis' fourth try; Cooper had another penalty goal; Wilson chased Timu's kick-ahead for his second try and Cooper converted; Marc Ellis touched down after making the most of a spilled pass resulting from a heavy Brooke tackle on Shiel and Cooper converted; and the final word was left to Jeff Wilson who ran in for his hat-trick and for good measure added the conversion as well. Scotland's points came from a further two Hastings penalty goals.

It had been, as they say in these parts, a 'right howking'. New Zealand had recorded their highest ever score in Europe and their biggest winning margin against Scotland. Gavin Hastings's four successful shots at goal took his international points tally to 502 (436 for Scotland and 66 for the Lions), leaving him behind only Michael Lynagh and Hugo Porta in the all-time greatest list. However, that was no consolation on an afternoon which belonged to Sean Fitzpatrick's All Blacks and, in particular, to the man his mates call 'Goldy', New Zealand's golden boy Jeff Wilson.

The All Blacks departed south, leaving Scottish rugby bruised, battered and maybe even a little bewildered. However, there was little time in which to lick wounds. By the first week of the New Year Scotland's international aspirants were on parade at the Murrayfield Trial and there were questions of personnel needing answers virtually across the board as the selectors sat down to choose a side for the Five Nations campaign.

The opening salvo in that campaign came against Wales at Cardiff less than a fortnight later. But even before the Scots had left home territory the gremlins – which seemed to be never far away all season – struck again. There had been much speculation within rugby circles as to the medical treatment which Craig Chalmers had received prior to the All Blacks match six weeks previously. Specifically, there was conjecture over the nature of an injection which had been administered to ease a calf-muscle problem on the morning of the All Blacks match. Had the injection been of a prohibited painkiller? That was the question to which the media now demanded an answer. The brouhaha erupted just as the Cardiff party was preparing to fly out of Edinburgh. The press posse which met the Scots at the airport took even the most seasoned campaigners by surprise.

An SRU statement quickly followed in which it was declared that Chalmers had, indeed, received an injection on the morning of the match but it had been of a non-steroidal, anti-inflammatory agent that was intended to ease his calf-muscle strain. It had not been a painkiller and nor had the medication been of such a nature that without it he could not have played.

The SRU said that the scheduled medication had been given by injection rather than tablet. This routine consultation and the decision to change from a tablet to an injection had taken place without the knowledge or involvement of the other members of the team management, said the statement.

'Mr Chalmers did not require the injection in order to take the field but was merely completing his course of medication. As always, the final decision on whether to play was the player's. Mr Chalmers declared himself fit to play for Scotland.'

End of story. Nevertheless, the episode had been at once a distraction from the rugby business in hand and a salutory warning that, with the high profile and celebrity status which many international rugby players now seek and enjoy, the switch from the sports pages to a prominent slot on Page One can take place within the bat of an eyelid.

And so to the National Stadium, Cardiff. It rained . . . and it rained . . . and it rained! The afternoon was, in short, miserable. Just to compound that misery Scotland lost 29–6 and the side's evil luck continued when both Chalmers and Iain Morrison were replaced hurt and Andy Nicol was crocked in the dying seconds of the game.

There had been some changes after All Black Saturday. Scott Hastings was out with a heel injury and Gregor Townsend came into the side at centre as did Kenny Logan on the left wing. The pack was shuffled, too, with Peter Wright, Neil Edwards, Derek Turnbull and Morrison being recalled to the national cause and Shade Munro winning his first cap. But once again the Scots never really got out of their blocks.

The game was marred early on by an outbreak of fighting between the two sets of forwards. The Scots were, though, to an extent which surprised many onlookers, non-combatants. The principal culprit was the Welsh hooker Garin Jenkins who flailed away like a demented windmill. The main recipient of his largely ineffective blows was the Scottish flanker Derek Turnbull who was moved to remark later that he had been hit so many times he was waiting for the bell to sound.

In one sense the fact that the Scots chose to abide by the laws and not retaliate was commendable. However, this collective 'decision' was symptomatic of an afternoon where the Welsh forwards played the lax French referee Patrick Robin to perfection and the Scots did not.

Monsieur Robin did not have a good game. As a Frenchman, he knows better than any Scot the meaning of the term *laissez faire* and, like many French referees, that is how he officiates. However, the Scots should have known this and should have been able to adapt their play to suit the conditions prevailing on the day. Additionally, Scottish supporters had a justifiable and major grouse against the ref for his refusal to award a perfectly good drop-goal by Gregor Townsend. Had he done so then the Welsh lead would have been cut to 17–6 with 25 minutes yet to play. But, in truth, it must have seemed to even the most dyed-in-the-wool Scotsman that Wales simply wanted the win more than the Scots and it is unlikely that Robin's error affected the eventual outcome.

It wasn't much of a game. The truly atrocious weather conditions saw to that. The first try of the afternoon wasn't scored until the 52nd minute, Mike Rayer doing the honours. Up until then all the points had come from penalty goals; Neil Jenkins with four and Hastings with one. Just over the hour mark Hastings kicked his second penalty. This time the award had come about after Phil Davies had been caught loitering with intent on the wrong side of a ruck as the ball came back. It was the kind of 'professional foul' which the All Blacks had honed to near perfection and which referees only really cottoned on to as their tour was nearing its end.

The Scots were disrupted by the departures of Chalmers and, in particular, Morrison who suffered a bad leg injury. The up-side of Morrison's replacement, however, was that their lineout work improved with the arrival of Doddie Weir. Doug Wyllie came on for Chalmers who had taken a blow to the face. Gregor Townsend switched from centre to fly-half and this seemed to give the backline more bite and penetration.

Hastings's kick made it 17–6 but thereafter the points all came from the Welsh. And from tries too. Rayer, who had come on for the injured Nigel

Walker, underlined his 'super-sub' status with a second try which Jenkins converted and Ieuan Evans brought proceedings to a close with an 'aquaplane' try in injury time. At the same time Scotland's third casualty of the afternoon was preparing to head for the dressing-room. Andy Nicol had damaged his ribs and would be out for two to three weeks. It was desperately bad luck on Nicol but a rugby nation's prayers were about to be answered. Gary Armstrong was about to come in from the cold.

Armstrong had watched the Welsh defeat on TV after turning out for Jed-Forest against Langholm. Significantly, he had played in the No.9 shirt that day. His self-imposed exile had been gradually broken, firstly for the District Select side against Auckland and then for the Barbarians against the All Blacks. In the latter game, when he showed that he had lost none of his scrumhalf prowess, he had sustained a rib injury ironically not dissimilar to that which had laid low Nicol.

The Scottish selectors now made their move to entice Armstrong back to the national cause. Team manager Duncan Paterson made the telephone call in which Armstrong agreed that he would once again be available for selection in the scrumhalf berth.

However, when the team for the Calcutta Cup match was announced, that old stand-by A.N. Other was pencilled in at scrumhalf. Armstrong had wanted to prove that he was fit enough not to make a fool of himself at international level. There then followed a fortnight's hard graft at Riverside Park under the tutelage of Jed trainer Chico Woods. Armstrong was given the afternoons off by his employers, Mainetti UK, during which he further honed his already impressive natural fitness. He played for his club against Gala a fortnight before the England game and proved to everyone's satisfaction (but most importantly his own) that he was up to the task.

Murrayfield itself looked a treat on Saturday 5 February. Contractors had worked around the clock to bring almost all of the new West stand into commission. As per schedule, only the wing sections remained to be completed and through it all, thanks to careful nurturing by head groundsman Bill Elwood and his staff, the Murrayfield playing surface looked as billiard-table good as it had ever done.

Armstrong wasn't the only fresh face in the side for the Royal Bank of Scotland International against England. The selectors had been hard at work since the Cardiff defeat. Doug Wyllie and Scott Hastings made up an unusual pairing in the centre. The Northampton flanker Peter Walton (all 17½-stone of him) was brought in to add some punch to the back-row where Doddie Weir, only a replacement in Cardiff but still the Scots' most reliable ball-provider, was restored to No.8. The trio was completed by Rob Wainwright who was to have his most satisfying (although curtailed) game in a Scottish jersey. Also winning his first cap (a year after his initial injury-jinxed selection) was the rugged Bristol prop-forward Alan Sharp, and Andy Reed made his Five Nations Championship return after injury.

But, Armstrong aside, the biggest talking point wasn't who was in the team. The major topic of conversation in rugby clubs and taverns around the land concerned the omission of Craig Minto Chalmers. 'Chic' had been a virtually permanent fixture in the side since his debut against Wales in 1989. Subsequently he played in 35 of the next 36 cap internationals. However, throughout the season he had battled unsuccessfully against injury and adversity. The edge and control which he had invariably shown just weren't there and Chalmers stepped aside to make way for Gregor Townsend, the Gala youngster who had switched to fly-half when Chalmers had sustained a facial knock in Cardiff. There was a bitter irony in the fact that with Armstrong rescued from his self-imposed exile there would be no 'Chic' around to be on the receiving end of his passes.

The Scottish camp had been under extreme pressure during the lead-up to the game. The fans and the players were desperate for a restoration of the passion which had been missing from the previous two outings. On that score at least nobody was to be disappointed.

It was an emotional roller-coaster of a game. The lead changed hands on six occasions as first one side and then the other took control. The atmosphere, too, was of a different order to that which had prevailed on All Black Saturday. Then, the West stand had been out of commission, a temporary affair having been constructed on the West touchline for VIPs. Now, though, all four sides of the ground were back in play and the almost claustrophobic atmosphere which is a virtual requirement of any big sporting occasion was back with a vengeance.

England began well; so well, in fact, that for 10 or 15 minutes it seemed as though Scotland would be on another hiding to nothing. The visitors took the lead after five minutes when Jonathan Callard, who was to play such a crucial role in the afternoon's proceedings, slotted home the first of his five penalty goals. Scotland were still under intense English pressure when Gavin Hastings missed the first of several kicks at goal in the 14th minute.

However, a storming run by Armstrong and an unsuccessful drop-goal effort by Townsend gave the first indication that the tide was turning in Scotland's favour. Then, in the 23rd minute, the Scots forced a scrummage near the England line. Armstrong, who was playing as if he had never been away, broke from the rear of the scrum, dummied, and almost evaded John Hall's crucial tackle. The crowd were sure that Armstrong had scored but the ball had been grounded initially just two or three inches short of the line.

Four minutes later Hastings missed with his second penalty-goal attempt but from the restart Rob Andrew kicked the ball straight back to the Scotland fullback who initiated Scotland's second real try-scoring opportunity of the afternoon.

Hastings put up the 'bomb', Andrew Reed secured possession and set Stanger off on a storming run which caused panic in English ranks. Rob Wainwright took the ball on the inside and pinned back his ears for a 22-metre dash to the line. Phil de Glanville covered across but the 6 ft 4 ins Scottish flanker rode the centre's tackle and went over for the try. Murrayfield was ecstatic. Scotland had taken the lead after 28 minutes. Callard and Andrew both missed with penalty-goal attempts before the interval and Scotland went into the second half with a slim, two-point cushion.

Three minutes later Hastings kicked his side further ahead with a huge penalty goal from just inside the England half and at last there was daylight between the two evenly matched sides.

Armstrong, who had forever been found where the action was thickest, left the field for five minutes to have a head wound swathed in bandages but he was soon back to take over once again from temporary replacement Bryan Redpath.

In the 52nd minute Callard kicked England back on terms with another penalty goal and seven minutes later put his side in front with a similar effort. The lead changed hands again on the hour mark when Hastings was successful with a penalty kick awarded as the off-side England backs had thwarted a Townsend drop-goal attempt.

Scotland's injury jinx struck again as Wainwright, who had been an inspiration, succumbed to facial damage and Iain Smith came on as replacement. Meanwhile Hastings had missed with two more penalty kicks and the family misery was compounded as brother Scott was forced to retire with a leg injury.

But the drama wasn't over even yet. In fact the final act was just about to begin. Callard kicked England back into an 11–12 lead with a penalty goal six minutes from the end and both sides still had everything to play for.

Scotland continued to press and, with 79 minutes 59 seconds showing on the clock, Gregor Townsend was finally successful with the drop-goal that he had been threatening to send between the uprights all afternoon. Gasps of joy and relief echoed around the tense Murrayfield stadium. Surely Scotland couldn't lose now, could they? Well yes, they could and they did.

England rushed to restart and Townsend blocked an Andrew drop at goal. Then, with only seconds remaining, the referee Lindsay McLachlan awarded England a penalty after Scotland were adjudged to have handled in a ruck. The seemingly contradictory signals which Mr McLachlan gave as he blew his whistle were only the forerunners of the controversy which was to ensue. The referee appeared to indicate that the ball had been swept to his left, i.e. towards English ranks. At once the Scotland players seemed to be bamboozled by the decision. Subsequently, far from conclusive video evidence appeared to show that the guilty hand had belonged to England's Rob Andrew and not to Ian Jardine who had come on as a replacement for Scott Hastings. But in reality it mattered not. The referee is not equipped with action-replay equipment and to carp about refereeing errors on the basis of what freeze-frame TV evidence might or might not show serves only to make a difficult job even harder. One cannot help but feel that the old maxim which has it that the referee is never more right than when he is wrong is the correct one for the good of the game.

However, the controversy which subsequently enveloped the referee's decision has tended to diminish the fact that Jon Callard's match-winning penalty goal must rank as one of the greatest pressure kicks of all time. In such circumstances and from a distance of some 42 or 43 metres it was far from a foregone conclusion. The ball flew high in the air, toppling end over end as it sped straight and true between the uprights. The England players whooped in delight while the Scots stood and stared in shocked disbelief. Immediately Mr McLachlan blew for no-side and England had won by a single point. The final scoreline of 15–14 reflected an engrossing contest which had showed that the Scottish side had restored pride in themselves. And that this was, indeed, the case was evidenced by the fact that both sides, but particularly the Scots, were given a standing ovation as they left the field.

The game had been played at an emotional intensity seldom seen even at international level. Afterwards, a delighted Will Carling said that it had been a 'hell of a game' and that he would probably be buying Jon Callard beer for the rest of his life!

The joy and relief so evident in the England camp was in direct contrast to the disbelief and deep disappointment felt by the Scots. They felt that they had done enough to win, which they had, and that to have lost in such circumstances, to a debateable refereeing decision with the final kick of the game, was just too hard to take.

None felt the despair worse than the skipper Gavin Hastings. Appearing on nationwide TV just moments after the game Hastings was distraught. His face drawn and grey from the physical and emotional effort of the previous 80 minutes, Hastings broke down and was unable to continue the interview. 'I don't think I've ever experienced so many highs and lows in a game and when Gregor put over that kick . . .', his voice cracking with emotion, trailed away to nothing. Then he struggled to add: '. . . just to lose it in the last minute . . . you saw the real Scotland out there.'

The interview was curtailed. In recent years TV has become ever more intrusive with microphones and cameras stuck under the noses of sportsmen and women just as they have finished competing. The practice began in athletics where athletes still gasping for breath were asked the inevitable question: 'How did it feel?' Perhaps in light of Hastings's breakdown, TV companies should reflect upon the need to allow a decent interval to elapse before sportsmen still on an emotional high or low are asked to share their thoughts with the watching public.

With the exception of a clumsily callous column in a London-based Sunday newspaper there was widespread sympathy for Hastings. This was emotion in the raw with no hint of the cynicism which often bedevils top-class sport. The message was clear. Losing hurts. In defeat the Scots had done much to restore morale and pride but still that desperately sought-after win eluded them. The feeling was that the Calcutta Cup performance had provided a platform on which to build and that the next outing, against the Irish, would bring a win.

Scotland had a month in which to reflect on the season thus far. And in the interim Ireland went to Twickenham and won. The prospect of travelling to Dublin to meet an Irish side with their confidence on a new-found high prompted coach Dougie Morgan to observe (with more sincerity than the usual coaching mantra that the next game's the most important one) that the Lansdowne Road sojourn could be the hardest of the season.

But in sharp contrast to the sun-dappled Murrayfield which had played host to the Calcutta Cup cliff-hanger, Lansdowne Road was seemingly at the eye of an Irish hurricane. The wind and rain howled down the pitch and blew away the pre-match plans of both sides. So atrocious were the conditions that rugby football in the proper sense of the term was impossible.

The gale snatched at kicks, passes were blown astray but Scotland seemed set to secure second-half victory after an opening period in which the forwards more than matched their Irish counterparts. Nevertheless, the Scots reached the interval 3–0 adrift after an Eric Elwood penalty goal. Two penalty goals from the Scottish skipper saw Scotland in the lead and there was just the slightest hint that Scotland were about to secure their first win of the season. Then, some ten minutes before the end, Elwood booted over the equalising penalty and the spoils were shared.

Scotland had failed to capitalise on what passed for swirling wind advantage in the second period but at least, with just a share of the spoils, some badly needed Championship points had accrued.

Then it emerged that the injury hoodoo had struck again. And it did so against the player that Scotland could most ill afford to lose. Gary Armstrong – alongside Reed and the Scots' front row – had been the man of the match. He had been at his terrier-like best. However, an injury to a thumb which Armstrong had tried to ignore and 'play through' turned out to be much worse than expected. And when the true severity of the injury became apparent his team-mates wondered how on earth he had managed to complete the game. The right thumb had been wrenched back and simultaneously twisted. The tendons had become detached from the bone and within 36 hours the Jed scrumhalf was on an operating table in Edinburgh. His re-emergence on to the international stage had been like a breath of fresh Border air. But now he was out for the remainder of the Championship season and Scotland's selectorial problems continued.

So, a strangely lacklustre Championship season was drawing to a conclusion. The quality of the rugby played by all five contenders had been far short of that normally expected. Tries (only 20 in total) were almost an endangered species while the penalty goal surely played a greater role in the outcome of many games than ever it was the intention of the legislators.

Some indication of just how ordinary a season it had been can be gathered from the fact that on the final Championship Saturday, as Scotland entertained France at Murrayfield and tried to keep the Wooden Spoon at bay, Wales were going for a Grand Slam at Twickenham. This is not to denigrate the Welsh performance. Their recovery from the dark days of the 1991 World Cup has been quite remarkable. And yet they never looked like a Grand Slam side should.

For the Hastings brothers, the Royal Bank of Scotland International against the French saw the passing of a family milestone. The duo – great servants to Scottish rugby both – notched up the unique achievement of 50 caps apiece, a record unlikely to be repeated.

The Scots found themselves ten points adrift after 18 minutes with the French scoring a try through Jean-Luc Sadourny and a conversion and penalty by Thierry Lacroix. Three penalty goals by the Scottish skipper saw the home side back on terms but Lacroix kicked the French into a 9–13 half-time lead with his second penalty goal.

In the 54th minute came one of those moments which has the crowd uttering a collective sigh. Gregor Townsend telegraphed his intention to transfer the ball to Gavin Hastings. The French skipper Phillipe Saint-Andre, presumably unable to believe his good fortune, snapped up the interception like a startled rabbit and (if such a thing is possible!) hared off for the line. Pierre Montlaur's conversion made it 9–20 and Scotland were in deep trouble. A Hastings penalty goal served only to narrow the deficit to 12–20 and France secured their first Murrayfield win since 1978.

Down at Twickenham England were dashing Welsh Grand Slam hopes by winning 15–8. Wales won the Championship but were denied the Grand Slam. The Welsh would not agree but to most neutral observers that seemed about right.

What then could Scotland take from a such a season? The emergence of Peter Walton augurs well for the future as does the belated appearance in a Scotland jersey of his fellow Exile Alan Sharp. Rob Wainwright played with style and panache and marked himself out as a likely future Scotland captain. Andy Reed was back on song, Doddie Weir continues to improve with age and Shade Munro has all the makings of a hard-grafting lock.

Behind the scrum, Gregor Townsend was more comprehensively blooded and the selectors now have a better idea of what he is capable of. In which regard it might well be that, in the short term, inside-centre alongside a recalled Craig Chalmers at fly-half might be the optimum choice. And finally, Gary Armstrong was wooed back from self-imposed exile.

- Armstrong seemed a certainty for further Scottish honours and looked likely to be the mainstay of Scotland's effort in the 1995 World Cup. However, a desperate training injury to his left knee of the eve of the 1994–95 season has cast the future in doubt. Scotland can ill afford to be without him for one of the busiest international seasons in the history of the game.

FINAL TABLE

	P	W	D	L	F	A	Pt
Wales	4	3	0	1	78	51	6
England	4	3	0	1	60	49	6
France	4	2	0	2	84	69	4
Ireland	4	1	1	2	49	70	3
Scotland	4	0	1	3	38	70	1

Stirling County's hooker Kevin McKenzie flourished in A Team guise. Here, for Scotland A against New Zealand, he performs above and beyond the call of duty with a daring attempt to stop 'Inga the Winga' in his tracks (The Herald)

McKenzie's Men Take Two from Four

THE A TEAM SEASON

By Graham Law

SPONSORSHIP is far from a novelty in rugby these days but it said much for the driving force behind the renaissance of the Scotland A rugby team in the past season that he was to be feted like some multi-capped, pretty-boy wing instead of cold-shouldered as a denizen of the front-row still seeking that coveted first cap.

The advertising slogan says: 'You can with a Nissan.' Hooker Kevin McKenzie was to discover because *he could* on the rugby pitch, particularly in the colours of Scotland A, whom he led to their two victories in 1993–94, that a car was presented to him by the Weir Nissan garage at Cambusbarron.

McKenzie duly attained full-cap status playing in both Tests on Scotland's summer tour to Argentina. In the second Test, he had something of a brainstorm, attempting and missing a drop-goal in the game's closing stages as the tourists sought to overturn a 17–19 deficit. Even to contemplate a drop-goal would have had most hookers drummed out of the front-row union. Typical of McKenzie, he did not duck the issue. 'I wish I had never attempted it. But at least I had the bottle to have a go,' he mused. The incident spawned one of those lovely tour nicknames as McKenzie was christened 'Lescarboura' by unsympathetic colleagues.

There again, McKenzie is something of a mould-breaker. When Glasgow won the Inter-District title in 1989–90, SRU president Jimmy McNeil popped in to offer his congratulations. McKenzie, irreverently (though without any malice) ordered his cohorts: 'Quiet for the bufty.' McKenzie's irrepressible nature was very much in evidence during the A campaign in which he played in all four matches – against New Zealand, Italy, Ireland and France. He

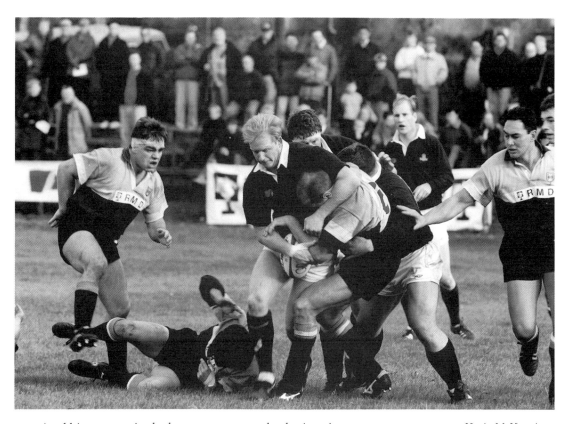

captained his country in the last two contests, both victories.

Here was an individual who had played at every level for Scotland since he first surfaced as an eight-year-old convert to mini-rugby at the prodigious Stirling County nursery.

His introduction was not without problems, however. On his first day at Stirling, he was banned from the club! He admitted: 'It's become part of club folklore but it's true. An army major, Ian Nelson, was looking after my age-group. I was sent off and made matters worse by swearing at Major Nelson. They told me to leave and never come back because they did not need my type there. But all my pals were there and I was really keen to play, so I apologised to Major Nelson and was allowed back.'

The discipline which McKenzie found in rugby was a godsend. He was transformed from being a 'right wee reprobate' in his early years at Dunblane High School to the deputy head boy who twice captained the Scottish Schools rugby team in 1985–86, including a rare success (10–7) against England.

It's a discipline, McKenzie asserts, he needs even now. 'I have tried easing back on my training and staying away from the gym for a few days but I just get so crabbit sitting about the house that my wife, Fiona, will tell me to go out for a run,' he explained.

McKenzie began weight-training under the guidance of his former Sunday school teacher, Dave Crofts. At first, he attended more out of loyalty to his

Kevin McKenzie again. This time in typically belligerent form for Glasgow against Edinburgh (The Herald)

Andy Nicol is well into his running in this shot from the Scotland A v Ireland A encounter (The Herald)

Stirling County team-mate, Chris Brown, but as the latter's interest waned, McKenzie ploughed on. 'When you are only 5 ft 6 ins, it's very appealing to try to build up,' he related. Crofts's job with the Ministry of Defence took him to Bristol, where he is weights advisor to the Courage League first division club. 'Not long after he went down, he phoned me about this really strong prop they had and reckoned it would be great if we could both play together for Scotland,' McKenzie recounted.

That prop was Alan Sharp and the vision materialised, initially in the colours of Scotland A in Italy, then in the full team on the Argentine tour. 'One thing Dave was spot-on about was Sharpie's strength. He's just awesome,' McKenzie volunteered.

Long before the pair combined, though, McKenzie had known the vicissitudes of international selection and was much the wiser for it.

He had graduated through the under-19 and -21 ranks and appeared in the 22–22 draw against Ireland in the 1989 B international at Murrayfield before the national representative well ran dry.

For four years, McKenzie had to simmer on the sidelines as he continued to demonstrate his worth for club and district. He could understand (well, almost) when players whom he respected, such as Jim Hay, Martin Scott or Ian Corcoran were preferred. Yet he had to button his lip when Harry Roberts, the South African Scot who had a brief flirtation with the land of his

granny, won a B cap in 1990.

No one, other than those privy to the machinations of the selectors, would be able to explain McKenzie's prolonged absence. That said, he tried hard to dismiss thoughts that he had missed the boat. 'I sought to concentrate on my games for the club and I always believed that if given the chance, I would be good enough,' he stated.

The first concrete signs of a return to favour came during the 1993 Scotland tour to the South Pacific. When Martin Scott suffered rib damage in Tonga, manager Allan Hosie, the former international referee, tried to summon McKenzie from home. But to McKenzie's dismay, he was unable to take up the chance, having just started a new sales post with Taylor Maxwell Timber, a company which McKenzie praises for the amount of time it allows him to devote to rugby. At that stage, though, time off was just not feasible.

The new season dawned and McKenzie, by his own admission, was intent on 'sticking in', purely to advance the cause of the club. Road-running and weight-training had seen his mighty-atom frame bulk up to almost 15 stones and when he was named in the autumn in a 24-strong Scotland squad as understudy to British Lion Kenny Milne, he hoped the wheel of fortune had turned.

The oft-voiced criticisms that he was too small, or gave away too many penalties, were forgotten. Instead, the consensus, as outlined by the A team manager, Kelso's Arthur Hastie, was that McKenzie was 'prepared to put his life on the line for the cause'. How such indomitable qualities were needed when New Zealand arrived at Old Anniesland for the first A game of the

Boroughmuir celebrate Cup success. Advocates of a competitive Scottish Cup competition maintain it will further hone player skills en route to District, A Team and full International honours
(The Herald)

season. Three days before the match, the South, Scotland's District champions, had been blitzed 84–5 and the Scottish rugby community was reeling.

McKenzie viewed the contest from a different perspective. 'Sure, we were only too well aware of what had happened to the South. But, for me, at that stage, it was my biggest occasion. For the first time in my life, I had a chance to play against an established international hooker, in an international. Better than that, I was not going to be compared to any old Joe Bloggs, but to Sean Fitzpatrick, the most-capped hooker in the world.'

McKenzie won more than favourable comparisons to the illustrious Fitzpatrick as the Scotland A pack gave a stirring display which earned four of its members – Alan Watt, Andy Macdonald, David McIvor and Rob Wainwright – promotion to the full Scotland team the following week.

The clean lineout count – against an All Black pack which showed only one change the next week, Zinzan Brooke for Paul Henderson on the flank – was 26–13 in Scotland A's favour, while the passion which McIvor and Wainwright, especially, brought to loose play was equally encouraging.

The Scots could not notch a try – Marc Ellis crossed for the lone All Blacks try – and their goal-kicking did not keep pace with Matthew Cooper's five penalties from eight attempts.

The Scots' points in a 9–20 demise stemmed from two drop-goals from captain Douglas Wyllie and a Michael Dods penalty. The backs might have done better, on occasions, to have kept the ball in hand, but Ian Jardine's typically pulverising weight of tackle was just what the doctor ordered and he was another to deserve his promotion to the senior team.

Douglas Wyllie's leadership of the A team that day – he had replaced the

Ian Jardine, one of the many who emerged from the A Team to secure full international status. Here in action against Ireland A (The Herald)

Rob Wainwright, Gary Armstrong, Shade Munro, Andrew Reed, Peter Walton and Doddie Weir admire Kyran Bracken's service (The Herald)

That's it: Ian Smith, in common with almost the entire Murrayfield crowd, thinks victory is assured after Gregor Townsend's late drop-goal (The Herald)

Jonathan Callard kicks the last-second penalty goal which was to break Scottish hearts . . . (The Herald)

. . . and the ball speeds straight and true to give England a 15–14 win (The Herald)

Andrew Reed cuts a sad and lonely figure as the reality of Calcutta Cup defeat sinks in (The Herald)

The spray flies from a sodden Lansdowne Road as Gavin Hastings, bandaged after a clash of heads with Gary Armstrong, slots home a successful penalty attempt (The Herald)

Now, now, boys: the referee steps in as Weir, Reed, Burnell and Milne look on
(The Herald)

Sleight of hand from Ian Smith as he is brought to ground by a pair of Irishmen
(The Herald)

*The Northampton flanker Peter Walton made a bold impression during his first season in
Scottish colours* (The Herald)

The French scrumhalf Alain Macabiau serves his stand-off as Smith, Munro and Burnell await developments (The Herald)

Zoot alors! *Gavin Hastings with no place to go as the Frenchmen pile in* (The Herald)

Lineout leap: Andy Reed soars skyward with just a little help from his friends
(The Herald)

A grimly determined Gregor Townsend makes for the gain line (The Herald)

Shade Munro, grandson of the former Scottish skipper J.M. Bannerman, opts for the direct route and takes the game to the Frenchmen (The Herald)

*The international
trial continues to
form an integral part
of the Scottish
season. Here Peter
Walton stakes a
successful claim for
higher honours*
(The Herald)

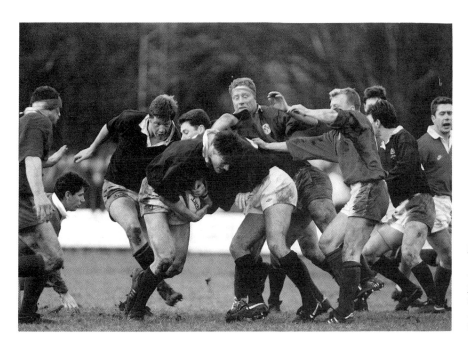

*The Scotland A
pack, with
Wainwright and
Munro to the fore,
prove more than a
handful for their
Irish counterparts*
(The Herald)

injured Craig Chalmers both as skipper and stand-off after the South's débâcle – won plaudits from the hierarchy. Not least for his hard-nosed assertion that it would be wrong to over-enthuse as the Scots had still lost the game.

Before the New Zealand international at Murrayfield, the newly constituted Scotland Development XV had to entertain the All Blacks at Myreside. The result – a 12–31 loss – was not surprising. The benefit for Scottish rugby, however, came again in the ability of a pack to take the battle to the enemy in the close-quarter exchanges. Four of the pack – lock Stewart Campbell and the entire back-row of Peter Walton, Fergus Wallace and Ian Smith – were to go on Scotland's summer tour, while the flankers both appeared for Scotland in the Five Nations Championship.

Australian Kent Bray – whose appearance trying out kilts on television's *Rugby Special* did not endear him to many whose nationality is not perceived as a badge of convenience – claimed the Development XV's points through four penalties. Eric Rush, Liam Barry and John Mitchell led the All Blacks' response with tries, Shane Howarth converting two and goaling four penalties.

The next month was a desperate time for Scottish rugby. A record defeat (15–51) by New Zealand at Murrayfield was followed by a 15–18 setback for the A team against Italy in Rovigo, where the forwards' performance did not dip much below the customary standard – Walton excelling in the nitty-gritty – but the backs failed to unlock a flat Italian defence, either through guile or through kicking from hand at half-back, an area where the Italians were well-served by their Argentine-born stand-off, Diego Dominguez.

It was of no consolation that Italy had fielded effectively their full national team and that advertising in the town ignored the A status of the Scotland side. The lack of spark had omens for the rest of the season. Dominguez goaled six penalties from nine attempts for the hosts and Michael Dods five from seven for Scotland and that summed up an unedifying match to which the selectors reacted by switching captaincy to McKenzie and including an additional six full caps for the home A match against Ireland in late December. Victory was badly needed to restore morale and it arrived courtesy of a three tries to nil, 24–9 scoreline, tries emanating from Iain Morrison, Wainwright and Shade Munro.

Morrison, the openside flanker, had made a tremendous recovery from knee cartilage damage which had affected him from March 1993. It was hard to believe that prior to the match he had played only a handful of club games, the majority for junior XVs at London Scottish, and it was a major blow to Scotland's progress in the Five Nations Championship when he broke his leg against Wales. It somehow seemed appropriate that as the A match had been switched from its original venue of Hughenden in Glasgow to Ayr's Millbrae ground – a stone's throw from Robert Burns's cottage – that Morrison should rove relentlessly in Scotland's cause.

Another player recently returned from injury, Gala stand-off Gregor Townsend, made a considerable impact. Townsend had by no means an entirely flawless day with his goal-kicking – he landed three conversions and a penalty from nine attempts at goal – but he did kick well from hand and had his outside backs involved in something more aesthetic than the pursuit of high kicks. Scottish relief was tempered by the knowledge that the Irish had given such a disjointed display, their only points emanating from three penalties from stand-off Alan McGowan.

At least, as McKenzie reflected at the post-match dinner, the duck had been broken, the forwards continued to chug and the efforts of coaches David Johnston and Hugh Campbell had been rewarded.

It was two months before the next A international – Scotland's last of the season – in the capital of Brittany, and birthplace of the French Revolution, Rennes. Only five of the team who had beaten the Irish remained, but there were some significant additions: David McIvor and Carl Hogg in the back-row and Craig Chalmers at stand-off.

The Scots entered the fray having lost their opening two matches in the Five Nations Championship, 6–29 to Wales in Cardiff and then 14–15 in the climactic Calcutta Cup clash at Murrayfield.

The A team were again having to adopt the mantle of standard bearers – a task they did proudly.

The Scots certainly were fortunate that on match day it rained incessantly and that the pitch quickly became a quagmire – conditions alien to many of the French backs, raised on the firm pitches in the deep south of the country. No matter, the Scottish pack, in Johnston's phrase, were 'collectively outstanding'. They had had their alarms pre-match, Alan Watt, the 6 ft 5 ins, GHK forward, suffering food poisoning after he had eaten a sandwich from a local café. His place was taken by Boroughmuir's Peter Wright, while the Gloucester prop, Peter Jones, had to catch an early morning flight from Heathrow to fulfil replacement duties.

Watt's absence placed a heavy onus on Stewart Campbell to produce lineout ball, but the Dundee student responded magnificently and with McIvor, Hogg and Stuart Reid, embellishing Scotland's first-phase possession with a unity, spine-in-line, on the drive in the loose, it only needed the backs to complement the forwards' endeavours for success to follow.

Chalmers, keeping his forwards going forward, dropped a goal, and Michael Dods was on target with three penalties out of four. His most crucial effort with the old-fashioned Wallaby ball, which was caked in mud, came ten minutes from no-side. It was close to the left touchline, from a distance of 40 metres, angle included, but Dods kept the trajectory low and the ball just made it. Scotland still had to defend feverishly in the remaining time but the French did not add to their three penalties from fullback Laurent Labit.

McKenzie reflected at the lavish after-match celebrations, to which it seemed every rugby club in the area had been invited, that he hoped the selectors would remember what so many of the uncapped players had achieved in the A victories. The message was not lost. By the end of the season, six players who featured in the matches against Ireland and France had been added to the list of full Scotland caps – Michael Dods, Scott Nichol, Alan Sharp, Shade Munro, Peter Walton and McKenzie.

One forward who had seen McKenzie's captaincy at close-quarters noted: 'I'm not a player who has to indulge in anything heavy before a game to get myself motivated. All I need is to pull on the jersey and I'm up and running. But for those who have to be fired up, I don't think there is anyone in a Scottish context more suited to that than Kevin McKenzie. He may not always say exactly the right thing but you can never doubt the sincerity with which it is expressed and how much it all means to him.'

'Guid Fun' and Hard Knocks

GARY ARMSTRONG PROFILE

By Derek Douglas

The Reluctant Hero's Comeback Season

❛I HAD made my mind up in the summer. I had discussed it with my dad and the family and sent a letter to the SRU saying that I really needed a fresh challenge, that I was going to try playing somewhere other than scrumhalf.

It didn't turn out the way that I wanted it to of course because Jed were struggling in the League and we were in the relegation zone for a while. I then came under pressure from different sources to go back to scrumhalf.

Jed were always asking me to go back to scrumhalf but I didn't want to do that while Grant Farquharson was still there. He had come back from Gala to take over from me at scrumhalf. But before Christmas we were second bottom in the league and really struggling for points. Things ▷

LANSDOWNE Road, Dublin, 5 March 1994. Scotland have just recorded a 6–6 draw against the Irish. The first Championship win of the season still evades them, but, arguably, of even greater significance is the hand injury suffered by Gary Armstrong. The full extent of the problem is not immediately apparent and seems not to have affected Armstrong's performance that afternoon in Dublin which has been that of a thoroughbred. A thoroughbred Border Terrier perhaps, but a thorougbred nonetheless. He has played a game of such distinction that the former Irish flanker Fergus Slattery is moved to observe that if Armstrong hadn't been on parade then the crowd could have demanded their money back.

Three days later the Scotland scrumhalf is undergoing surgery at the Edinburgh Royal Infirmary and the news isn't good.

The official bulletin is delivered by SRU chief executive Bill Hogg: 'Gary Armstrong has torn ligaments at the base of his thumb and he'll be out for six to eight weeks. It's very sad. Gary has made the most tremendous impact in the two matches he has played since his return.'

Scotland coach Douglas Morgan is less prosaic: 'Well, that's it. He's out and with the French game still to come we have no option but to look forward. Still, it maybe proves he's not from another planet after all!'

The coach makes the extra-terrestrial observation with a rueful smile flickering on his furrowed features. Morgan, in his playing days a British Lion and an uncompromisingly competitive scrumhalf, knows more than most about the life of hard knocks experienced by

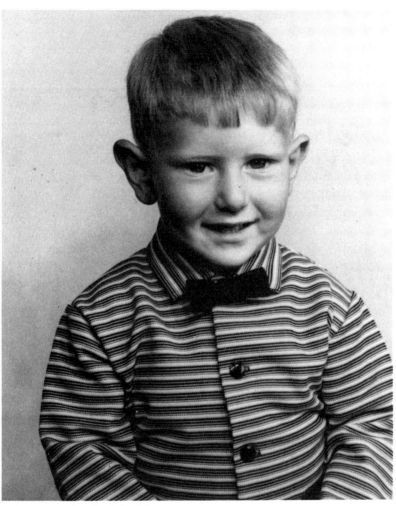

Who's a pretty boy then? Aged four

wearers of the No. 9 jersey. He knows, too, that Armstrong's enforced absence from the final game of the Championship season will be a bitter, bitter blow.

GARY Armstrong, a son of Jedburgh but born on 30 September 1966 in Edinburgh, is in rugby terms a man apart. Currently, he is without doubt the best scrumhalf in the world. And more, he is one of the best scrumhalves the world has seen, ever. But why stop there. Gary Armstrong is, pound for pound, one of the best players ever to have graced the sport of rugby union football.

There are now no technical flaws in his game. He has more than mastered the un-Holy Trinity of scrumhalf play. He can pass. He can run. He can kick. But that's just for starters. Armstrong possesses a

▷ were beginning to look really grim.

The situation with Grant was tricky. But the way things turned out the team wasn't playing worth a damn. This is nothing against Grant. There was a definite problem, though.

At the end of the day it was left up to the club. They said that either Grant was to be replaced by somebody else or I was going back to scrumhalf. I was coming under a lot of pressure and I decided that I would go back to scrumhalf because the selectors had said that they were going to replace Grant anyway.

During the break away from scrumhalf I had got my appetite for the game back. I was enjoying my rugby again but I wasn't enjoying all the mucking about. I was only getting a couple of games in a position before I was being moved again. I had said to the selectors at the beginning of the season that I would have been quite happy to have started off in the seconds and to have worked my way up but they didn't want that. I was chopping and changing all the time. It wasn't any good for me or the club. I played at stand-off, inside-centre, outside-centre and even at fullback for half a game. After that I was back to scrumhalf.

The change happened after I was approached by the District Select asking if I would play scrumhalf for them against Auckland at Mansfield Park. They were short of players because of the All Blacks being across at the same time and the games against the South and the A Team and so on. I said that I would play.

It went OK. I enjoyed it. It ▷

▷ took ten minutes or so to get back into the way of it. I didn't find the pace of the game a problem. It was just getting back into the way of operating at the base of the scrum again. After ten minutes, though, it was as if I had never been away.

That was the first time I'd played at scrumhalf that year. I really enjoyed it. Then I got an invite to go down to play against the All Blacks for the Barbarians at Cardiff. That was after Scotland had had their drubbing.

My position was just as it had always been. I was always available to play international rugby but I didn't want to play scrumhalf. OK, maybe they were never going to pick me anywhere else and at the end of the day maybe it was just a break away that I needed, to recharge the batteries, that kind of thing. But after watching Scotland being drubbed by the All Blacks that got me fired up and then, with the Barbarians, I actually got the chance to play against them. Because of what had happened at Murrayfield I really wanted to have a go at the New Zealanders. The Baa Baas had a good side and I really thought that we could have beaten them.

I watched the All Blacks game at Murrayfield from the stand. I thought the reason for the defeat was simple. We were feart o' them. OK, the All Blacks were a good team but we showed them far too much respect. We should have got stuck in about them. By the end they were just taking the mickey out of us. If you think that you're up there with the big boys then no side should beat you 51–15. It was just embarrassing. Then, ▷

tactical awareness that can sometimes be just plain scary. Instinctively, it seems, he just knows what's going to happen next. It's almost as if he has read the script. This sixth sense gives him the uncanny ability to pop up anywhere; to make the try-saving tackle; to make the try-scoring link; or to take the final pass at the line.

In defence he is rock-solid and in attack he seems to have computed the options and made the right selection while opponents are still mentally and physically struggling to get on the pace.

Armstrong is also immensely strong and fantastically – sometimes rashly – brave. His 5 ft 8 ins, 13 st 10 lb frame has taken a terrible pounding over the years. During that 5 March game at Lansdowne Road he had been involved in a collision with Gavin Hastings. The Scotland skipper is no shrinking violet himself but he came off decidedly second-best with a head wound that required four of those new-fangled staples. 'Gary's hewn from a block of granite,' Hastings later remarked.

Outwith the rugby environment Gary Armstrong is, to put it mildly, of a retiring disposition. But on the field of play he comes alive. He is in his natural element. For Scotland, the Lions or Jed he never gives second best. But removed from the cauldron of international rugby he is just a regular guy; a family man who drives a lorry for Mainetti (UK) in Jedburgh. He won't use two words when one will do and he is unfazed to the point of embarrassment by the praise of those who recognise and laud his singular rugby talents. He has shunned approaches from Rugby League, thus turning his back on a way of life that would have earned him some big bucks in a sporting environment for which he seems to have been tailor-made. Why?

Mini rugby at Jed. Gary is in the back row, extreme left

Seven-a-side success with Jed-Thistle

▷ when I was walking out of
the stand at the end, I heard
somebody shouting: "It's all
your fault Gary Armstrong."
OK, maybe they were only
kidding but that got me to
thinking.

Sitting watching the boys
taking a drubbing like that you
would have to be made of
wood if it didn't get to you.
You're Scottish through and
through and it really hurts to
see Scotland being howked like
that. So when I got the phone-
call from the Baa Baas
secretary Mickey Steele-
Bodger after the Auckland
game asking if I was available
for selection I said that I was.
Later on he phoned back to say
that I'd been picked. The other
Scots in the side were Scott
Hastings and Rob
Wainwright. The Baa Baas had
a good team out and I
genuinely thought we could
have taken the All Blacks. As it
was we went down – but I
think we gave a good account
of ourselves.

I was really enjoying playing
in front of a big crowd again
and, from a personal point of
view, everything was going
OK until about 15 minutes
into the second half when I
sprung a rib cartilage and that
was me out for five weeks. It
was a bit of a sickener but
you've just got to get up and
get on with it. I don't really
know what happened. I fell
awkwardly and the cartilage
just popped.

I'd just come back from the
groin injury and I'd been out
with the knee injury the season
before so all of that does flash
through your mind and you
think here we go again. I tried
to play on but every time I was
tackled the cartilage would just
pop out again. It was getting ▷

▷ sorer and sorer and so I just had to call it a day.

I wasn't fit again until after the New Year. I came back for Jed against Langholm on the day that Scotland lost to Wales in Cardiff. I watched the Welsh game on the telly. There didn't seem to be any get–up and go about the boys. It was just flat. Wales took advantage of the mistakes that Scotland made and there didn't seem to be any fire about them. They were just flat. Cardiff is always a hard place to go to and win. Even when we won the Grand Slam in 1990 it was a close game down there.

Andy Nicol damaged his ribs in the last minutes of the game and he was out. After that I got the call from the SRU asking if I was available. Actually Alistair McIntosh, my boss at Mainetti, took the first call from Duncan Paterson because I was away.

At the end of the summer in 1993 I had phoned Duncie to tell him what the position was and Duncie had said that if they needed me in an emergency could they call on me. I had said that I wanted to leave my options open but if they were struggling then of course they should get in touch.

When my boss told me that Duncan was looking for me I said that I wasn't anywhere near fit enough to play international rugby. Alistair, who's a Dundee HSFP man, said that they would get me fit. Duncie telephoned me that night and it all happened from there.

I had three weeks to get ready between the Welsh game and the English game and Mainetti gave me every afternoon off to train with ▷

Early recognition with Dunferline HS. Gary is seated front row, extreme right

'Well, I like Jedburgh. I like playing for Jed–Forest. I like the crack wi' the lads. I'm happy here with Shona and the kids. And, ee ken, there's mair tae life than money,' he says.

Such is the extent of Armstrong's unpretentiousness that, in conversation, it is often difficult to appreciate that here is a sportsman of genuine world class. If he were a football player, an athlete or a racing driver then he would be lauded from the roof-tops with a lifestyle to match. None of which is to say that Gary Armstrong doesn't know how good he is. He does. Or at least one suspects he does. But he doesn't see the point, or feel it necessary, to tell people how good he is. It's a sporting cliché but it's true nonetheless. He doesn't come even close to talking a good game. But on the field of play, where he lets his boots and his body do the talking, he is as articulate as the world's greatest orator.

All of which is why when, during the late summer of 1993, Armstrong told Scotland team manager Duncan Paterson that he didn't want to play scrumhalf for Scotland any more it came as such a hammer-blow not only to Paterson but to the Scottish rugby nation at large. In the past two seasons Scotland had lost Calder, Jeffrey, White, Sole, Lineen, Tuklo and Dods. Others had been tried and tested and had come and gone. The team was in transition but Armstrong had seemed like the granite foundation block on which a new side could be built.

Now, he, too, had opted for voluntary exile. What he had told Duncan Paterson was not that he didn't want to play for Scotland but that he didn't want to play scrumhalf for Scotland. From anybody else

Jed-Thistle collect the spoils. Gary is kneeling second from the right in the front row

such a seemingly selfish statement of intent would have been dismissed as star-struck arrogance. But from the Scottish rugby public there was never even a hint that this was their verdict. There was just surprise and disappointment that Gary – always 'Gary' never 'Armstrong' – had come to this decision. From Paterson, too, there was understanding and the privately elicited promise that if, *in extremis*, his country really needed him then approaches could be made.

When Armstrong took the decision – after consultation with Shona and his mum and dad – his batteries were low after two years of hard rugby and injury-induced disappointment. He missed the 1992 Championship season after all but severing the medial ligament of the left knee in a game for Jed against Currie.

He was back in Scottish colours for 1993 but played throughout the Five Nations Championship with a groin injury sustained in the Murrayfield opener against Ireland. The injury was treated throughout the season and in the summer of that year the Lions trip to New Zealand beckoned. Still, though, the injury had not healed. It had become so troublesome and painful that often Armstrong had difficulty climbing out of bed in the morning.

Lions coach Ian McGeechan said that Armstrong's name had been the first to go down on the team-sheet when the touring party was selected. But he wouldn't be going. Shortly before the tourists flew out Armstrong failed a fitness test and was told by the medics that rest would be the most effective cure.

The groin injury, following on from the knee-ligament tear and

▷ Jed's Chico Woods. We trained at Riverside and at the gym. I did a lot of sprinting and wore a two-stone weights-jacket to build up my stamina.

The Scottish team to play against England was announced with A.N. Other at scrumhalf and I had to prove my fitness in Jed's game against Gala two weeks before the Calcutta Cup match. I suppose I was in the team but I didn't want to be selected until I had proved myself. I'd only had a couple of games since coming back from the Baa Baas cartilage injury and so it was important to me that I proved to myself that the ribs were OK and I wanted to test out my general fitness after the work that I'd been doing with Chico.

On the day against England I felt OK. The atmosphere at Murrayfield was great but, if anything, maybe I had done too much training in the lead-up to the game. I was still doing fitness work right up until the Wednesday when we got together as a squad.

It was a game which we should have won. There's no doubt about that. To lose 15–14 with the last kick of the game was really hard to take. With just a few minutes to go we all thought we had the game won. But the English took a quick kick-off and we weren't quite ready. If we'd got the ball then there was so little time left that it would have been blootered into the stands and that would have been it. That was where it was heading if we had got possession but we never got the ball back. Then England got their penalty and Callard kicked the goal.

It was a real sickener. We ▷

▷ had all put a lot of effort into winning that game after what had happened in Wales and then to be beaten by the last kick of the game was a bit of a disaster. If nothing else, though, we had proved to ourselves and to the Scottish public that we were capable of coming back after bad defeats by the New Zealanders and the Welsh.

The boys were really sick in the dressing-room because we knew we should have won. Gav was the worst because he'd missed a few penalties. But that's what rugby's all about. I was lying in the bath when he went away to do some TV interviews. When he came back he said he'd "Done a Gazza", I didn't know what the hell he was on about. Then he explained what had happened. It was understandable from his point of view. We all felt really cut up about what had happened. We were all feeling depressed and upset because we had lost a game that we should have won. But Gavin was so distressed that maybe the telly folk shouldn't have shown it.

We just had to pick ourselves up, though. It was Ireland next and we went across there with a game-plan that we were going to move it wide but it was howling a gale and belting down rain and we had to change the plan again. We aimed to keep it tight in the first half. It was a gale howling straight down the park. We played well. I think in the second half if we had played the same then we would have won but it was just the mental thing. You always feel that when you've got a strong wind behind you then you're going to win without any problems ▷

previous serious damage to elbows, ankles and knees must take a mental toll. Was it any wonder that Armstrong fancied a crack at a position away from the base of the scrummage? Now, though, and despite the 1994 injuries to the ribs and thumb, Armstrong has regained his appetite for the game and for the scrumhalf berth. He says that he is keen to add to his tally of 30 caps ('Is it 30? I'm not too sure really') and, barring unforeseen developments, is more than willing to put his hat into the selection ring for next season.

THE road which led to a current tally of 30 Scottish caps, a British Lions tour and recognition as the world's best scrumhalf began with a wife and mother's plaintive plea: 'Don't dare bring those boys home covered in glaur again.'

'Those boys' were the Armstrong brothers, Gary and Kevin. The speaker was mum Margaret and the target of her oft-repeated Sunday morning reproaches was dad Lawrence who at the time coached Jed-Forest's still burgeoning 'mini' section at Riverside Park.

Lawrence, in his playing days a Jed-Forest flanker-cum-centre, recalls: 'The boys would come down to Riverside with me when I was coaching the minis. Boys being boys they would usually end up filthy. Margaret said that if they were going with me then they would be as well joining in. So we got them kitted out and it didn't matter any more whether they got covered in glaur or not.'

Jed-Forest has been the bedrock of Armstrong's rugby life. Seen here in a 1993 game against Boroughmuir (The Herald)

The dressing-room aftermath of 1990 Grand Slam success (The Herald)

The comeback game: wooed back to the No9 jersey for the Scottish Districts' win over Auckland (The Herald)

▷ but it didn't happen.

The draw wasn't good enough and it looked like we were going to be playing for the wooden spoon. I'd never been in that situation before but in any case I knew after the Lansdowne Road game that I probably wouldn't be in the side to play the French at Murrayfield.

I had torn ligaments and tendons in my thumb. I can't even remember how it happened. There was just a general mêlée and I came out of it with a sair thumb. It felt at first like a bad stave but the pain was murder. It was worse than anything I had ever experienced before.

I went into hospital on the Monday and was operated on on the Tuesday. The surgeon reckoned that the thumb must have been bent back and twisted. The tendons were ripped off the bone. He said the injury was particularly common among skiers, in particular skiers who fall on the artificial slope at Hillend, near Edinburgh. The surgeon called it Hillend Thumb. But that was it for me. The international season was over. The medics said that I'd be out for six weeks but I was back after five. Looking back, it was a strange season for me. I definitely needed a break. I don't think folk have any real idea of the pressures that international rugby players are under these days. There's just not enough time in the day to fit in everything that you're supposed to do and hold down a full-time job, spend time with your family and do what's expected through the rugby as well. I think if something's not done about it soon then something's definitely going to give.' ●

Back in the old routine. Armstrong is recalled to the colours for the one-point defeat by England (The Herald)

As a result, the Armstrong boys started out on the rugby trail a year or two before they should have done. Both would play for Jed-Forest, both would play age-group rugby for Scotland and Kevin would go on to take part in Scotland's 1993 tour to the South Seas.

'Until I was old enough to actually take part I just used to muck about with a ball, and try to join in with the bigger boys. I really enjoyed it,' says Gary.

But Lawrence's work in insurance took the family away from Jedburgh to Coldstream and then Dunfermline where the boys made their mark in the Dunfermline HS side. Early recognition came with representative honours at both District and Scotland under-15 level but by the time Gary was old enough to leave school the lure of the Borderland was beckoning again.

'When I was old enough I came back to the Borders and stayed with my grandmother at Pinnacle Farm, near Ancrum. I kept up the rugby by joining the Jedburgh semi-junior side Jed Thistle,' recalls Gary.

A Scotland under-18 cap followed and, for the first and last time in his career, young Armstrong found himself sidelined through selectorial dictat. The selector preferred the Biggar scrumhalf Rob Young and Armstrong was dropped.

'There's nothing really that you can do about it. You can only give 100 per cent. Nothing less will do. If the selectors decide then that they want somebody else then you just have to accept their decision. That doesn't mean, though, that you don't go out to prove them wrong!'

The people's champion. Gary is voted Player of the Year for the second time in
succession by readers of The Herald. If he wins again he gets to keep the paper!
(The Herald)

The next step up the rugby ladder came with promotion to Jed-
Forest seconds where he played in the South District Union league
and where he first made the acquaintance of his future international
partner Craig Chalmers who was at this time playing for Melrose
seconds.

At Riverside Park the young and ambitious Armstrong had a
perfect role-model on which to base his drive for full international
honours. Roy Laidlaw was the king-pin of the Jed effort while Gary
was learning his craft on the back pitches. But, in 1987, with the club
toiling near the bottom of Division One, the decision was taken to
give them both a run in the side. Roy moved to stand-off to
accommodate Gary but the Scottish selectors deemed that this wasn't
conducive to the national cause and the experiment lasted only long
enough to ease Jed's plight.

Further representative honours came Gary's way with outings for
the national youth and under-21 sides and when Laidlaw retired at the
end of the 1988 season the Scotland selectors called up his young
Riverside protégé.

By then Armstrong had already tasted success at senior international level with two outings in the B side (scoring a debut hat-trick
in the 37–0 win over the Italians) and in the autumn of 1988 Gary
donned the Scotland No. 9 jersey for the first time at full international
level for the 32–13 defeat by the touring Wallabies.

'For the first two or three games in the national side you are really
just finding your feet. The pace of the game is just unlike anything
you've ever experienced before. I enjoyed my first cap, and although

Close but no cigar! Gary is just inches short with a comeback try against England in 1994 (The Herald)

it would have been nice to have got a win, I had proved to myself that I could do it. I was back in the side for the Five Nations Championship and we got a win first time out against Wales.'

Despite his relative inexperience Armstrong was already being noticed furth of Scotland. He was a member of Finlay Calder's victorious British Lions party to Australia in 1989. He was kept out of the Test side by Robert Jones, the Welshman who was to become such a firm friend, but even so he was the tourists' second top try-scorer with five touchdowns to his name.

Then came what Armstrong still reckons is the highlight of his career: 17 March 1990 at Murrayfield when David Sole's Scots tasted Grand Slam glory, sending Will Carling and his men hameward tae think again.

'That was special. Even now when I watch the video it makes the hairs stand up on the back of my neck. We just wanted it more than the English boys. When we went out on to the pitch before the kick-off the English were standing around with their wives signing autographs and doing TV interviews. They looked so arrogant it really got our backs up. I think they had begun to believe all the pre-match publicity about how invincible they were. At the end of the day, though, we wanted it more than they did.'

Armstrong played immaculately that afternoon and it was his scrummage break which led to Tony Stanger's match-winning try. The Scotland scrum-half was lauded at home and abroad but he was also attracting attention from Rugby League. On several occasions he was sounded out as to his availability to cross over into the professional code.

'Yes, there were some serious approaches and I thought about it very carefully. I discussed it with Shona and with the family but at the end of the day I decided against going. It would have meant moving Shona and the kids out and I didn't want to leave Jed.'

Lawrence, too, recalls these family summit meetings. 'We talked the whole thing through but at the end of the day it was Gary and Shona's decision. There's very little goes by that isn't discussed by us all, Margaret and me and the two boys. Rugby is everybody's life in this family. At one stage Kevin had more caps than Gary with the under-21s, -18s and -15s. We were always a close family but rugby has brought us closer together still. We were out in Australia with Gary and the Lions in 1989 and we went out to New Zealand in 1993 even though at the end of the day Gary didn't make it. We had to come home early because Margaret's father died. So all in all that was a year we would rather forget.

'I take great pride in the boys' achievements. We all do. They've both done much, much more than I ever did on the rugby field. I played twice for the Co-optimists and once for a so-called Scottish Select when Berwick opened their clubrooms. A lot of our life now is just spent following the boys.

'That's why when Gary told me that he had had enough at the top and had to have a break it was very difficult for me just to stand back and say to him that he would have to think it through and make the decision himself; basically that it was up to him and Shona. Like nearly every other rugby fan in Scotland I was very disappointed that, to all intents and purposes, he had decided to call it quits at the top level but I had to stand back and not put any pressure on because having seen the pressures that already exist on Gary, and the other Scottish players, I didn't want to add to them.'

Lawrence adds: 'With all the changes being planned in rugby, Scottish Cups and mid-week games and Sunday sevens, there's not enough folk asking the players whether or not they can cope and something's going to give.'

But for now Gary, who in 1994 was named *The Herald* Player of the Year for the second time in succession, is content just to take each day and each match as it comes.

'I'm enjoying my rugby again. I'm enjoying playing for Jed and even though I say that there's nothing really left for me to do in rugby one thing that I haven't done is tour with the club. Maybe that's something that I should be aiming for in the future. I think that would be relaxing and guid fun.'

And there's the nub of the matter. Far too many folk have forgotten that rugby should be 'guid fun'. Gary Armstrong hasn't forgotten it, though, and it's a hard fact that all rugby folk will forget only at their peril.

- Armstrong's injury jinx re-appeared just as the 1994–95 season was about to get underway. A training accident saw the unfortunate Jed man suffer serious damage to his left knee, and the early prognosis was that he would be out of the game for a considerable time.

The Royal Bank
of Scotland

Nobody Ever Said It Would Be Easy!

THE 1994 TOUR TO ARGENTINA

By Alan Lorimer

ALL tours are ultimately judged on their results. The verdict on Scotland's tour to Argentina in May and June which showed only one victory in six games can only be one of overall disappointment, albeit that a number of circumstances made success only a distant possibility.

When the Stewart's-Melville FP centre Doug Wyllie withdrew from the tour it must have seemed the final bombshell for an already beleaguered tour management that in the weeks before departure for Argentina had been hit by an unprecedented run of bad luck with injuries to top players.

It was hard enough for the tour management that the most senior of Scotland's players – Gavin Hastings, Scott Hastings, Gary Armstrong, Doddie Weir, Ken Milne and Tony Stanger – had all decided that their best preparation for the World Cup would be a rest from international rugby over the summer months but to then have the tour party weakened further by a spate of injuries that removed *en bloc* virtually the remainder of the experienced core was really more than any touring side could be expected to bear.

In the weeks between the selection of the tour party and its departure to Argentina, injuries robbed the Scotland party of Derek Stark, Andy Nicol and Craig Chalmers from the backs and Iain Morrison and Rob Wainwright from the forwards. The loss of Wainwright was a particularly bitter blow, both in terms of his playing skills and of his ability to lead. In the event the selectors were forced to look for a new captain and decided that the safest choice would be the Bath and British Lions lock Andy Reed.

Chris Dalgleish, Derrick Patterson and Duncan Hodge were the respective replacements for Stark, Nicol and Chalmers, while there were call-ups for

David McIvor and Fergus Wallace to take the places of Morrison and Wainwright. The final change to the party was the replacement of Doug Wyllie by Rowen Shepherd.

In many ways the absence of Chalmers was the most crucial loss to the Scots who, without a real general to control matters behind the scrum, never quite realised the 15-man game that had been anticipated. Gregor Townsend assumed the pivotal role at stand-off in both Tests but the young Gala player never reproduced the form that had earned him such acclaim when he played in Sydney during the summer of 1993.

One sensed, however, that Townsend, who came in for coaching criticism, looked happier when played at centre in the match against Rosario, when his natural running skills had a chance to be expressed.

Nor did a rather inflexible approach to alignment help Townsend and those outside him. True, the Australian method of attacking has shown to be most effective when it is carried out with slick passing and with players – particularly the blindside wing and fullback – running on to the ball at pace. Scottish rugby, however, is not quite at that stage and to a large extent the possibilities for practising such moves in the domestic game are limited by weather and ground conditions.

Yet it seemed as though Scotland had given notice of their intent to play attacking rugby in the opening game against Buenos Aires, the Argentine provincial champions. The sunny and warm conditions at the Ferro Carril Oeste stadium for the opening game of the tour almost demanded an open game of rugby from the two sides. In the event, both obliged, the Scots less generously, though, than the hosts.

The result was a 24–24 draw – Scotland only just avoiding defeat with a penalty goal on full time by Mike Dods – but the inescapable conclusion was that the tourists won enough good ball to win comfortably. The Scots, however, denied themselves victory by kicking away hard-won possession when moving the ball perhaps offered more profitable outcomes.

That said, Scotland could take much from the fact that all three tries were scored by the threequarters, which, in itself, was an indication that after several seasons of adopting a limited approach the Scots were seeking to play a more expansive game. That policy translated into two fine tries by Chris Dalgleish of Gala and a third by Scott Nichol of Selkirk.

Nichol's try was the result of a splendid break by the Scotland stand-off Gregor Townsend who again demonstrated his searing pace and the ability to beat opponents. It was Mike Dods's velocity in coming into the line that made the first try for his Gala clubmate Chris Dalgleish.

Apart from his crucial penalty goal to level the scores at the end of the game, Mike Dods was successful with two other penalty kicks but the Gala fullback missed all three conversion attempts.

Ironically, it was the Scottish-sounding Duncan Forrester who proved the thorn in the tourists' side by putting over four penalty kicks and converting the try by Rivarola from a run out of defence by the left wing Albanese. The other Buenos Aires points came from a try by Lerga after a 'cavalry charge' by the forwards in a penalty move.

The trip to Mendoza should have proved a tonic. The cooler and cleaner air of the attractive city nestling in the shadow of the majestic Andes was a welcome contrast with the vast metropolis of Buenos Aires with its heavily exhaust-polluted atmosphere.

A large crowd of excited fans was waiting at the door of the Plaza Hotel in Mendoza. Had rugby really made inroads into Argentina's popular culture? Alas, no. The fans were waiting for the River Plate soccer team who were staying at the same hotel as the Scots.

For the game against Cuyo the tour management picked all those players who had not played in the first game, the one exception being Carl Hogg whose injured back forced him to withdraw from the side. The match in many ways proved to be the nadir of the tour as Scotland, beaten in most areas of the game, finished losers by 25–11.

Disappointingly, the Scotland forwards failed to achieve any measure of control and this in turn had a knock-on effect behind the scrum where 19-year-old Duncan Hodge made a nervous start to his tour, the Watsonian missing all his kicks at goal, albeit atoning with the tourists' only try of the game. It was left to Rowen Shepherd, taking over as kicker, to add the other points with two second-half penalty goals.

If Scotland, who were led by Paul Burnell, learned anything from this game then it was surely the effectiveness of moving the ball through the hands. Cuyo showed this skill admirably and, with their dynamic scrumhalf Diaz ready to ignite offensive moves and a lively back-row eager to join in, Cuyo scored three tries in their comprehensive win.

Eleven of the side defeated by Cuyo were asked to play a second successive game for the match against Cordoba, the final chance for the tour management to look at several possible Test selections. With Mike Dods nursing a slight injury, the tour selectors turned to Rowen Shepherd to play at fullback; the other major change was in the captaincy, which was entrusted to Jeremy Richardson.

There was little doubt that Scotland went into their third tour game knowing that a win was necessary to provide the psychological boost for the first Test. After the less than satisfactory performances in the first two matches few would have forecast such a massive win by the tourists, who ran in six tries for a 40–14 victory.

A delighted tour manager Fred McLeod summed up the Scots' achievement against Cordoba when he said, 'The tour has really taken off. We badly needed a win. We got it in real style.'

Scotland looked a transformed side from the team that had lost against Cuyo. Most of what the Scotland forwards had been practising in training was realised on the field as the pack, playing with considerably more fire, out-rucked their opponents to produce quick, quality possession for the backs. 'We played the game off second-phase possession,' commented Richie Dixon, the Scotland assistant coach.

Only in the set scrums were the Scots put under pressure; in the loose play, however, the Scotland forwards excelled with fine performances from the back-row trio of Carl Hogg, playing his first tour game, Fergus Wallace and Dave McIvor, and lock Jeremy Richardson who proved an inspirational captain.

Richardson, in combination with Stewart Campbell and Carl Hogg, won some priceless possession in the lineout but the crucial difference at the touchline was the way the Scots contested at their opponents' throw-in.

Duncan Hodge, the 19-year-old Watsonian stand-off singled out by coach Morgan as one of the outstanding players, was able to regain his confidence after a difficult first outing three days earlier. The beneficiaries of Hodge's play were the outside backs who accounted for four of the Scots' six tries – one apiece by wingers Craig Joiner and Ken Logan, fullback Rowen Shepherd and centre Ian Jardine.

Scotland's other tries were scored by Alan Watt and Dave McIvor, both the forward scores being created by Carl Hogg, whose return at No. 8 after missing the first two games did much to help the Scottish effort.

The tourists named two new caps in their side for the first Test against Argentina at the Ferro Carril Oeste stadium in Buenos Aires. Kevin McKenzie, the Stirling County hooker, had served a long apprenticeship before winning national honours, whereas Craig Joiner, the 20-year-old Melrose wing was, it seemed, fresh from the junior ranks.

Overall, the tour selectors opted for safety by choosing players who had experienced international rugby. The one position that seemed to be 'open' was scrumhalf. The selectors, however, turned down the claims of Derrick Patterson and stuck with Bryan Redpath who had shown up well against Cordoba.

Doug Morgan had spoken in the days prior to the Test of his concern that three warm-up matches were insufficient for such a vital game. In fact 11 of the Test side would be playing only their second tour game and, moreover, the Pumas had played together on the previous weekend in their World Cup qualifier win over the USA.

Despite these misgivings, Scotland went into the first Test against the Pumas in optimistic mood, having had their confidence lifted by the 40–14 midweek win over Cordoba. But the effervescent style which the tourists displayed in their first tour victory was not to be repeated as the Scots became entangled in a dour struggle with an overcautious Pumas team to finish losers by 16–15.

While much of what was poor play by Scotland could be attributed to the genuine lack of preparation time, there is little doubt that the Scots, despite competing on equal terms upfront, failed because of their cautious attitude and in the view of Doug Morgan, the Scotland coach, 'bad decision-making', which was a point that he controversially made to the media after the game.

The Gala stand-off Gregor Townsend did not have a good game but he was not helped by the reluctance of Bryan Redpath, the Scotland scrumhalf, to attempt any breaks, although the Melrose player compensated with a swift service. The lack of probing runs round the fringes of the scrum in turn meant that the back-row rarely became involved in offensive moves, the only way it seemed that the tourists could break up the static pattern of play imposed by the Pumas.

The other major area Morgan pointed the finger at was goal-kicking. Mike Dods finished the game with five penalty goals from ten attempts and other opportunities were missed by Gregor Townsend who sent two drop-goals wide of the posts as the Scots tried hard to overtake the Pumas in the final few minutes of the game.

Scotland's tactics were matched by the Pumas who were also afflicted by a safety-first attitude. The result was a thoroughly unedifying game of rugby that lacked any flow and *de facto* was just a series of set-pieces punctuated by penalties.

Argentina, however, did score the only try of the game when Martin Teran, the right wing, booted the ball forward from a spilled catch to touch down under the posts, leaving Santiago Meson with a simple conversion kick. Meson, who had put over two first-half penalties, added to Scotland's discomfort with a second-half goal, leaving the tourists trailing 16–3 at one point. Dods, however, pulled the Scots back into the game with four penalties but just when the Gala fullback had the chance to win the game he proved fallible.

The question uppermost in the coaches' mind was obviously what to do about the stand-off position. The fifth tour game against Rosario at the magnificent Jockey Club provided the last opportunity for experimentation and for looking closely at alternative solutions. The possibilities for the second Test were keeping Townsend at stand-off, risking the young Duncan Hodge or moving Graham Shiel from inside-centre.

The match also afforded those who would not win Test selection their last opportunity to play against Argentine opposition. In many ways Rosario represent the best in Argentine rugby, as their record against touring sides amply bears out. Scotland were to find out only too quickly why Rosario are held in such high repute.

Rosario, winners over Queensland and the New Zealand development side, added Scotland to their list of victims with a 27–16 victory and in the process gave the tourists a lesson in running rugby. On an ideal surface for the handling game Scotland revealed once again the main symptom of their current malaise by kicking away far too much hard-won possession. Only when the match was out of reach did the Scots finally abandon caution and in doing so showed what might have been with some effective running rugby that produced two late tries.

By contrast Rosario, whose backs were guided by man of the match Guillermo del Castillo, the Pumas stand-off, moved the ball at every opportunity to create constant problems for the Scotland defence. Del Castillo not only accounted for three drop-goals but also opened up the defence for two fine tries by the Rosario backs Caffaro-Rossi and Crexell.

Scotland's forwards failed to dominate the frontal battle despite good performances from flanker Dave McIvor and try-scorer Alan Watt. Behind the scrum Derrick Patterson put in a lively performance to challenge for a Test place and Gregor Townsend exorcised the stinging criticism which had earlier come his way with several good breaks late in the game, two of which led to tries by Ken Logan and Alan Watt.

The other good performance was from Rowen Shepherd, playing his second game at fullback. Shepherd's adventurous running out of defence perhaps convinced the Scots, and particularly Townsend, to abort the safety-first strategy and go for the game that comes naturally.

The defeat by Rosario prompted a no-change policy by the tour selectors who announced an unchanged Test side for the second match against Argentina. It also had the effect of putting pressure on the Test side who were only too well aware of the criticism already mounting back home of the poor overall showing.

There was pressure, too, on the Test team from the knowledge that Scotland had gone seven international matches without a win and in that period had scored only one try. But there was pressure also on the Pumas who knew that defeat by what they saw as a Scotland A team would be unacceptable.

Argentina made two changes from the side that won against Scotland on the previous Saturday. Frederico Mendez, the young prop who is best remembered for landing a punch on Paul Ackford, the England lock, during the Pumas 1990 tour, came in at loosehead and in the back row Jose Santamarina was the preferred choice at No. 8.

Despite drawing first blood in the two-match international series, the Pumas were unhappy about the way they had performed against Scotland. Their tense and negative style of play was attributed to the fact that Argentina were in the middle of a World Cup qualifying series against the USA – a less inhibited type of game was anticipated from the Pumas in the second match.

In the event the Pumas continued their winning run, finishing 19–17 victors over the Scots. 'It does not get any easier. We lost to England by one point, drew with Ireland, lost to Argentina by one point in the first Test and then by just two points in the second Test,' a frustrated Douglas Morgan commented after the game.

It was, however, a vastly improved performance by the Scots and one which contributed to an exciting game that Scotland did not deserve to lose. But the message was once again one of converting opportunities into points. The consistently fallible area in the Scotland game has been goal-kicking and in the second Test at the Ferro Carril Oeste Stadium that again proved the critical weakness.

Graham Shiel, entrusted with the goal-kicking duties, looked to have been the right choice as he put Scotland into the lead with two well-struck penalty goals. But the Melrose centre lost his composure after failing first with a long-range attempt and then with a relatively simple kick just outside the 22-metre area. Two further misses prompted a change of kicker, Mike Dods taking over and succeeding with one goal from two attempts.

The Gala fullback, however, could not rescue the game for the tourists when he was presented with a difficult long-range kick right on full time.

More than just kicking, however, let down the Scots. Too often in the Pumas 22-metre area they lost their composure and made several bad decisions, the most palpable of which being Kevin McKenzie's rush of blood to the head in attempting a drop-goal.

Encouragingly for the coaches, Scotland's forwards produced a more dynamic performance that helped to make the game a much less static affair than in the first Test. Behind the scrum Ian Jardine looked the most forceful of the Scots but as a unit the backline did not have the poise of the Pumas who, when required to do so, moved the ball delightfully and at speed.

The Scotland backs at least stopped the try famine when Ken Logan squeezed in at the corner. Logan, however, was forced to retire soon after with an Achilles tendon injury, allowing replacement Scott Nichol to win his first cap.

The Scots' try was matched by an equally good score for the Pumas by

Rolando Martin, their blindside flanker, after Diego Cuesta-Silva had made the all-important break.

The disappointment of losing yet again was painful to bear but the truth of the matter was that Scotland, with an understrength tour party, could hardly have expected to succeed where other countries had failed. Jim Telfer, the Scotland Director of Rugby, summed it up succinctly when he said, 'the results reflected the quality of players on the tour'.

Argentina is a difficult country in which to tour, largely because of the problems of language. Scotland's task was made all the more difficult by the late decision to condense the tour from eight to six matches, leaving the tourists with too short a build-up time before going into the first Test. But the compensation was the overwhelmingly generous hospitality, the fondest memories of which were visits to the Monte Grande Club (founded by Scots) and to a large ranch near Rosario.

But despite a heap of mitigating factors the blunt truth was that Scotland underperformed in the forward battle and behind the scrum were unnecessarily cautious.

All the same, there were some plusses. Youngster Craig Joiner proved that he is capable of playing at international level, Derrick Patterson impressed at scrumhalf, and Rowen Shepherd showed that he could become the successor at fullback to Gavin Hastings. Their day will surely come.

Tour results

25 May – Buenos Aires 24, Scotland 24; 28 May – Cuyo 25, Scotland 11; 31 May – Cordoba 14, Scotland 40; 4 June – Argentina 16, Scotland 15; 7 June – Rosario 27, Scotland 16; 11 June – Argentina 19, Scotland 17.

First Test: Scotland – M. Dods (Gala); C. Joiner (Melrose), I. Jardine (Stirling County), G. Shiel (Melrose), K. Logan (Stirling County); G. Townsend (Gala), B. Redpath (Melrose); A. Sharp (Bristol), K. McKenzie (Stirling County), P. Burnell (London Scottish), S. Munro (Glasgow High/Kelvinside), A. Reed (Bath) captain, P. Walton (Northampton), C. Hogg (Melrose), I. Smith (Gloucester).
Argentina – S. Meson; M. Teran, D. Cuesta-Silva, M. Loffreda captain, G. Jorge, G. del Castilla, N. Miranda; M. Corral, J. Angelillo, P. Noriego, P. Sporleder, G. Llanes, C. Viel, P. Camerlinckx, P. Temperley.
Referee W. Erickson (Australia).

Second Test: Scotland – M. Dods (Gala); C. Joiner (Melrose), I. Jardine (Stirling County), G. Shiel (Melrose), K. Logan (Stirling County) replaced by S. Nichol (Selkirk) 70 mins; G. Townsend (Gala), B. Redpath (Melrose); A. Sharp (Bristol) replaced by A. Watt (Glasgow High/Kelvinside) 74 mins, K. McKenzie (Stirling County), P. Burnell (London Scottish), S. Munro (Glasgow High/Kelvinside), A. Reed (Bath) captain, P. Walton (Northampton), C. Hogg (Melrose), I. Smith (Gloucester).
Argentina – S. Meson; M. Teran, D. Cuesta-Silva, M. Loffreda captain, G. Jorge, G. del Castilla, N. Miranda; F. Mendez, J. Angelillo, P. Noriego, P. Sporleder, G. Llanes, R. Martin, J. Santamarina, C. Viel-Temperley.
Referee W. Erickson (Australia).

Scotland tour party: Backs – C. Dalgleish (Gala), M. Dods (Gala), D.

Hodge (Watsonians), I. Jardine (Stirling County), C. Joiner (Melrose), K. Logan (Stirling County), S. Nichol (Selkirk), D. Patterson (Edinburgh Academicals), B. Redpath (Melrose), R. Shepherd (Edinburgh Academicals), G. Shiel (Melrose), G. Townsend (Gala). Forwards – S. Brotherstone (Melrose), P. Burnell (London Scottish), S. Campbell (Dundee HSFP), S. Ferguson (Peebles), C. Hogg (Melrose), D. McIvor (Edinburgh Academicals), K. McKenzie (Stirling County), S. Munro (Glasgow High/Kelvinside), A. Reed (Bath) captain, S. Reid (Boroughmuir), J. Richardson (Edinburgh Academicals), A. Sharp (Bristol), I. Smith (Gloucester), F. Wallace (Glasgow High/Kelvinside), P. Walton (Northampton), A. Watt (Glasgow High/Kelvinside).

Hon. coaches: D. Morgan, R. Dixon.

Hon. manager: F. McLeod. Manager's assistant: C. Bisset.

Hon. doctor: J. Graham. Hon. physiotherapist: J. Robson.

The Royal Bank of Scotland

Scotland's International Players in Season 1993–94

Profiles by Bill McMurtrie

(Ages and caps as at the end of the 1994 Five Nations Championship)

GARY ARMSTRONG (Jed-Forest)
Age 27, 5 ft 8 in, 13 st 10 lb, 30 caps

Gary Armstrong is arguably the best scrumhalf in the world, reflected by his election as *The Herald* readers' player of the year for two successive seasons, but he dropped into voluntary exile early in 1993–94, preferring to play as an outside-back with Jed-Forest. He returned as Scotland's scrumhalf for the matches against England and Ireland, though a hand injury in Dublin confined his national comeback to those two matches.

PAUL BURNELL (London Scottish)
Age 28, 6 ft 1 in, 16 st 8 lb, 34 caps

Paul Burnell has firmly established himself as Scotland's tight-head since his debut as a 22-year-old in 1989. He was on the Lions 1993 New Zealand tour, playing in the first Test, and though he has been criticised for not imposing himself on the game as a senior player he is a much-respected scrummager. During the 1994 Championship campaign he gave sterling performances, especially against England and Ireland.

CRAIG CHALMERS (Melrose)
Age 25, 5 ft 10 in, 13 st 6 lb, 35 caps

Craig Chalmers has fallen from grace after five seasons of international rugby before he was 25. He was only 20 when he scored a try and a drop-goal on his debut in the Murrayfield win over Wales in 1989. He was also on the Lions tour to Australia later that year, playing in the first Test, and he had appeared in 35 out of 36 internationals for Scotland before he lost his place to a fellow Borderer, Gregor Townsend, in the 1994 Championship.

DAMIAN CRONIN (London Scottish)
Age 30, 6 ft 6 in, 17 st 10 lb, 29 caps

Damian Cronin was a regular in Scotland's second row from 1988 until the 1991 Championship, playing in 22 out of 23 internationals, including the 1990 Grand Slam, and he made such an impression with his scrummaging as well as his lineout game on his return to the national team in 1993 that he was selected for the Lions tour to New Zealand later that year. His 1993–94 season, however, was cut short by injury against the All Blacks.

MIKE DODS (Gala)
Age 25, 5 ft 11 in, 11 st 12 lb, 1 cap

Mike Dods, younger brother of Gala's former international fullback, earned the dubious tag of having the shortest international career on record when he gained his first cap as temporary replacement for Gavin Hastings for only a handful of seconds before half-time in the Dublin international against Ireland in March. Though lightweight, he is an outstanding prospect, with electrifying pace and a sharp sense of intrusion timing, qualities by which Gala have profited in seven-a-side rugby.

NEIL EDWARDS (Northampton)
Age 29, 6 ft 4 in, 17 st 5 lb, 5 caps

Neil Edwards shot to the fore in 1992 as a wily, front-jumping lock, making his international debut against England at Murrayfield and scoring the try that helped Scotland to beat France at the same ground. He also went on Scotland's Australian tour that year, playing in the first Test, but he did not reappear in the national XV until he was selected for the 1994 Cardiff match against Wales.

GAVIN HASTINGS (Watsonians) captain
Age 32, 6 ft 2 in, 14 st 8 lb, 50 caps

Gavin Hastings has been a solidly secure, forcefully attacking fullback for Scotland since his debut in 1986 as well as being a highly popular figure off the field. He has been Scotland's captain for the past two seasons, and he also led the Lions in New Zealand in 1993. He has scored 436 points for Scotland, and he is now his country's most-capped fullback.

SCOTT HASTINGS (Watsonians)

Age 29, 6 ft 1 in, 14 st 4 lb, 50 caps

Scott Hastings, like his elder brother, Gavin, reached a notable milestone in his rugby career by winning his fiftieth cap in Scotland's international against France in March 1994. Their first, eight years earlier, was also against France, and in the interim Scott has been Scotland's regular first-choice outside-centre as well as going on two Lions tours. Who could forget his try-saving tackle on Rory Underwood in the 1990 Grand Slam decider?

CARL HOGG (Melrose)

Age 24, 6 ft 4½ in, 15 st 7 lb, 3 caps

Carl Hogg is a versatile forward who played lock for Scotland in the 1991 B international against France and appeared in all three back-row positions during the 1992 tour in Australia. It was on that tour that he won his first cap, playing at blindside in the two Tests, and later that year, with international experience behind him, he was a key member of the Scottish team who reached the quarter-finals of the Students World Cup in Italy. His only subsequent cap was as a replacement against New Zealand in November 1993.

IAN JARDINE (Stirling County)

Age 28, 6 ft 1 in, 13 st 7 lb, 3 caps

Ian Jardine was with Scotland in North America in 1991, but it was the 1993 tour to the South Pacific that projected him into the international XV. He played in the non-cap Tests against Fiji, Tonga, and Western Samoa, giving secure performances in defence, especially with his weighty tackling in the last of those matches, and after the Scotland A match against the All Blacks in November that year he was promoted to the international XV for the game against New Zealand a week later.

KENNY LOGAN (Stirling County)

Age 21, 6 ft 1 in, 13 st 8 lb, 7 caps

Kenny Logan became Stirling County's first home-bred cap when, deputising for the injured Gavin Hastings, he switched from his intended debut position on the right wing to play fullback in the Brisbane Test on Scotland's 1992 tour in Australia, though he played on the left wing in all of Scotland's matches in the 1994 Five Nations Championship. He is happy to play in either position for Scotland, but the best of his powerful running has yet to be seen most effectively in international rugby.

ANDY MACDONALD (Heriot's FP)

Age 28, 6 ft 8 in, 17 st 10 lb, 1 cap

Andy Macdonald had been a potential international lock from his days in Scotland's under-21 team, and his progress continued with a Cambridge Blue in 1989. B and A internationals and selection for the non-cap Tests against the USA and Canada on the 1991 tour kept him in the selectors' eyes – not that anyone could miss a player of his height. But it was not until after the Scotland A game against New Zealand at Old Anniesland in November 1993 that he was promoted to the national XV the following week.

DAVID McIVOR (Edinburgh Academicals)
Age 30, 6 ft 1 in, 16 st 9 lb, 5 caps
David McIvor has been acknowledged as a reliable blindside wing-forward since his debut for North and Midlands in 1986, and he has never been dropped by Edinburgh Academicals during his six seasons with the club. He had a full season in Scotland's XV for the 1992 Championship, though after his omission for the Tests on the tour to Australia that year he did not return to the national team until the match against New Zealand in November 1993.

KENNY MILNE (Heriot's FP)
Age 32, 6 ft, 15 st 2 lb, 20 caps
Kenny Milne, Scotland's undisputed first-choice hooker since 1992, is the youngest of three brothers who have played in Scotland's front row. He was Scotland's 1990 Grand Slam hooker as well as being on the Lions 1993 tour in New Zealand, playing in the first Test, though perhaps a more famous day in the Milne family was when the three brothers played together for the Barbarians.

IAIN MORRISON (London Scottish)
Age 31, 6 ft 1 in, 15 st 11 lb, 5 caps
Iain Morrison came to international prominence late in his rugby life as he was 30 when he made his debut in the 1993 victory over Ireland at Murrayfield. Before then, though, he was respected as a sevens expert, and in the 1993 Championship he established himself as a rare genuine open-side flanker. Injury prevented him from playing against New Zealand in November that year, and misfortune struck again when he returned for Scotland against Wales in January 1994 as he broke a leg early on in that Cardiff match.

SHADE MUNRO (Glasgow High/Kelvinside)
Age 27, 6 ft 6 in, 17 st, 4 caps
Few international debuts can have been more eagerly awaited and thoroughly deserved than Shade Munro's was when he played against Wales in January 1994, following in the footsteps of his grandfather, John Bannerman, who was capped 37 times for Scotland between the wars. A severe knee injury in 1990 had kept Munro out of rugby for two years, but even before then he had established himself as a hard-working forward with considerable footballing potential.

ANDY NICOL (Dundee High School FP)
Age 23, 5 ft 11 in, 13 st 4 lb, 8 caps
Andy Nicol was only the second player to have three seasons in the Scottish Schools XV, and he went on to prove his potential when he had to stand in for the injured Gary Armstrong throughout Scotland's 1992 international campaign. The Dundee scrumhalf had the rare experience of playing in a winning team against the All Blacks, when he was in the World XV for New Zealand rugby's centenary celebrations in 1992, and he deservedly won a Lions blazer when he temporarily joined the British Isles 1993 tour of New Zealand as a replacement immediately after he had led Scotland on the South Pacific tour.

BRYAN REDPATH (Melrose)
Age 22, 5 ft 7 in, 10 st 10 lb, 3 caps

Bryan Redpath, the youngest of three brothers who have played rugby for Melrose, won caps as a temporary replacement against both New Zealand and England in 1993–94 before he was chosen for the first time against France, after Gary Armstrong's Dublin injury. Basil, as he is known, is a combative, pawky little competitor who relishes a challenge, and he has probably the fastest service of any scrumhalf in Scottish rugby.

ANDY REED (Bath)
Age 24, 6 ft 7 in, 17 st 2 lb, 7 caps

Andy Reed, capped by England as a colt, came a long way in his first year of international rugby, playing in all four of Scotland's 1993 Championship matches as well as the first Test of the Lions New Zealand tour. A knee injury kept him out of the national XV against New Zealand and Wales in 1993–94, but on his return against England he so justified the selectors' faith in him that they made him pack leader for the two remaining Championship matches.

ALAN SHARP (Bristol)
Age 24, 5 ft 10 in, 16 st 7 lb, 3 caps

Alan Sharp has won international honours on both sides of the border, with English Schools then Scotland Colts and England B, but since his decision to throw his lot in with Scotland he has been an undoubted asset as a secure, technically sound scrummager on the loose-head. His debut against England, however, was a year later than it ought to have been as injury had denied him a first cap, against Ireland, in 1993.

GRAHAM SHIEL (Melrose)
Age 23, 5 ft 10 in, 12 st 10 lb, 7 caps

Graham Shiel signalled his undoubted international potential as a talented midfield back when he played in the non-cap Tests against the USA and Canada on the 1991 tour to North America, and later that year he scored a vital try when he made his cap debut for Scotland as stand-off replacement for his injured club colleague, Craig Chalmers, in the World Cup match against Ireland at Murrayfield. He established himself at centre in the national XV in 1993, but after Scotland's defeat by New Zealand injury kept him out of rugby throughout the 1994 Five Nations Championship.

IAN SMITH (Gloucester)
Age 29, 5 ft 1 in, 14 st, 8 caps

Ian Smith, who, like his father, has captained Gloucester, was capped five times for Scotland as open-side wing-forward in 1992 after having played for England B in 1989, but he was displaced from the national XV by Iain Morrison in 1993. Injuries to Morrison and Rob Wainwright allowed Smith back into Scotland XV in 1994, and especially against Ireland he responded by looking better than third choice.

TONY STANGER (Hawick)
Age 25, 6 ft 2 in, 15 st 2 lb, 35 caps

Tony Stanger played in every one of Scotland's internationals from his debut against Fiji in 1989 to the Championship match against France in March 1994. He scored two tries in his first international and three in his next (against Romania). He is now joint second in Scotland's try-scoring list with 15, and undoubtedly the most memorable of them was in the 13–7 win over England in the 1990 Grand Slam decider.

GREGOR TOWNSEND (Gala)
Age 20, 5 ft 11 in, 12 st 7 lb, 5 caps

Gregor Townsend was destined for international rugby when his precocious talent flourished while he was a pupil at Galashiels Academy. He made his international debut as a 19-year-old replacement against England at Twickenham in 1993, and he was latterly preferred to the previously well-established Craig Chalmers as Scotland's stand-off for the 1994 Championship.

DEREK TURNBULL (Hawick)
Age 32, 6 ft 4 in, 15 st 6 lb, 15 caps

Derek Turnbull had the toughest of international baptisms when he played in the 1987 World Cup quarter-final against New Zealand in Christchurch. He also had one game in the 1991 World Cup, and he was in famous company when he won a replacement cap in the 1990 Grand Slam decider against England. Only in 1991 and 1993, however, has he commanded a regular place as blindside flanker through the Championship series.

ROB WAINWRIGHT (Edinburgh Academicals)
Age 28, 6 ft 4 in, 15 st 4 lb, 7 caps

Rob Wainwright – a Cambridge Blue, as his father was before him – is such a versatile footballer that he has played international rugby as both open-side flanker and No. 8 as well as one game as replacement lock. He scored Scotland's only try of 1993–94, running in from outside the English 22 in the Calcutta Cup match, but a fractured jaw put him out of rugby for the remainder of the international season.

PETER WALTON (Northampton)
Age 24, 6 ft 3 in, 17 st 7 lb, 3 caps

Peter Walton, Scottish Schools captain in 1987 while he was at Merchiston, looks too bulky to be a top-rate flanker, but he showed up particularly well in the defeat Scotland A suffered in Italy and justified his promotion to the senior national XV with strong performances against England (on his debut) and Ireland, especially in the first half in the Dublin match.

ALAN WATT (Glasgow High/Kelvinside)
Age 26, 6 ft 6 in, 18 st 12 lb, 3 caps

Alan Watt was arguably the best mid-lineout jumper in Scottish rugby before he was converted to an international prop, but he has played only three matches in the front row for Scotland since his debut at tight-head in the 1991 World Cup against Zimbabwe at Murrayfield. His two other caps have been at loose-head. He replaced the injured Alan Sharp for the 1993 Murrayfield match against Ireland before he himself fell ill, though he returned for the international against New Zealand in November that year.

DODDIE WEIR (Melrose)
Age 23, 6 ft 6 in, 15 st 6 lb, 23 caps

George Wilson Weir, better known as Doddie, made his international debut against Argentina in 1990 and established himself in the national XV during the World Cup the following year. Since then he has become undisputably Scottish rugby's best mid-lineout jumper, and though he went off the boil early in season 1993–94, initially omitted from the January international against Wales, he came good, especially against England.

PETER WRIGHT (Boroughmuir)
Age 26, 6 ft, 17 st 2 lb, 6 caps

Peter Wright has played on both sides of the front row for Scotland, making his debut in his club position at tight-head on the 1992 tour to Australia. He went through that tour with hardly a hint of his reputation for being hot-headed, and the following year he added to his credits as emergency loose-head in three internationals for Scotland. He adapted so well that he also went with the Lions to New Zealand. Since then, however, his only international was in the Cardiff defeat in January 1994.

DOUGLAS WYLLIE (Stewart's-Melville FP)
Age 30, 6 ft 1 in, 13 st 10 lb, 18 caps

Douglas Wyllie has had an international career lasting almost ten years since his debut as stand-off against Australia in 1984, though only six of the 14 games he has started for Scotland have been at fly-half. He enjoyed an international revival at centre in 1994 after a gap following the 1991 World Cup, and for the first time he played in all four matches in a Five Nations Championship programme.

The Royal Bank of Scotland

Scotland's A Team Players in Season 1993–94

Profiles by Graham Law

STEWART CAMPBELL (Dundee HSFP)
Lock, born 25.4.72 in Glasgow, 6 ft 6 in, 15 st 8 lb, uncapped
Stewart Joseph Campbell has played international rugby in three age-groups as well as representing Scottish Students. A former pupil of Balfron High, he played his early rugby with West of Scotland and it was from the Burnbrae club that he was capped at under-18 level. When studies took him to Dundee, he enlisted at Mayfield and he enjoyed three seasons in the national under-19 team and two with the national under-21s. He has had 11 games for North and Midlands and in the past season he played for the Scotland Development team against the All Blacks, Scotland A in France and on the national tour to Argentina. His great-grandfather, John May, was a Scottish football internationalist. He is an architecture student in Dundee.

CRAIG CHALMERS *See* international player profile.

MICHAEL DODS *See* international player profile.

NEIL EDWARDS *See* international player profile.

DANNY HERRINGTON (Dundee HSFP).
Prop, born 28.5.61, 5 ft 11 in, 16 st, uncapped
Danny William Herrington made the breakthrough to the Scotland A team in the past season, playing in the matches against New Zealand and France. He began as a No. 8 at Alva Academy and it was not until his early 20s that Herrington made the switch to prop, while he was with the Hillfoots club, whom he helped to win promotion from Division VI. The first hint that he was destined for higher things came when he guested for Boroughmuir in a victory over Pontypool in Wales in 1990. The following season he joined Dundee High School FP, and district honours for North and Midlands followed. He is a part-time milkman.

CARL HOGG *See* international player profile.

IAN JARDINE *See* international player profile.

KENNY LOGAN *See* international player profile.

ANDY MACDONALD *See* international player profile.

DALE McINTOSH (Pontypridd)
Flanker/No. 8, born 23.11.69 in Turangi, New Zealand, 6 ft 3 in, 16 st, uncapped
Dale Lynsay Manawa McIntosh added his second A cap (against Italy) in the past season to the Scottish honours he had already secured at B and under-21 levels. Qualifying through an Edinburgh-born grandfather, McIntosh has represented King Country, Counties and Hawkes Bay in his native New Zealand. Injury has often struck at the most inopportune moments, a fractured arm forcing him to miss Scotland's 1993 South Pacific tour. He has played for the Scottish Exiles and is an employee with the Just Rentals television firm in Pontypridd.

DAVID McIVOR *See* international player profile.

KEVIN McKENZIE (Stirling County)
Hooker, born 22.1.68 in Stirling, 5 ft 6 in, 14 st 1 lb, 2 caps
Kevin Duncan McKenzie, as reserve to Kenny Milne, broke through in the past season to become a member of Scotland's squad, having represented his country at every level by the time he won his two caps on the Argentina tour. He played in all four of the Scotland A matches in the past season, captaining the side in the wins against their Irish and French counterparts. While at Dunblane High School, McKenzie played for the Scottish Schools in 1985-86, captaining the team in two matches, including a 10-7 win against England. Honours at under-19, under-21 and B level duly materialised. He is a sales representative with Taylor Maxwell Timber Limited.
International record: 1994 Arg (1, 2)

KENNY MILLIGAN (Stewart's-Melville)
Wing/centre, born 19.7.72 in Edinburgh, 5 ft 10 in, 12 st 7 lb, uncapped
Kenneth Robert Milligan, known to his friends as Spike, had two seasons – in the Scottish Schools XV, leading the side in all five matches in 1989–90, then graduating through the ranks of national under-19 and under-21 teams to Scotland A, for whom he made his debut against France A in Aberdeen in 1993. As a follow-up he played in three of Scotland's four A internationals in the past season, all on the wing. He was chosen for the Rugby World Cup Sevens at Murrayfield in 1993 but a hamstring injury prevented him participating and its recurrence saw him return from the South Pacific tour. He is a student at Heriot-Watt University.

IAIN MORRISON *See* international player profile.

SHADE MUNRO *See* international player profile.

SCOTT NICHOL (Selkirk)
Centre, born 18.6.70 in Selkirk, 5 ft 10 in, 11 st 7 lb, 1 cap
Scott Alan Nichol won Scottish Schools caps as a wing in 1987–88, by which time he had already played club rugby for Selkirk. He played in the A internationals against New Zealand, Italy and Ireland in the past season to add to an impressive list of representative honours, including national under-19 and under-21s, 13 games for the South, appearances for Scotland at the 1991 and 1994 Hong Kong Sevens, the 1993 summer tour to the South Pacific and the 1994 Argentina tour. Nichol – a former holder of the Borders under-15 tennis title – is a fireman with the Lothian and Borders Brigade.
International record: Arg (2) (r)

ANDY NICOL *See* international player profile.

GARY PARKER (Melrose)
Winger/utility back, born 3.3.66 in Galashiels, 5 ft 6 in, 11 st 7 lb, uncapped
Gary Alexander Parker is a former footballer who spent 17 months with Hearts, two months with Berwick Rangers, six years in New Zealand with Napier City and a season in Australia before he resumed his rugby career which had seen him collect Scottish Schools caps at scrumhalf while he was a pupil at Galashiels Academy. Since his return to Scotland, he has maintained a prodigious scoring record: in the past season, he notched 417 points, featuring 28 tries, including the first for the South against the All Blacks in 58 years in the 84–5 drubbing at Netherdale. He made his A international debut against New Zealand three days after that defeat. He is a financial representative with Royscot Trust.

BRYAN REDPATH *See* international player profile.

STUART REID (Boroughmuir)
Flanker/No 8, born 31.1.70, in Kendal, 6 ft 3 in, 15 st 7 lb, uncapped

Although Stuart James Reid was born in England, his parents came from Hawick and he has been immersed in the Scottish set-up from national under-19 and under-21 levels. His early club rugby was with the Lancaster club, Vale of Lune, before he joined Boroughmuir in 1989. He has played 19 games as a regular in the Edinburgh district side over the last five years and his honours have included three B caps, three A caps – the most recent, the 1994 win against the French and national tours to North America in 1991, where he played in both non-cap Tests, Australia in 1992 and Argentina (1994). He is a police constable with the Lothian and Borders force.

ALAN SHARP *See* international player profile.

ROWEN SHEPHERD (Edinburgh Academicals)
Stand-off/centre/fullback, born 25.12.70 in Edinburgh, 6 ft, 13 st 7 lb, uncapped

Rowen James Stanley Shepherd was called into Scotland's 1994 Argentina tour squad less than one week before departure. During the tour he played one game in his recognised berth of centre but, thereafter, settled so comfortably at fullback, where he had limited experience, that it seems he is intent on pressing for more honours from that berth. A graduate of Thurso High School and the Caithness club, he also played for Scotland at under-18, under-19 and under-21 and was on the 1991 national tour to North America. He has played 16 games for North and Midlands and made his A debut in the 12–9 win over France in February 1994. He is a rugby development officer with Dunfermline District Council.

DEREK STARK (Boroughmuir)
Wing, born 13.4.66 in Johnstone, 6 ft 2 in, 14 st 2 lb, 4 caps

Derek Alexander Stark added three A caps and an outing for the Scotland Development XV to his representative honours last season, although a groin injury, which he had been fighting since December 1992, flared up towards the end of the season, causing him to miss the tour to Argentina. Stark scored on his Five Nations debut against Ireland in 1993, demonstrating the Midas touch which has seen him notch six tries in seven under-21 appearances. He toured Zimbabwe (1988) and Australia (1992) with Scotland, though in the interim he took time out to concentrate on athletics and has a personal best of 10.6 secs for the 100 m. He shares the running of the family hotel, The Foxbar, in Kilmarnock.
International record: 1993 I, F, W, E. 5 points – 1 try.

GREGOR TOWNSEND *See* international player profile.

ROB WAINWRIGHT *See* international player profile.

PETER WALTON *See* international player profile.

ALAN WATT *See* international player profile.

DODDIE WEIR *See* international player profile.

PETER WRIGHT *See* international player profile.

DOUGLAS WYLLIE *See* international player profile.

Statistics and Fixtures

Compiled by Bill McMurtrie

I – CLUB CHAMPIONSHIP AND DISTRICT LEAGUE TABLES 1993–94

McEWAN'S 70/- NATIONAL LEAGUE

Division 1	P	W	D	L	F	A	Pts
Melrose	13	12	0	1	410	192	24
Gala	12	9	0	3	274	214	18
Edinburgh Academicals	13	8	1	4	265	183	17
Heriot's FP	12	7	0	5	230	224	14
Watsonians	13	7	0	6	276	337	14
Stirling County	12	6	1	5	227	163	13
Hawick	12	6	1	5	218	178	13
Jed-Forest	13	6	0	7	231	199	12
Currie	12	6	0	6	230	285	12
Stewart's-Melville FP	13	5	1	7	157	190	11
Boroughmuir	12	5	0	7	214	228	10
West of Scotland	13	4	1	8	235	279	9
Kelso	13	4	0	9	175	296	8
Selkirk	13	0	1	12	138	312	1

Champions: Melrose.
Relegated: Kelso, Selkirk.

Division 2	P	W	D	L	F	A	Pts
Glasgow High/ Kelvinside	13	13	0	0	440	115	26
Dundee HSFP	12	11	0	1	395	80	22
Kirkcaldy	13	10	0	3	277	150	20
Edinburgh Wanderers	13	8	0	5	214	251	16
Musselburgh	13	7	0	6	204	185	14
Peebles	13	6	0	7	206	219	12
Glasgow Academicals	13	5	1	7	237	276	11
Wigtownshire	13	5	0	8	172	241	10
Haddington	12	5	0	7	146	220	10
Grangemouth	13	4	1	8	201	293	9
Biggar	13	3	2	8	203	240	8
Preston Lodge FP	13	4	0	9	158	291	8
Clarkston	13	4	0	9	158	357	8
Ayr	13	3	0	10	168	261	6

Promoted: GHK (champions), Dundee HSFP.
Relegated: Clarkston, Ayr.

Division 3

	P	W	D	L	F	A	Pts
Gordonians	13	10	1	2	263	123	21
Corstorphine	13	10	0	3	237	161	20
Kilmarnock	13	9	1	3	277	129	19
Hillhead/Jordanhill	13	9	0	4	223	109	18
Hutcheson's/ Aloysians	13	8	0	5	216	159	16
Langholm	12	7	0	5	224	124	14
East Kilbride	13	7	0	6	190	192	14
Royal High	13	6	0	7	176	169	12
Stewartry	13	4	2	7	125	168	10
Portobello FP	13	5	0	8	172	237	10
Dunfermline	12	4	1	7	153	228	9
Dumfries	13	4	1	8	148	240	9
Howe of Fife	13	3	0	10	161	309	6
Perthshire	13	1	0	12	86	303	2

Promoted: Gordonians (champions), Corstorphine.
Relegated: Howe of Fife, Perthshire.

Division 4

	P	W	D	L	F	A	Pts
Trinity Academicals	13	11	0	2	293	149	22
Edinburgh University	13	10	1	2	287	155	21
Dalziel HS FP	12	9	0	3	176	144	18
Livingston	12	8	0	4	215	157	16
Ardrossan Academicals	12	7	1	4	145	148	15
Cambuslang	12	7	0	5	214	183	14
St Boswells	12	6	0	6	144	194	12
Morgan Academy FP	12	5	0	7	179	173	10
Highland	13	5	0	8	191	239	10
Alloa	13	5	0	8	163	217	10
Aberdeen GS FP	13	4	0	9	251	249	8
North Berwick	13	4	0	9	158	267	8
Cartha Queen's Park	13	3	1	9	158	216	7
Leith Academicals	13	2	1	10	122	205	5

Promoted: Trinity Academicals (champions), Edinburgh University.
Relegated: Cartha Queen's Park, Leith Academicals.

Division 5

	P	W	D	L	F	A	Pts
Duns	13	9	2	2	328	153	20
Glenrothes	13	10	0	3	288	168	20
Linlithgow	13	10	0	3	225	138	20
Falkirk	13	7	2	4	195	130	16
Berwick	13	8	0	5	184	138	16
Penicuik	13	7	0	6	241	209	14
Clydebank	13	5	1	7	134	176	11
Paisley	13	5	0	8	201	195	10
Irvine	13	5	0	8	158	198	10
Lismore	13	5	0	8	167	219	10
Madras College FP	13	5	0	8	208	295	10
Hillfoots	13	5	0	8	160	275	10
Lenzie	13	4	0	9	204	296	8
Aberdeenshire	13	3	1	9	117	220	7

Promoted: Duns (champions), Glenrothes.
Relegated: Lenzie, Aberdeenshire.

Division 6

	P	W	D	L	F	A	Pts
Allan Glen's	13	12	0	1	372	96	24
Cumbernauld	13	12	0	1	270	106	24
Forrester FP	13	7	0	6	231	205	14
St Andrews University	13	7	0	6	197	328	14
Greenock Wanderers	13	6	1	6	322	250	13
Dunbar	13	6	1	6	230	184	13
Ross High	13	6	1	6	213	178	13
Murrayfield	13	6	0	7	301	225	12
Marr	13	6	0	7	215	191	12
Earlston	13	5	1	7	163	249	11
Waysiders/ Drumpellier	13	5	0	8	180	312	10
Harris Academy FP	13	4	1	8	149	218	9
Moray	13	4	0	9	150	284	8
Lasswade	13	2	1	10	126	293	5

Promoted: Allan Glen's (champions), Cumbernauld.
Relegated: Moray, Lasswade.

Division 7

	P	W	D	L	F	A	Pts
Annan	12	12	0	0	501	78	24
Aberdeen University	12	8	0	4	312	170	16
Holy Cross	12	8	0	4	299	167	16
Garnock	12	8	0	4	184	121	16
Whitecraigs	12	6	1	5	158	177	13
Hyndland FP	12	6	1	5	149	220	13
Waid Academy FP	12	6	0	6	236	195	12
Broughton FP	12	6	0	6	175	189	12
Panmure	12	4	2	6	194	228	10
Walkerburn	12	4	0	8	214	254	8
RAF Kinloss	12	4	0	8	160	245	8
Dalkeith	12	3	2	7	90	211	8
Montrose	12	0	0	12	99	516	0

Promoted: Annan (champions), Aberdeen University.
Relegated: Dalkeith, Montrose.
Stirling University expelled from national league for failing to fulfil fixtures.

District League Champions (promoted to Division 7):
Glasgow: Cumnock
Edinburgh: Edinburgh Northern
North and Midlands: Lochaber (North League champions, who won play-off against Rosyth and District, winners of Midlands District League)

BANK OF SCOTLAND BORDER LEAGUE

	P	W	D	L	F	A	Pts
Melrose	11	10	0	1	355	119	20
Jed-Forest	12	7	1	4	289	139	15
Hawick	10	7	1	2	219	113	15
Gala	8	5	0	3	123	169	10
Kelso	12	4	0	8	209	265	8
Selkirk	10	2	0	8	124	200	4
Langholm	9	0	0	9	39	353	0

RMD GLASGOW AND DISTRICT LEAGUE

Division 1

	P	W	D	L	F	A	Pts
Cumnock	13	11	0	2	276	86	22
Strathendrick	13	11	0	2	257	75	22
Glasgow University	13	9	1	3	296	146	19
Hamilton Academicals	13	7	1	5	158	123	15
Strathaven	12	7	1	4	126	181	15
Mull	13	7	0	6	161	147	14
Strathclyde Police	12	6	1	5	153	143	13
Mid Argyll	12	6	0	6	206	189	12
St Mungo/Turnbull	13	4	1	8	146	218	9
Newton Stewart	12	3	2	7	140	179	8
Oban Lorne	13	4	0	9	168	245	8
McLaren FP	13	3	1	9	184	284	7
Bute	13	3	1	9	115	226	7
Carrick	13	3	1	9	171	315	7

Promoted to national league: Cumnock.
Relegated: Carrick.

Division 2

	P	W	D	L	F	A	Pts
Uddingston	13	13	0	0	327	54	26
Strathclyde University	14	11	1	2	459	90	23
Vale of Leven	14	11	1	2	314	148	23
Arran	12	8	0	4	283	109	16
Helensburgh	13	8	0	5	215	123	16
Birkmyre	14	8	0	6	197	144	16
Kintyre	12	8	0	4	156	138	16
Linwood	14	7	0	7	257	210	14
Clydesdale	13	5	0	8	76	193	10
Craigielea	14	5	0	9	159	326	10
Dumbarton	13	4	0	9	115	193	8
St Modans	14	4	0	10	129	213	8
Bearsden	13	3	0	10	87	271	6
Shawlands	14	2	0	12	60	293	4
Cowal	13	2	0	11	112	441	4

Promoted: Uddingston, Strathclyde University.

EDINBURGH AND DISTRICT LEAGUE

	P	W	D	L	F	A	Pts
Edinburgh Northern	11	10	0	1	288	38	20
Heriot-Watt University	10	7	0	3	304	77	14
Moray House	10	6	0	4	157	157	12
Lanark	9	4	0	5	111	206	8
Royal (Dick) Vet College	10	3	0	7	118	155	6
Ferranti	10	3	0	7	133	229	6
Liberton	8	1	0	7	31	280	2

Champions: Edinburgh Northern (promoted to national league).

MIDLANDS DISTRICT LEAGUE

	P	W	D	L	F	A	Pts
Rosyth and District	18	15	1	2	510	89	31
Kinross	14	12	0	3	401	117	24
Carnoustie HS FP	16	11	0	5	351	242	22
Stobswell	13	8	1	4	235	164	17
Dundee University	15	8	0	7	372	155	16
Strathmore	16	7	0	9	198	239	14
Dalgety Bay	15	6	0	9	139	425	12
Crieff	15	3	0	12	115	542	6
West Fife	13	2	0	11	120	349	4

Champions: Rosyth (beaten by Lochaber, North District League champions, in play-off for promotion to national league).

NORTH DISTRICT LEAGUE

	P	W	D	L	F	A	Pts
Lochaber	12	12	0	0	358	60	24
Orkney	12	10	1	1	235	83	21
Mackie Academy FP	12	8	1	3	161	76	17
RAF Lossiemouth	12	7	0	5	253	121	14
Ellon	12	5	1	6	170	111	11
Garioch	11	5	1	5	149	152	11
Aberdeen Wanderers	10	5	0	5	99	107	10
Banff	11	4	1	6	138	146	9
Dyce	13	4	1	7	112	255	9
Caithness	9	4	0	5	95	124	8
Aboyne	11	3	0	8	71	184	6
Moray College	10	2	0	8	65	198	4
Ross-Sutherland	10	0	0	10	52	341	0

Champions: Lochaber (promoted to national league by winning play-off against Rosyth and District, Midlands District League champions).

ABERDEEN AND DISTRICT LEAGUE

	P	W	D	L	F	A	Pts
Grampian Police	8	6	0	2	152	72	12
Peterhead	8	5	1	2	95	87	11
RAF Buchan	8	5	0	3	101	41	10
3rd Aberdeen GS FP	8	5	0	3	115	103	10
2nd Moray	8	3	1	4	116	132	7
3rd Gordonians	8	3	1	4	102	125	7
Huntly	8	3	0	5	71	114	6
3rd Aberdeenshire	8	2	1	5	93	132	5
2nd RAF Kinloss	8	2	0	6	90	129	4

LEADING SCORERS IN SCOTTISH RUGBY IN 1993–94

(Points and try totals are for all matches. Where a player has scored for more than one team his club total is shown in brackets.)

Points

417 Gary Parker (Melrose) (287)

354 Harry Bassi
   (Glasgow High/Kelvinside)

318 Duncan Hodge
   (Watsonians) (193)

293 Bryan Easson
   (Boroughmuir) (245)

278 Jon Newton
   (Dundee HS FP) (260)

269 John Mitchell (Kirkcaldy)

255 Graeme Aitchison (Kelso)

230 Dave Barrett
   (West of Scotland) (152)

229 Brian Hay-Smith
   (Edinburgh Academicals)

220 Ally Donaldson
   (Currie) (205)

218 Mike Dods (Gala) (116)

196 Cliff Livingstone
   (Musselburgh) (172)

177 Mark McKenzie
   (Stirling County)

161 Gavin Hastings
   (Watsonians) (56)

161 Murray Thomson
   (Stewart's-Melville FP)

151 Robbie Bremner
   (Edinburgh Wanderers) (133)

145 Derek Stark
   (Boroughmuir) (95)

142 Dennis Lavery (Biggar)

139 Tony Greenshields
   (Clarkston) (110)

132 Cameron Glasgow
   (Heriot's FP) (113)

118 Gavin Rennie
   (Grangemouth)

117 Calum MacGregor
   (Glasgow Academicals)

113 Martin Hose (Wigtownshire)

112 Scott Welsh (Hawick)

110 Bryan Craig (Haddington)

105 Robbie Kemp (Ayr)

105 Keith Suddon (Hawick)

102 Rowen Shepherd
   (Edinburgh Academicals) (66)

100 Scott Brownlee
   (Haddington)

100 Stuart Lang (Kelso) (47)

Tries

29 Derek Stark
   (Boroughmuir) (19)

28 Gary Parker (Melrose) (17)

21 Keith Suddon (Hawick) (20)

19 John Price (Clarkston)

17 Gordon Waddell (Gala)

16 Mike Cousin
   (Dundee HS FP) (15)

16 Gerry Hawkes
   (Glasgow High/Kelvinside)

16 Kenny Logan
   (Stirling County) (8)

15 Ross Brown (Melrose) (13)

15 Fergus Henderson
   (Watsonians) (14)

15 Cameron Little
   (Glasgow High/Kelvinside)

15 Peter Manning
   (Glasgow High/Kelvinside)

14 Craig Joiner (Melrose) (8)

13 Colin Gillan
   (Edinburgh Wanderers) (12)

13 Lindsay Graham (Biggar)

13 John Mitchell (Kirkcaldy)

13 Kenny Nisbet (Peebles)

13 Neil White (Melrose)

12 Chris Dalgleish (Gala) (8)

12 Alan Drysdale
   (Wigtownshire)

12 Alan Kittle
   (Stewart's-Melville FP) (11)

12 Craig Macdonald
   (Kirkcaldy) (10)

12 Neill Renton (Kirkcaldy)

11 Hugh Gilmour (Heriot's FP)
   (9)

11 Scott Hastings
   (Watsonians) (7)

11 Stuart Lang (Kelso) (7)

11 Dave Wilson (Currie)

10 Calum ('Howler') Brown
   (Jed-Forest)

10 John Kerr (Watsonians)

10 Sean Lineen
   (Boroughmuir) (6)

10 Craig McGreary
   (Haddington) (9)

10 Stuart Munro (West of
   Scotland)

10 Andy Nicol (Dundee HS FP)

10 Rowen Shepherd
   (Edinburgh Academicals) (7)

10 Kevin Whitaker (Heriot's FP)

II – INTER-DISTRICT AND CLUB CHAMPIONS

INTER-DISTRICT CHAMPIONS

1953–54
  Edinburgh W3
1954–55
  South W3
1955–56
  Glasgow W2: D1
1956–57
  Edinburgh-South W2: L1
1957–58
  Edinburgh-South W2: D1
1958–59
  Edinburgh-South W2: L1
1959–60
  Edinburgh-North and Midlands-South
  W2: L1
1960–61
  Edinburgh W3
1961–62
  Edinburgh-South W2: D1
1962–63
  Edinburgh W3
1963–64
  South W3

1964–65
  Glagow-South W2: L1
1965–66
  South W3
1966–67
  South W2: D1
1967–68
  Edinburgh-Glasgow-South W2: L1
1968–69
  South W3
1969–70
  South W2: D1
1970–71
  South W3
1971–72
  Edinburgh W2: L1
  (Edinburgh beat Glasgow 20–16 in a
  play-off at Murrayfield)
1972–73
  Edinburgh-Glasgow W2: L1
1973–74
  Glasgow W3

1974–75
  Glasgow-North and Midlands W2: L1
1975–76
  Edinburgh-Glasgow-South W2: L1
1976–77
  South W3
1977–78
  Edinburgh-Glasgow-South W2: L1
1978–79
  South W3
1979–80
  Edinburgh W3
1980–81
  South W3
1981–82
  Edinburgh-South W3: D1
1982–83
  South W4
1983–84
  South W4
1984–85
  South W4

1985–86
  South W4
1986–87
  Edinburgh W4
1987–88
  Edinburgh W4
1988–89
  Edinburgh W4
1989–90
  Glasgow W3: D1
1990–91
  South W3: D1
1991–92
  No championship because of the World Cup
1992–93
  South W3: L1
1993–94
  South ★
(★ Knock-out competition: South beat
  Glasgow 28–14 in the final)

INTER-CITY SERIES

(since the first match in 1872)
Edinburgh won 57, Glasgow won 38, with 19 drawn.

UNDER-21 INTER-DISTRICT CHAMPIONS

1979–80
  Edinburgh W3
1980–81
  South W3
1981–82
  Edinburgh W2: D1
1982–83
  South W3
1983–84
  South W2: D1
1984–85
  South W3
1985–86
  South W3
1986–87
  Glasgow W3

1987–88
  South W3
1988–89
  Unfinished
1989–90
  South W3: D1
1990–91
  South-Glasgow W3: L1
1991–92
  Glasgow W4
1992–93
  Edinburgh W4
1993–94
  South W3
(Anglo-Scots, later Scottish Exiles, played in
the competition from 1989–90 until 1992–93)

UNDER-18 INTER-DISTRICT CHAMPIONS

1982–83
 Edinburgh W3
1983–84
 Edinburgh W3
1984–85
 South W3
1985–86
 South W3
1986–87
 South W3
1987–88
 Glasgow W2: D1

1988–89
 Glasgow W3
1989–90
 South W3
1990–91
 North and Midlands W3
1991–92
 Edinburgh W3
1992–93
 South W3
1993–94
 North and Midlands-South W2

SCOTTISH UNOFFICIAL CLUB CHAMPIONS

1865–66   Edinburgh Academicals
1866–67   Edinburgh Academicals
1867–68   Edinburgh Academicals
1868–69   Edinburgh Academicals
1869–70   Edinburgh Academicals
1870–71   Edinburgh Academicals
1871–72   Glasgow Academicals and
  Edinburgh University
1872–73   Glasgow Academicals
1873–74   Glasgow Academicals and
  Edinburgh Academicals
1874–75   Edinburgh Academicals
1875–76   Glasgow Academicals
1876–77   Glasgow Academicals
1877–78   Edinburgh Academicals
1878–79   Edinburgh Academicals
1879–80   Edinburgh Academicals
1880–81   Edinburgh Institution FP
1881–82   Edinburgh Institution FP
1882–83   Glasgow Academicals and
  West of Scotland
1883–84   Royal High School FP
1884–85   West of Scotland
1885–86   Edinburgh Academicals and
  West of Scotland
1886–87   Edinburgh Academicals
1887–88   Edinburgh Academicals
1888–89   West of Scotland
1889–90   Edinburgh Academicals and
  West of Scotland
1890–91   West of Scotland
1891–92   Watsonians and West of Scotland
1892–93   Watsonians
1893–94   Watsonians

1894–95   Watsonians and West of Scotland
1895–96   Hawick
1896–97   Clydesdale, Jed-Forest and
  Watsonians
1897–98   Edinburgh Academicals
1898–99   Edinburgh Academicals
1899–1900   Edinburgh Academicals and
  Edinburgh University
1900–01   Edinburgh Academicals
1901–02   Edinburgh University
1902–03   Edinburgh University and
  Watsonians
1903–04   Edinburgh University and
  Glasgow Academicals
1904–05   Glasgow Academicals
1905–06   Edinburgh Academicals
1906–07   Jed-Forest
1907–08   Edinburgh University
1908–09   Hawick and Watsonians
1909–10   Watsonians
1910–11   Watsonians
1911–12   Edinburgh University and
  Watsonians
1912–13   Glasgow Academicals
1913–14   Watsonians
1914–19   No competition (First World War)
1919–20   Heriot's FP
1920–21   Watsonians
1921–22   Glasgow Academicals
1922–23   Heriot's FP
1923–24   Glasgow Academicals and
  Glasgow High School FP
1924–25   Glasgow Academicals
1925–26   Glasgow Academicals

1926–27	Hawick		1952–53	Selkirk
1927–28	Heriot's FP		1953–54	Glasgow High School FP
1928–29	Heriot's FP		1954–55	Boroughmuir
1929–30	Glasgow Academicals		1955–56	Edinburgh Academicals
1930–31	Dunfermline		1956–57	Edinburgh Academicals and Jed-Forest
1931–32	Gala		1957–58	Stewart's College FP
1932–33	Dunfermline and Hawick		1958–59	Langholm
1933–34	Hillhead High School FP and Royal High School FP		1959–60	Hawick
1934–35	Watsonians		1960–61	Hawick
1935–36	Glasgow High School FP		1961–62	Glasgow High School FP
1936–37	Hillhead High School FP and Watsonians		1962–63	Melrose
1937–38	Stewart's College FP		1963–64	Hawick
1938–39	Allan Glen's FP		1964–65	Hawick and West of Scotland
1939–46	No competition (Second World War)		1965–66	Hawick
			1966–67	Melrose
1946–47	Stewart's College FP		1967–68	Hawick
1947–48	Aberdeen GS FP and Kelso		1968–69	Jordanhill College
1948–49	Hawick		1969–70	Watsonians
1949–50	Heriot's FP		1970–71	West of Scotland
1950–51	Glasgow High School FP		1971–72	Hawick
1951–52	Melrose		1972–73	Boroughmuir

SCOTTISH RUGBY UNION CLUB CHAMPIONSHIP WINNERS

1973–74	Hawick		1984–85	Hawick
1974–75	Hawick		1985–86	Hawick
1975–76	Hawick		1986–87†	Hawick
1976–77	Hawick (after play-off with Gala)		1987–88	Kelso
1977–78*	Hawick		1988–89	Kelso
1978–79	Heriot's FP		1989–90	Melrose
1979–80	Gala		1990–91	Boroughmuir
1980–81	Gala		1991–92	Melrose
1981–82	Hawick		1992–93	Melrose
1982–83	Gala		1993–94	Melrose
1983–84	Hawick			

(* Championship sponsored by Schweppes for nine years)
(† McEwan's sponsorship introduced)

BORDER LEAGUE CHAMPIONS

1901–02	Hawick		1908–09	Hawick
1902–03	Jed-Forest		1909–10	Hawick and Jed-Forest
1903–04	Jed-Forest		1910–11	Melrose (after play-off with Hawick at Riverside Park)
1904–05	Jed-Forest			
1905–06	Gala		1911–12	Hawick
1906–07	Jed-Forest (first season of cup)		1912–13	Hawick
1907–08	Jed Forest		1913–14	Hawick

1914–19	First World War		1958–59	Langholm
1919–20	Jed-Forest		1959–60	Hawick
1920–21	Hawick (after play-off with Jed-Forest at the Greenyards)		1960–61	Hawick
			1961–62	Hawick
1921–22	Gala		1962–63	Melrose
1922–23	Hawick		1963–64	Hawick
1923–24	Hawick		1964–65	Hawick
1924–25	Hawick		1965–66	Hawick
1925–26	Hawick (after play-off with Kelso at the Greenyards)		1966–67	Gala
			1967–68	Hawick
1926–27	Hawick		1968–69	Hawick
1927–28	Hawick		1969–70	Hawick
1928–29	Hawick		1970–71	Melrose
1929–30	Hawick		1971–72	Hawick
1930–31	Kelso		1972–73	Hawick
1931–32	Hawick		1973–74	Hawick
1932–33	unfinished		1974–75	Hawick
1933–34	Kelso		1975–76	Hawick
1934–35	Selkirk		1976–77	Hawick
1935–36	unfinished		1977–78	Hawick
1936–37	Kelso		1978–79	Hawick
1937–38	Selkirk		1979–80	Gala
1938–39	Melrose		1980–81	Gala
1939–46	Second World War		1981–82	Hawick
1946–47	unfinished		1982–83	Hawick
1947–48	unfinished		1983–84	Hawick
1948–49	Hawick		1984–85	Hawick
1949–50	Gala and Melrose		1985–86	Kelso
1950–51	Hawick		1986–87	Kelso
1951–52	unfinished		1987–88*	Jed-Forest
1952–53	Selkirk		1988–89	Hawick
1953–54	Melrose		1989–90	Melrose
1954–55	Hawick		1990–91†	Melrose
1955–56	Hawick		1991–92	Melrose
1956–57	Jed-Forest		1992–93	Melrose
1957–58	Melrose		1993–94	Melrose

(* Sponsored by Scotch Beef for three seasons)
(† Bank of Scotland sponsorship introduced)

SCOTTISH RUGBY UNION YOUTH LEAGUE CHAMPIONS

1980–81*	Kirkcaldy		1987–88	Melrose Colts
1981–82	Kirkcaldy		1988–89	Stirling County
1982–83	Melrose Colts		1989–90†	Gala Wanderers
1983–84	Melrose Colts		1990–91	West of Scotland
1984–85	Jed Thistle		1991–92	Kelso Harlequins
1985–86	Stirling County		1992–93	Kelso Harlequins
1986–87	Hawick PSA		1993–94	Biggar

(* Sponsored by Royal Bank for 10 years)
(† Digital sponsorship introduced)

Statistics & Fixtures

III – SCOTLAND INTERNATIONAL PLAYERS

List of Abbreviations

Playing Positions

fb	fullback
rw	right wing
c	centre
so	stand-off
lw	left wing
sh	scrumhalf
lh	loose-head
h	hooker
th	tight-head
l	lock
wf	wing forward
8	no. 8
r	replacement
t	temporary replacement
★	captain

Scores

t	try
g	goal
pg	penalty goal
dg	drop goal

Countries

A	Australia
Arg	Argentina
E	England
EC	Centenary match against England (non-championship)
F	France
Fj	Fiji
I	Ireland
NSW	New South Wales
NZ	New Zealand
P-SRU	President's Overseas XV
R	Romania
SA	South Africa
W	Wales
WC	World Cup
WS	Western Samoa
Z	Zimbabwe

INTERNATIONAL PLAYERS IN 1993–94

	New Zealand	Wales	England	Ireland	France
Hastings, A.G. (Watsonians)	fb★	fb★	fb★	fb★	fb★
Dods, M. (Gala)				(t)	
Stanger, A.G. (Hawick)	rw	rw	rw	rw	rw
Jardine, I.C. (Stirling County)	c	c	(r)		
Shiel, A.G. (Melose)	c				
Townsend, G.P.J. (Gala)		c	so	so	so
Wyllie, D.S. (Stewart's–Melville FP)	(r)	(r)	c	c	c
Hastings, S. (Watsonians)	lw		c	c	c
Logan, K.M. (Stirling County)	(t)	lw	lw	lw	lw
Chalmers, C.M. (Melrose)	so	so			
Nicol, A.D. (Dundee HS FP)	sh	sh			
Armstrong, G. (Jed-Forest)			sh	sh	
Redpath, B.W. (Melrose)	(t)		(t)		sh
Watt, A.G.J. (GHK)	lh				
Wright, P.H. (Boroughmuir)		lh			
Sharp, A.V. (Bristol)			lh	lh	lh
Milne, K.S. (Heriot's FP)	h	h	h	h	h
Burnell, A.P. (London Scottish)	th	th	th	th	th
Cronin, D.F. (London Scottish)	l				
Macdonald, A.E.D. (Heriot's FP)	l				
Edwards, N.G.B. (Northampton)		l			
Munro, D.S. (GHK)		l	l	l	l
Reed, A.I. (Bath)			l	l	l
McIvor, D.J. (Edinburgh Academicals)	wf				
Wainwright, R.I. (Edinburgh Academicals)	wf	8	wf		

Statistics & Fixtures

	New Zealand	Wales	England	Ireland	France
Turnbull, D.J. (Hawick)		wf			
Morrison, I.R. (London Scottish)		wf			
Walton, P. (Northampton)			wf	wf	wf
Smith, I.R. (Gloucester)			(r)	wf	wf
Weir, G.W. (Melrose)	8	(r)	8	8	8
Hogg, C.D. (Melrose)	(r)				

SCOTLAND A TEAM PLAYERS IN 1993–94

	New Zealand	Italy	Ireland A	France A
Dods, M. (Gala)	fb	fb		fb
Logan, K.M. (Stirling County)	rw	lw	fb	
Milligan, K.R. (Stewart's-Melville FP)		rw	rw	rw
Nichol, S.A. (Selkirk)	c	c	c	
Jardine, I.C. (Stirling County)	c	c	c	c
Shepherd, R.J.S. (Edinburgh Academicals)				c
Parker, G.A. (Melrose)	lw			
Stark, D.A. (Boroughmuir)			lw	lw
Wyllie, D.S. (Stewart's-Melville FP)	so★	so★		
Townsend, G.P.J. (Gala)			so	
Chalmers, C.M. (Melrose)				so
Redpath, B.W. (Melrose)	sh	sh		sh
Nicol, A.D. (Dundee HS FP)			sh	
Watt, A.G.J. (GHK)	lh			
Sharp, A.V. (Bristol)		lh	lh	
McKenzie, K.D. (Stirling County)	h	h	h★	h★
Herrington, D.W. (Dundee HS FP)	th			th

	New Zealand	Italy	Ireland A	France A
Wright, P.H. (Boroughmuir)		th	th	lh
Munro, D.S. (GHK)	l		l	l
Macdonald, A.E.D. (Heriot's FP)	l		l	
Weir, G.W. (Melrose)			l	
Edwards, N.G.B. (Northampton)				l
Campbell, S.J. (Dundee HS FP)				l
McIvor, D.J. (Edinburgh Academicals)	wf			wf
Walton, P. (Northampton)		wf	wf	
Wainwright, R.I. (Edinburgh Academicals)	wf		8	
Morrison, I.R. (London Scottish)			wf	
Reid, S.J. (Boroughmuir)				wf
Hogg, C.D. (Melrose)	8	wf		8
McIntosh, D.L.M. (Pontypridd)		8		

FULL LIST OF INTERNATIONAL PLAYERS

When Scotland played against a country more than once in one year the figures (1) and/or (2) denote whether the player appeared in the first and/or second match.

Abercrombie, C.H., United Services, London Scottish – 1910 *I, E,* 1911 *F, W,* 1913 *F, W*

Abercrombie, J.G., Edinburgh U. – 1949 *F, W, I,* 1950 *F, W, I, E*

Agnew, W.C.C., Stewart's College FP – 1930 *W, I*

Ainslie, R., Edinburgh Institution FP – 1879 *I, E,* 1880, *I, E,* 1881 *E,* 1882 *I, E*

Ainslie, T., Edinburgh Institution FP – 1881 *E,* 1882 *I, E,* 1883 *W, I, E,* 1884 *W, I, E,* 1885 *W, I (1, 2)*

Aitchison, G.R., Edinburgh Wanderers – 1883 *I*

Aitchison, T.G., Gala – 1929 *W, I, E*

Aitken, A.I., Edinburgh Institution FP – 1889 *I*

Aitken, G.G., Oxford University – 1924 *W, I, E,* 1925 *F, W, I, E,* 1929 *F*

Aitken, J., Gala – 1977 *E, I, F,* 1981 *F, W, E, I, NZ (1, 2), R, A,* 1982 *E, I, F, W,* 1983 *F, W, E, NZ,* 1984 *W, E, I, F, R*

Aitken, R., London Scottish, Royal Navy – 1947 *W*

Allan, B., Glasgow Academicals – 1881 *I*

Allan, J., Edinburgh Academicals – 1990 *NZ (1),* 1991 *W, I, R, WC (J, I, WS, E, NZ)*

Allan, J.L., Melrose – 1952 *F, W, I,* 1953 *W*

Allan, J.L.F., Cambridge University – 1957 *I, E*

Allan, J.W., Melrose – 1927 *F,* 1928 *I,* 1929 *F, W, I, E,* 1930 *F, E,* 1931 *F, W, I, E,* 1932 *SA, W, I,* 1934 *I, E*

Allan, R.C., Hutchesons' GS FP – 1969 *I*

Allardice, W.D., Aberdeen GS FP – 1948 *A, F, W, I,* 1949 *F, W, I, E*

Allen, H.W., Glasgow Academicals – 1873 *E*

Anderson, A.H., Glasgow Academicals – 1849 *I*

Anderson, D.G., London Scottish – 1889 *I,* 1890 *W, I, E,* 1891 *W, E,* 1892 *W, E*

Anderson, E., Stewart's College FP – 1947 *I, E*

Anderson, J.W., West of Scotland – 1872 *E*

Anderson, T., Merchiston – 1882 *I*

Angus, A.W., Watsonians – 1909 *W*, 1910 *F, W, E*, 1911 *W, I*, 1912 *F, W, I, E, SA*, 1913 *F, W*, 1914 *E*, 1920 *F, W, I, E*

Anton, P.A., St Andrews University – 1873 *E*

Armstrong, G., Jed-Forest – 1988 *A*, 1989 *W, E, I, F, Fj, R*, 1990, *I, F, W, E, NZ* (1, 2), *Arg*, 1991 *F, W, E, I, R, WC (J, I, WS, E, NZ)*, 1993 *I, F, W, E*, 1994 *E, I*

Arneil, R.J., Edinburgh Academicals, Leicester, Northampton – 1968 *I, E, A*, 1969 *F, W, I, E, SA*, 1970 *F, W, I, E, A*, 1971 *F, W, I, E, EC*, 1972 *F, W, E*, 1973 *NZ*

Arthur, A., Glasgow Academicals – 1875 *E*, 1876 *E*

Arthur, J.W., Glasgow Academicals – 1871 *E*, 1872 *E*

Asher, A.G.G., Oxford University, Fettesian-Lorettonians, Edinburgh Wanderers – 1882 *I*, 1884 *W, I, E*, 1885 *W*, 1886 *I, E*

Auld, W., West of Scotland – 1889 *W*, 1890 *W*

Auldjo, L.J., Abertay – 1878 *E*

Bain, D. McL., Oxford University – 1911 *E*, 1912 *F, W, E, SA*, 1913 *F, W, I, E*, 1914 *W, I*

Baird, G.R.T., Kelso – 1981 *A*, 1982 *E, I, F, W, A* (1, 2), 1983 *I, F, W, E, NZ*, 1984 *W, E, I, F, A*, 1985 *I, W, E*, 1986 *F, W, E, I, R*, 1987 *E*, 1988 *I*

Balfour, A., Watsonians – 1896 *W, I, E*, 1897 *E*

Balfour, L.M., Edinburgh Academicals – 1872 *E*

Bannerman, E.M., Edinburgh Academicals – 1872 *E*, 1873 *E*

Bannerman, J.M., Glasgow HS FP, Oxford University – 1921 *F, W, I, E*, 1922 *F, W, I, E*, 1923 *F, W, I, E*, 1924 *F, W, I, E*, 1925 *F, W, I, E*, 1926 *F, W, I, E*, 1927 *F, W, I, E, NSW*, 1928 *F, W, I, E*, 1929 *F, W, I, E*

Barnes, I.A., Hawick – 1972 *W*, 1974 *F(r)*, 1975 *E(r), NZ*, 1977 *I, F, W*

Barrie, R.W., Hawick – 1936 *E*

Bearne, K.R.F., Cambridge University, London Scottish – 1960 *F, W*

Beattie, J.A., Hawick – 1929 *F, W*, 1930 *W*, 1931 *F, W, I, E*, 1932 *SA, W, I, E*, 1933 *W, E, I*, 1934 *I, W, E*, 1935 *W, I, E, NZ*, 1936 *W, I, E*

Beattie, J.R., Glasgow Academicals – 1980 *I, F, W, E*, 1981 *F, W, E, I*, 1983 *F, W, E, NZ*, 1984 *E (r), R, A*, 1985 *I*, 1986 *F, W, E, I, R*, 1987 *I, F, W, E*

Bedell-Sivright, D.R., Cambridge University, West of Scotland, Edinburgh University – 1900 *W*, 1901 *W, I, E*, 1902 *W, I, E*, 1903 *W, I*, 1904 *W, I, E*, 1905 *NZ*, 1906 *W, I, E, SA*, 1907 *W, I, E*, 1908 *W, I*

Bedell-Sivright, J.V., Cambridge University – 1902 *W*

Begbie, T.A., Edinburgh Wanderers – 1881 *I, E*

Bell, D.L., Watsonians – 1975 *I, F, W, E*

Bell, J.A., Clydesdale – 1901 *W, I, E*, 1902 *W, I, E*

Bell, L.H.I., Edinburgh Academicals – 1900 *E*, 1904 *W, I*

Berkeley, W.V., Oxford University, London Scottish – 1926 *F*, 1929 *F, W, I*

Berry, C.W., Fettesian-Lorettonians, Edinburgh Wanderers – 1884 *I, E*, 1885 *W, I* (1) 1887 *I, W, E*, 1888 *W, I*

Bertram, D.M., Watsonians – 1922 *F, W, I, E*, 1923 *F, W, I, E*, 1924 *W, I, E*

Biggar, A.G., London Scottish – 1969 *SA*, 1970 *F, I, E, A*, 1971 *F, W, I, E, EC*, 1972 *F, W*

Biggar, M.A., London Scottish – 1975 *I, F, W, E*, 1976 *W, E, I*, 1977 *I, F, W*, 1978 *I, F, W, E, NZ*, 1979 *W, E, I, F, NZ*, 1980 *I, F, W, E*

Birkett, G.A., Harlequins, London Scottish – 1975 *NZ*

Bishop, J.M., Glasgow Academicals – 1893 *I*

Bisset, A.A., RIE College – 1904 *W*

Black, A.W., Edinburgh University – 1947 *F, W*, 1948 *E*, 1950 *W, I, E*

Black, W.P., Glasgow HS FP – 1948 *F, W, I, E*, 1951 *E*

Blackadder, W.F., West of Scotland – 1938 *E*

Blaikie, C.F., Heriot's FP – 1963 *I, E*, 1966 *E*, 1968 *A*, 1969 *F, W, I, E*

Blair, P.C.B., Cambridge University – 1912 *SA*, 1913 *F, W, I, E*

Bolton, W.H., West of Scotland – 1876 *E*

Borthwick, J.B., Stewart's College FP – 1938 *W, I*

Bos, F.H. ten, Oxford University, London Scottish – 1959 *E*, 1960 *F, W, SA*, 1961 *F, SA, W, I, E*, 1962 *F, W, I, E*, 1963 *F, W, I, E*

Boswell, J.D., West of Scotland – 1889 *W, I*, 1890 *W, I, E*, 1891 *W, I, E*, 1892 *W, I, E*, 1893 *I, E*, 1894 *I, E*

Bowie, T.C., Watsonians – 1913 *I, E*, 1914 *I, E*

Boyd, G.M., Glasgow HS FP – 1926 *E*

Boyd, J.L., United Services – 1912 *E, SA*

Boyle, A.C.W., London Scottish – 1963 *F, W, I*

Boyle, A.H.W., St Thomas's Hospital,

London Scottish – 1966 *A*, 1967, *F*, *NZ*, 1968 *F*, *W*, *I*

Brash, J.C., Cambridge University – 1961 *E*

Breakey, R.W., Gosforth – 1978 *E*

Brewis, N.T., Edinburgh Institution FP – 1876 *E*, 1878 *E*, 1879 *I*, 1880 *I*, *E*

Brewster, A.K., Stewart's-Melville FP – 1977 *E*, 1980 *I*, *F*, 1986 *E*, *I*, *R*

Brown, A.H., Heriot's FP – 1928 *E*, 1929 *F*, *W*

Brown, A.R., Gala – 1971 *E*, *EC*, 1972 *F*, *W*, *E*

Brown, C.H.C., Dunfermline – 1929 *E*

Brown, D.I., Cambridge University – 1933 *W*, *E*, *I*

Brown, G.L., West of Scotland – 1969 *SA*, 1970 *F*, *W*(r), *I*, *E*, *A*, 1971 *F*, *W*, *I*, *E*, *EC*, 1972 *F*, *W*, *E*, *NZ*, 1973 *E*(r), *P*, 1974 *W*, *E*, *I*, *F*, 1975 *I*, *F*, *W*, *E*, *A*, 1976 *F*, *W*, *E*, *I*

Brown, J.A., Glasgow Academicals – 1908 *W*, *I*

Brown, J.B., Glasgow Academicals – 1879 *I*, *E*, 1880 *I*, *E*, 1881 *I*, *E*, 1882 *I*, *E*, 1883 *W*, *I*, *E*, 1884 *W*, *I*, *E*, 1885 (1, 2), 1886 *W*, *I*, *E*

Brown, P.C., West of Scotland, Gala – 1964 *F*, *NZ*, *W*, *I*, *E*, 1965 *I*, *E*, *SA*, 1966 *A*, 1969 *I*, *E*, 1970 *W*, *E*, 1971 *F*, *W*, *I*, *E*, *EC*, 1972 *F*, *W*, *E*, *NZ*, 1973 *F*, *W*, *I*, *E*, *P*

Brown, T.G., Heriot's FP – 1929 *W*

Brown, W.D., Glasgow Academicals – 1871 *E*, 1872 *E*, 1873 *E*, 1874 *E*, 1875 *E*

Brown, W.S., Edinburgh Institution FP – 1880 *I*, *E*, 1882 *I*, *E*, 1883 *W*, *I*, *E*

Browning, A., Glasgow HS FP – 1920 *I*, 1922 *F*, *W*, *I*, 1923 *W*, *I*, *E*

Bruce, C.R., Glasgow Academicals – 1947 *F*, *W*, *I*, *E*, 1949 *F*, *W*, *I*, *E*

Bruce, N.S., Blackheath, Army, London Scottish – 1958 *F*, *A*, *I*, *E*, 1959 *F*, *W*, *I*, *E*, 1960 *F*, *W*, *I*, *E*, *SA*, 1961 *F*, *SA*, *W*, *I*, *E*, 1962 *F*, *W*, *I*, *E*, 1963 *F*, *W*, *I*, *E*, 1964 *F*, *NZ*, *W*, *I*, *E*

Bruce, R.M., Gordonians – 1947 *A*, 1948 *F*, *W*, *I*

Bruce Lockhart, J.H., London Scottish – 1913 *W*, 1920 *E*

Bruce Lockhart, L., London Scottish – 1948 *E*, 1950 *F*, *W*, 1953 *I*, *E*

Bruce Lockhart, R.B., Cambridge University, London Scottish – 1937 *I*, 1939 *I*, *E*

Bryce, C.C., Glasgow Academicals – 1873 *E*, 1874 *E*

Bryce, R.D.H., West of Scotland – 1973 *I*(r)

Bryce, W.E., Selkirk – 1922 *W*, *I*, *E*, 1923 *F*, *W*, *I*, *E*, 1924 *F*, *W*, *I*, *E*

Brydon, W.R.C., Heriot's FP – 1939 *W*

Buchanan, A. Royal HS FP – 1871 *E*

Buchanan, F.G., Kelvinside Academicals, Oxford University – 1910 *F*, 1911 *F*, *W*

Buchanan, J.C.R., Stewart's College FP, Exeter – 1921 *W*, *I*, *E*, 1922 *W*, *I*, *E*, 1923 *F*, *W*, *I*, *E*, 1924 *F*, *W*, *I*, *E*, 1925 *F*, *I*

Buchanan-Smith, G.A.E., London Scottish – 1989 *R*(r), 1990 *Arg*

Bucher, A.M., Edinburgh Academicals – 1897 *E*

Budge, G.M., Edinburgh Wanderers – 1950 *F*, *W*, *I*, *E*

Bullmore, H.H. Edinburgh University – 1902 *I*

Burnell, A.P., London Scottish – 1989 *E*, *I*, *F*, *Fj*, *R*, 1990 *I*, *F*, *W*, *E*, *Arg*, 1991 *F*, *W*, *E*, *I*, *R*, *WC* (*J*, *Z*, *I*, *WS*, *E*, *NZ*), 1992 *E*, *I*, *F*, *W*, 1993 *I*, *F*, *W*, *E*, *NZ* 1994 *W*, *E*, *I*, *F*

Burnet, P.J., London Scottish – 1960 *SA*

Burnet, W., Hawick – 1912 *E*

Burnet, W.A., West of Scotland – 1934 *W*, 1935 *W*, *I*, *E*, *NZ*, 1936 *W*, *I*, *E*

Burnett, J.N., Heriot's FP – 1980 *I*, *F*, *W*, *E*

Burrell, G., Gala – 1950 *F*, *W*, *I*, 1951 *SA*

Cairns, A.G., Watsonians – 1903 *W*, *I*, *E*, 1904 *W*, *I*, *E*, 1905 *W*, *I*, *E*, 1906 *W*, *I*, *E*

Calder, F., Stewart's-Melville FP – 1986 *F*, *W*, *E*, *I*, *R*, 1987 *I*, *F*, *W*, *E*, *WC* (*F*, *Z*, *R*, *NZ*), 1988 *I*, *F*, *W*, *E*, 1989 *W*, *E*, *I*, *F*, *R*, 1990 *I*, *F*, *W*, *NZ* (1, 2), 1991 *R*, *WC* (*J*, *I*, *WS*, *E*, *NZ*)

Calder, J.H., Stewart's-Melville FP – 1981 *F*, *W*, *E*, *I*, *NZ* (1, 2), *R*, *A*, 1982 *E*, *I*, *F*, *W*, *A* (1, 2), 1983 *I*, *F*, *W*, *E*, *NZ*, 1984 *W*, *E*, *I*, *F*, *A*, 1985 *I*, *F*, *W*

Callander, G.J., Kelso – 1984 *R*, 1988 *I*, *F*, *W*, *E*, *A*

Cameron, A., Glasgow HS FP – 1948 *W*, 1950 *I*, *E*, 1951 *F*, *W*, *I*, *E*, *SA*, 1953 *I*, *E*, 1955 *F*, *W*, *I*, *E*, 1956 *F*, *W*, *I*

Cameron, A.D., Hillhead HS FP – 1951 *F*, 1954 *F*, *W*

Cameron, A.W., Watsonians – 1887 *W*, 1893 *W*, 1894 *I*

Cameron, D., Glasgow HS FP – 1953 *I*, *E*, 1954 *F*, *NZ*, *I*, *E*

Cameron, N.W., Glasgow University – 1952 *E*, 1953 *F*, *W*

Campbell, A.J., Hawick – 1984 *I*, *F*, *R*, 1985 *I*, *F*, *W*, *E*, 1986 *F*, *W*, *E*, *I*, *R*, 1988 *F*, *W*, *A*

Campbell, G.T., London Scottish – 1892 *W*, *I*, *E*, 1893 *I*, *E*, 1894 *W*, *I*, *E*, 1895 *W*, *I*, *E*, 1896 *W*, *I*, *E*, 1897 *I*, 1899 *I*, 1900 *I*

Campbell, H.H., Cambridge University, London Scottish – 1947 *I*, *E*, 1948 *I*, *E*.

Campbell, J.A., Merchiston, West of Scotland – 1878 *E*, 1879 *I*, *E*, 1881 *I*, *E*.

Campbell, J.A., Cambridge University – 1900 *I*

The Royal Bank of Scotland

Statistics & Fixtures

Campbell, N.M., London Scottish – 1956 *F*, *W*

Campbell-Lamerton, J.R.E., London Scottish – 1986 *F*, 1987 *WC* (*Z*, *R*(r))

Campbell-Lamerton, M.J., Halifax, Army, London Scottish – 1961 *F*, *SA*, *W*, *I*, 1962 *F*, *W*, *I*, *E*, 1963 *F*, *W*, *I*, *E*, 1964 *I*, *E*, 1965 *F*, *W*, *I*, *E*, *SA*, 1966 *F*, *W*, *I*, *E*

Carmichael, A.B., West of Scotland – 1967 *I*, *NZ*, 1968 *F*, *W*, *I*, *E*, *A*, 1969 *F*, *W*, *I*, *E*, *SA*, 1970 *F*, *W*, *I*, *E*, *A*, 1971 *F*, *W*, *I*, *E*, *EC*, 1972 *F*, *W*, *E*, *NZ*, 1973 *F*, *W*, *I*, *E*, *P*, 1974 *W*, *E*, *I*, *F*, 1975 *I*, *F*, *W*, *E*, *NZ*, *A*, 1976 *F*, *W*, *E*, *I*, 1977 *E*, *I*(r), *F*, *W*, 1978 *I*

Carmichael, J.H., Watsonians – 1921 *F*, *W*, *I*

Carrick, J.S., Glasgow Academicals – 1876 *E*, 1877 *E*

Cassels, D.Y., West of Scotland – 1880 *E*, 1881 *I*, 1882 *I*, *E*, 1883 *W*, *I*, *E*

Cathcart, C.W., Edinburgh University – 1872 *E*, 1873 *E*, 1876 *E*

Cawkwell, G.L., Oxford University – 1947 *F*

Chalmers, C.M., Melrose – 1989 *W*, *E*, *I*, *F*, *Fj*, 1990 *I*, *F*, *W*, *E*, *NZ* (1, 2), *Arg*, 1991 *F*, *W*, *E*, *I*, *R*, *WC* (*J*, *I*, *WS*, *E*, *NZ*), 1992 *E*, *I*, *F*, *W*, *A* (1, 2), 1993 *I*, *F*, *W*, *E*, *NZ*, 1994 *W*

Chalmers, T., Glasgow Academicals – 1871 *E*, 1872 *E*, 1873 *E*, 1874 *E*, 1875 *E*, 1876 *E*

Chambers, H.F.T., Edinburgh University – 1888 *W*, *I*, 1889 *W*, *I*

Charters, R.G., Hawick – 1955 *W*, *I*, *E*

Chisholm, D.H., Melrose – 1964 *I*, *E*, 1965 *E*, *SA*, 1966 *F*, *I*, *E*, *A*, 1967 *F*, *W*, *NZ*, 1968 *F*, *W*, *I*

Chisholm, R.W.T., Melrose – 1955 *I*, *E*, 1956 *F*, *W*, *I*, *E*, 1958 *F*, *W*, *A*, *I*, 1960 *SA*

Church, W.C., Glasgow Academicals – 1906 *W*

Clark, R.L., Edinburgh Wanderers, Royal Navy – 1972 *F*, *W*, *E*, *NZ*, 1973 *F*, *W*, *I*, *E*, *P*

Clauss, P.R.A., Oxford University, Birkenhead Park – 1891 *W*, *I*, *E*, 1892 *W*, *E*, 1895 *I*

Clay, A.T., Edinburgh Academicals – 1886 *W*, *I*, *E*, 1887 *I*, *W*, *E*, 1888 *W*

Clunies-Ross, A., St Andrews University – 1871 *E*

Coltman, S., Hawick – 1948 *I*, 1949 *F*, *W*, *I*, *E*

Colville, A.G., Merchistonians – 1871 *E*, 1872 *E*

Connell, G.C., Trinity Academicals, London Scottish – 1968 *E*, *A*, 1969 *F*, *E*, 1970 *F*

Cooper, M. McG., Oxford University – 1936 *W*, *I*

Corcoran, I., Gala – 1992 *A* (1(r))

Cordial, I.F., Edinburgh Wanderers – 1952 *F*, *W*, *I*, *E*

Cotter, J.L., Hillhead HS FP – 1934 *I*, *E*

Cottington, G.S., Kelso – 1934 *I*, *E*, 1935 *W*, *I*, 1936 *E*

Coughtrie, S., Edinburgh Academicals – 1959 *F*, *W*, *I*, *E*, 1962 *W*, *I*, *E*, 1963 *F*, *W*, *I*, *E*

Couper, J.H., West of Scotland – 1896 *W*, *I*, 1899 *I*

Coutts, F.H., Melrose, Army – 1947 *W*, *I*, *E*

Coutts, I.D.F., Old Alleynians – 1951 *F*, 1952 *E*

Cowan, R.C., Selkirk – 1961 *F*, 1962 *F*, *W*, *I*, *E*

Cowie, W.L.K., Edinburgh Wanderers – 1953 *E*

Cownie, W.B., Watsonians – 1893 *W*, *I*, *E*, 1894 *W*, *I*, *E*, 1895 *W*, *I*, *E*

Crabbie, G.E., Edinburgh Academicals – 1904 *W*

Crabbie, J.E., Edinburgh Academicals, Oxford University – 1900 *W*, 1902 *I*, 1903 *W*, *I*, 1904 *E*, 1905 *W*

Craig, J.B., Heriot's FP – 1939 *W*

Cramb, R.I., Harlequins – 1987 *WC* (*R* (r)), 1988 *I*, *F*, *A*

Cranston, A.G., Hawick – 1976 *W*, *E*, *I*, 1977 *E*, *W*, 1978 *F* (r), *W*, *E*, *NZ*, 1981 *NZ* (1, 2)

Crawford, J.A., Army, London Scottish – 1934 *I*

Crawford, W.H., United Services, RN – 1938 *W*, *I*, *E*, 1939 *W*, *E*

Crichton-Miller, D., Gloucester – 1931 *W*, *I*, *E*

Crole, G.B., Oxford University – 1920 *F*, *W*, *I*, *E*

Cronin, D.F., Bath – 1988 *I*, *F*, *W*, *E*, *A*, 1989 *W*, *E*, *I*, *F*, *Fj*, *R*, 1990 *I*, *F*, *W*, *E*, *NZ* (1, 2), 1991 *F*, *W*, *E*, *I*, *R*, *WC* (*Z*), *A* (2), 1993 *I*, *F*, *W*, *E*, *NZ*

Cross, M., Merchistonians – 1875 *E*, 1876 *E*, 1877 *I*, *E*, 1878 *E*, 1879 *I*, *E*, 1880 *I*, *E*

Cross, W., Merchistonians – 1871 *E*, 1872 *E*

Cumming, R.S., Aberdeen University – 1921 *F*, *W*

Cunningham, G., Oxford University, London Scottish – 1908 *W*, *I*, 1909 *W*, *E*, 1910 *F*, *I*, *E*, 1911 *E*

Cunningham, R.F., Gala – 1978 *NZ*, 1979 *W*, *E*

Currie, L.R., Dunfermline – 1947 *A*, 1948 *F*, *W*, *I*, 1949 *F*, *W*, *I*, *E*

Cuthbertson, W., Kilmarnock, Harlequins – 1980 *I*, 1981 *W*, *E*, *I*, *NZ* (1, 2), *R*, *A*, 1982 *E*, *I*, *F*, *W*, *A* (1, 2), 1983 *I*, *F*, *W*, *NZ*, 1984 *W*, *E*, *A*

Dalgleish, K.J., Edinburgh Wanderers, Cambridge University – 1951 *I, E,* 1953 *F, W*

Dallas, J.D., Watsonians – 1903 *E*

Davidson, J.A., London Scottish, Edinburgh Wanderers – 1959 *E,* 1960 *I, E*

Davidson, J.N.G., Edinburgh University – 1952 *F, W, I, E,* 1953 *F, W,* 1954 *F*

Davidson, J.P., RIE College – 1873 *E,* 1874 *E*

Davidson, R.S., Royal High School FP – 1893 *E*

Davies, D.S., Hawick – 1922 *F, W, I, E,* 1923 *F, W, I, E,* 1924 *F, E,* 1925 *W, I, E,* 1926 *F, W, I, E,* 1927 *F, W, I*

Dawson, J.C., Glasgow Academicals – 1947 *A,* 1948 *F, W,* 1949 *F, W, I,* 1950 *F, W, I, E,* 1951 *F, W, I, E, SA,* 1952 *F, W, I, E,* 1953 *E*

Deans, C.T., Hawick – 1978 *F, W, E, NZ,* 1979 *W, E, I, F, NZ,* 1980 *I, F,* 1981, *F, W, E, I, NZ* (1, 2), *R, A,* 1982 *E, I, F, W, A* (1, 2), 1983 *I, F, W, E, NZ,* 1984 *W, E, I, F, A,* 1985 *I, F, W, E,* 1986 *F, W, E, I, R,* 1987 *I, F, W, E, WC (F, Z, R, NZ)*

Deans, D.T., Hawick – 1968 *E*

Deas, D.W., Heriot's FP – 1947 *F, W*

Dick, L.G., Loughborough Colleges, Jordanhill, Swansea – 1972 *W* (r), *E,* 1974 *W, E, I, F,* 1975 *I, F, W, E, NZ, A,* 1976 *F,* 1977 *E*

Dick, R.C.S., Cambridge University, Guy's Hospital – 1934 *W, I, E,* 1935 *W, I, E, NZ,* 1936 *W, I, E,* 1937 *W,* 1938 *W, I, E*

Dickson, G., Gala – 1978 *NZ,* 1979 *W, E, I, F, NZ,* 1980 *W,* 1981 *F,* 1982 *W* (r)

Dickson, M.R., Edinburgh University – 1905 *I*

Dickson, W.M., Blackheath, Oxford University – 1912 *F, W, E, SA,* 1913 *F, W, I*

Dobson, J., Glasgow Academicals – 1911 *E,* 1912 *F, W, I, E, SA*

Dobson, J.D., Glasgow Academicals – 1901 *I*

Dobson, W.G., Heriot's FP – 1922 *W, I, E*

Docherty, J.T., Glasgow HS FP – 1955 *F, W,* 1956 *E,* 1958 *F, W, A, I, E*

Dods, F.P., Edinburgh Academicals – 1911 *I*

Dods, J.H., Edinburgh Academicals, London Scottish – 1895 *W, I, E,* 1896 *W, I, E,* 1897 *I, E*

Dods, M., Gala – 1994 *I* (t)

Dods, P.W., Gala – 1983 *I, F, W, E, NZ,* 1984 *W, E, I, F, R, A,* 1985 *I, F, W, E,* 1989 *W, E, I, F,* 1991 *I* (r), *R, WC (Z, NZ* (r))

Donald, D.G., Oxford University – 1914 *W, I*

Donaldson, R.L.H., Glasgow HS FP – 1921 *W, I, E*

Donaldson, W.P., Oxford University, West of Scotland – 1893 *I,* 1894 *I,* 1895 *E,* 1896 *I, E,* 1899 *I*

Don Wauchope, A.R., Cambridge University, Fettesian-Lorettonians – 1881 *E,* 1882 *E,* 1883 *W,* 1884 *W, I, E,* 1885 *W, I* (1, 2), 1886 *W, I, E,* 1888 *I*

Don Wauchope, P.H., Fettesian-Lorettonians, Edinburgh Wanderers – 1885 *I* (1, 2), 1886 *W,* 1887 *I, W, E*

Dorward, A.F., Cambridge University, Gala – 1950 *F,* 1951 *SA,* 1952 *W, I, E,* 1953 *F, W, E,* 1955 *F,* 1956 *I, E,* 1957 *F, W, I, E*

Dorward, T.F., Gala – 1938 *W, I, E,* 1939 *I, E*

Douglas, G., Jed-Forest – 1921 *W*

Douglas, J., Stewart's College FP – 1961 *F, SA, W, I, E,* 1962 *F, W, I, E,* 1963 *F, W, I*

Douty, P.S., London Scottish – 1927 *NSW,* 1928 *F, W*

Drew, D., Glasgow Academicals – 1871 *E,* 1876 *E*

Druitt, W.A.H., London Scottish – 1936 *W, I, E*

Drummond, A.H., Kelvinside Academicals – 1938 *W, I*

Drummond, C.W., Melrose – 1947 *F, W, I, E,* 1948 *F, I, E,* 1950 *F, W, I, E*

Drybrough, A.S., Edinburgh Wanderers, Merchistonians – 1902 *I,* 1903 *I*

Dryden, R.H., Watsonians – 1937 *E*

Drysdale, D., Heriot's FP, Oxford University, London Scottish – 1923 *F, W, I, E,* 1924 *F, W, I, E,* 1925 *F, W, I, E,* 1926 *F, W, I, E,* 1927 *F, W, I, E, NSW,* 1928 *F, W, I E,* 1929 *F*

Duff, P.L., Glasgow Academicals – 1936 *W, I,* 1938 *W, I, E,* 1939 *W*

Duffy, H., Jed-Forest – 1955 *F*

Duke, A., Royal High School FP – 1888 *W, I,* 1889 *W, I,* 1890 *W, I*

Duncan, A.W., Edinburgh University – 1901 *W, I, E,* 1902 *W, I, E*

Duncan, D.D., Oxford University – 1920 *F, W, I, E*

Duncan, M.D.F., West of Scotland – 1986 *F, W, E, R,* 1987 *I, F, W E, WC (F, Z, R, NZ),* 1988 *I, F, W, E, A,* 1989 *W*

Duncan, M.M., Fettesian-Lorettonians 1888 *W*

Dunlop, J.W., West of Scotland – 1875 *E*

Dunlop, Q., West of Scotland – 1971 *E, EC*

Dykes, A.S., Glasgow Academicals – 1923 *E*

Dykes, J.C., Glasgow Academicals – 1922 *F, E,* 1924 *I,* 1925 *F, W, I,* 1926 *F, W, I, E,* 1927 *F, W, I, E, NSW,* 1928 *F, I,* 1929 *F, W, I*

Dykes, J.M., Clydesdale, London Scottish, Glasgow HS FP – 1898 *I, E,* 1899 *W, E,* 1900 *W, I,* 1901 *W, I, E,* 1902 *E*

Edwards, D.B., Heriot's FP – 1960 *I, E, SA*

Edwards, N.G.B., Harlequins, Northampton – 1992 *E, I, F, W, A* (1), 1994 *W*

Elgie, M.K., London Scottish – 1954 *NZ, I, E, W*, 1955 *F, W, I, E*

Elliot, C., Langholm – 1958 *E*, 1959 *F*, 1960 *F*, 1963 *E*, 1964 *F, NZ, W, I, E*, 1965 *F, W, I*

Elliot, M., Hawick – 1895 *W*, 1896 *E*, 1897 *I, E*, 1899 *I, E*

Elliot, T., Gala – 1905 *E*

Elliot, T., Gala – 1955 *W, I, E*, 1956 *F, W, I, E*, 1957 *F, W, I, E*, 1958 *W, A, I*

Elliot, T.G., Langholm – 1968 *W.A.*, 1969 *F, W*, 1970 *E*

Elliot, W.I.D., Edinburgh Academicals – 1947 *F, W, E, A*, 1948 *F, W, I, E*, 1949 *F, W, I, E*, 1950 *F, W, I, E*, 1951 *F, W, I, E, SA*, 1952 *F, W, I, E*, 1954 *NZ, I, E, W*

Emslie, W.D., Royal High School FP – 1930 *F*, 1932 *I*

Evans, H.L., Edinburgh University – 1885 *I* (1, 2)

Ewart, E.N., Glasgow Academicals – 1879 *E*, 1880 *I, E*

Fahmy, E.C., Abertillery – 1920 *F, W, I, E*

Fasson, F.H., London Scottish, Edinburgh University – 1900 *W*, 1901 *W, I*, 1902 *W, E*

Fell, A.N., Edinburgh University – 1901 *W, I, E*, 1902 *W, E*, 1903 *W, E*

Ferguson, J.H., Gala – 1928 *W*

Ferguson, W.G., Royal High School FP – 1927 *NSW*, 1928 *F, W, I, E*

Fergusson, E.A.J., Oxford University – 1954 *F, NZ, I, E, W*

Finlay, A.B., Edinburgh Academicals – 1875 *E*

Finlay, J.F., Edinburgh Academicals – 1871 *E*, 1872 *E*, 1874 *E*, 1875 *E*

Finlay, N.J., Edinburgh Academicals – 1875 *E*, 1876 *E*, 1878 *E*, 1879 *I, E*, 1880 *I, E*, 1881 *I, E*

Finlay, R., Watsonians – 1948 *E*

Fisher, A.T., Waterloo, Watsonians – 1947 *I, F*

Fisher, C.D., Waterloo – 1975 *NZ, A*, 1976 *W, E, I*

Fisher, D., West of Scotland – 1893 *I*

Fisher, J.P., Royal High School FP, London Scottish – 1963 *E*, 1964 *F, NZ, W, I, E*, 1965 *F, W, I, E, SA*, 1966 *F, W, I, E, A*, 1967 *F, W, I, E, NZ*, 1968 *F, W, I, E*

Fleming, C. J. N., Edinburgh Wanderers – 1896 *I, E*, 1897 *I*

Fleming, G.R., Glasgow Academicals – 1875 *E*, 1876 *E*

Fletcher, H.N., Edinburgh University – 1904 *E*, 1905 *W*

Flett, A.B., Edinburgh University – 1901 *W, I, E*, 1902 *W, I*

Forbes, J.L., Watsonians — 1905 *W*, 1906 *I, E*

Ford, D.St.C., United Services, RN – 1930 *I, E*, 1931 *E*, 1932 *W, I*

Ford, J.R., Gala – 1893 *I*

Forrest, J.E., Glasgow Academicals – 1932 *SA*, 1935 *E, NZ*

Forrest, J.G.S., Cambridge University – 1938 *W, I, E*

Forrest, W.T., Hawick – 1903 *W, I, E*, 1904 *W, I, E*, 1905 *W, I*

Forsayth, H.H., Oxford University – 1921 *F, W, I, E*, 1922 *W, I, E*

Forsyth, I.W., Stewart's College FP – 1972 *NZ*, 1973 *F, W, I, E, P*

Forsyth, J., Edinburgh University – 1871 *E*

Foster, R.A., Hawick – 1930 *W*, 1932, *SA, I, E*

Fox, J., Gala – 1952 *F, W, I, E*

Frame, J.N.M., Edinburgh University, Gala – 1967 *NZ*, 1968, *F, W, I, E*, 1969, *W, I, E, SA*, 1970, *F, W, I, E, A*, 1971, *F, W, I, E, EC*, 1972 *F, W, E*, 1973 *P* (r)

France, C., Kelvinside Academicals – 1903 *I*

Fraser, C.F.P., Glasgow University – 1888 *W*, 1889 *W*

Fraser, J.W., Edinburgh Institution FP – 1881 *E*

Fraser, R., Cambridge University – 1911 *F, W, I, E*

French, J., Glasgow Academicals – 1886 *W*, 1887 *I, W, E*

Frew, A., Edinburgh University – 1901 *W, I, E*

Frew, G.M., Glasgow HS FP – 1906 *SA*, 1907 *W, I, E*, 1908 *W, I, E*, 1909 *W, I, E*, 1910 *F, W, I*, 1911 *E*

Friebe, J.P., Glasgow HS FP – 1952 *E*

Fulton, A.K., Edinburgh University, Dollar Academicals – 1952 *F*, 1954 *F*

Fyfe, K.C., Cambridge University, Sale, London Scottish – 1933 *W, E*, 1934 *E*, 1935 *W, I, E, NZ*, 1936 *W, E*, 1939 *I*

Gallie, G.H., Edinburgh Academicals – 1939 *W*

Gallie, R.A., Glasgow Academicals – 1920 *F, W, I, E*, 1921 *F, W, I, E*

Gammell, W.B.B., Edinburgh Wanderers – 1977 *I, F, W*, 1978 *W, E*

Geddes, I.C., London Scottish – 1906 *SA*, 1907 *W, I, E*, 1908 *W, E*

Geddes, K.I., London Scottish – 1947 *F, W, I, E*

Gedge, H.T.S., London Scottish, Edinburgh Wanderers – 1894 *W, I, E*, 1896 *E*, 1899 *W, E*

Gedge, P.M.S., Edinburgh Wanderers – 1933 *I*

Gemmill, R., Glasgow HS FP – 1950 *F, W, I, E*, 1951 *F, W, I*

Gibson, W.R., Royal High School FP – 1891 *I, E*, 1892 *W, I, E*, 1893 *W, I, E*, 1894 *W, I, E*, 1895 *W, I, E*

Gilbert-Smith, D.S., London Scottish – 1952 *E*

Gilchrist, J., Glasgow Academicals – 1925 *F*

Gill, A.D., Gala – 1973 *P*, 1974 *W, E, I, F*

Gillespie, J.I., Edinburgh Academicals – 1899 *E*, 1900 *W, E*, 1901 *W, I, E*, 1902 *W, I*, 1904 *I, E*

Gillies, A.C., Watsonians, Carlisle – 1924 *W, I, E*, 1925 *W, E*, 1926 *F, W*, 1927 *F, W, I, E*

Gilray, C.M., Oxford University, London Scottish – 1908 *E*, 1909 *W, E*, 1912 *I*

Glasgow, R.J.C., Dunfermline – 1962 *F, W, I, E*, 1963 *I, E*, 1964 *I, E*, 1965 *W, I*

Glen, W.S., Edinburgh Wanderers – 1955 *W*

Gloag, L.G., Cambridge University – 1949 *F, W, I, E*

Goodfellow, J., Langholm – 1928 *W, I, E*

Goodhue, F.W.J., London Scottish – 1890 *W, I, E*, 1891 *W, I, E*, 1892 *W, I, E*

Gordon, R., Edinburgh Wanderers – 1951 *W*, 1952 *F, W, I, E*, 1953 *W*

Gordon, R.E., Royal Artillery – 1913 *F, W, I*

Gordon, R.J., London Scottish – 1982 *A* (1, 2)

Gore, A.C., London Scottish – 1882 *I*

Gossman, B.M., West of Scotland – 1980 *W*, 1983 *F, W*

Gossman, J.S., West of Scotland – 1980 *E* (r)

Gowans, J.J., Cambridge University, London Scottish – 1893 *W*, 1894 *W, E*, 1895 *W, I, E*, 1896 *I, E*

Gowlland, G.C., London Scottish – 1908 *W*, 1909 *W, E*, 1910 *F, W, I, E*

Gracie, A.L., Harlequins – 1921 *F, W, I, E*, 1922 *F, W, I, E*, 1923 *F, W, I, E*, 1924 *F*

Graham, I.N., Edinburgh Academicals – 1939 *I, E*

Graham, J., Kelso – 1926 *I, E*, 1927, *F, W, I, E, NSW*, 1928 *F, W, I, E*, 1930, *I, E*, 1932 *SA, W*

Graham, J.H.S., Edinburgh Academicals – 1876 *E*, 1877 *I, E*, 1878 *E*, 1879 *I, E*, 1880 *I, E*, 1881 *I, E*

Grant, D., Hawick – 1965 *F, E, SA*, 1966 *F, W, I, E, A*, 1967 *F, W, I, E, NZ*, 1968 *F*

Grant, D.M., East Midlands – 1911 *W, I*

Grant, M.L., Harlequins – 1955 *F*, 1956 *F, W*, 1957 *F*

Grant, T.O., Hawick – 1960 *I, E, SA*, 1964 *F, NZ, W*

Grant, W.St.C., Craigmount – 1873 *E*, 1874 *E*

Gray, C.A., Nottingham – 1989 *W, E, I, F, Fj, R*, 1990 *I, F, W, E, NZ* (1, 2), *Arg*, 1991 *F, W, E, I*, WC (*J, I, WS, E, NZ*)

Gray, D., West of Scotland – 1978 *E*, 1979 *I, F, NZ*, 1980 *I, F, W, E*, 1981 *F*

Gray, G.L., Gala – 1935 *NZ*, 1937 *W, I, E*

Gray, T., Northampton, Heriot's FP – 1950 *E*, 1951 *F, E*

Greenlees, H.D., Leicester – 1927 *NSW*, 1928 *F, W*, 1929 *I, E*, 1930 *E*

Greenlees, J.R.C., Cambridge University, Kelvinside Academicals – 1900 *I*, 1902 *W, I, E*, 1903 *W, I, E*

Greenwood, J.T., Dunfermline, Perthshire Academicals – 1952 *F*, 1955 *F, W, I, E*, 1956 *F, W, I, E*, 1957 *F, W, E*, 1958 *F, W, A, I, E*, 1959 *F, W, I*

Greig, A., Glasgow HS FP – 1911 *I*

Greig, L.L., Glasgow Academicals, United Services – 1905 *NZ*, 1906 *SA*, 1907 *W*, 1908 *W, I*

Greig, R.C., Glasgow Academicals – 1893 *W*, 1897 *I*

Grieve, C.F., Oxford University – 1935 *W*, 1936 *E*

Grieve, R.M., Kelso – 1935 *W, I, E, NZ*, 1936 *W, I, E*

Gunn, A.W., Royal High School FP – 1912 *F, W, I, SA*, 1913 *F*

Hamilton, A.S., Headingley – 1914 *W*, 1920 *F*

Hamilton, H.M., West of Scotland – 1874 *E*, 1875 *E*

Hannah, R.S.M., West of Scotland – 1971 *I*

Harrower, P.R., London Scottish – 1885 *W*

Hart, J.G.M., London Scottish – 1951 *SA*

Hart, T.M., Glasgow University – 1930 *W, I*

Hart, W., Melrose – 1960 *SA*

Harvey, L., Greenock Wanderers – 1899 *I*

Hastie, A.J., Melrose – 1961 *W, I, E*, 1964 *I, E*, 1965 *E, SA*, 1966 *F, W, I, E, A*, 1967 *F, W, I, NZ*, 1968 *F, W*

Hastie, I.R., Kelso – 1955 *F*, 1958 *F, E*, 1959 *F, W, I*

Hastie, J.D.H., Melrose – 1938 *W, I, E*

Hastings. A.G., Cambridge University, Watsonians, London Scottish – 1986 *F, W, E, I, R*, 1987 *I, F, W, E*, WC (*F, Z, R, NZ*), 1988 *I, F, W, E, A*, 1989 *Fj, R*, 1990 *I, F, W, E, NZ* (1, 2), *Arg*, 1991 *F, W, E, I*, WC (*J, I, WS, E, NZ*), 1992 *E, I, F, W, A* (1), 1993, *I, F, W, E, NZ*, 1994 *W, E, I, F*

Hastings, S., Watsonians – 1986 *F, W, E, I, R*, 1987 *I, F, W*, WC (*R*), 1988 *I, F, W, A*, 1989 *W, E, I, F, Fj, R*, 1990 *I, F, W, E, NZ* (1, 2), *Arg*, 1991 *F, W, E, I*, WC (*J, Z, I, WS, E, NZ*), 1992 *E, I, F, W, A* (1, 2), 1993 *I, F, W, E, NZ*, 1994 *E, I, F*

Hay, B.H., Boroughmuir – 1975 *NZ, A*, 1976 *F*, 1978 *I, F, W, E, NZ*, 1979 *W, E, I, F, NZ*, 1980 *I, F, W, E*, 1981 *F, W, E, I, NZ* (1, 2)

Hay-Gordon, J.R., Edinburgh Academicals – 1875 *E*, 1877 *I*, *E*

Hegarty, C.B., Hawick – 1978 *I*, *F*, *W*, *E*

Hegarty, J.J., Hawick – 1951 *F*, 1953 *F*, *W*, *I*, *E*, 1955 *F*

Henderson, B.C., Edinburgh Wanderers – 1963 *E*, 1964 *F*, *I*, *E*, 1965 *F*, *W*, *I*, *E*, 1966 *F*, *W*, *I*, *E*

Henderson, F.W., London Scottish – 1900 *W*, *I*

Henderson, I.C., Edinburgh Academicals – 1939 *I*, *E*, 1947 *F*, *W*, *E*, *A*, 1948 *I*, *E*

Henderson, J.H., Oxford University, Richmond – 1953 *F*, *W*, *I*, *E*, 1954 *F*, *NZ*, *I*, *E*, *W*

Henderson, J.M., Edinburgh Academicals – 1933 *W*, *E*, *I*

Henderson, J.Y.M., Watsonians – 1911 *E*

Henderson, M.M., Dunfermline – 1937 *W*, *I*, *E*

Henderson, N.F., London Scottish – 1892 *I*

Henderson, R.G., Newcastle Northern – 1924 *I*, *E*

Hendrie, K.G.P., Heriot's FP – 1924 *F*, *W*, *I*

Hendry, T.L., Clydesdale – 1893 *W*, *I*, *E*, 1895 *I*

Henriksen, E.H., Royal High School FP – 1953 *I*

Hepburn, D.P., Woodford – 1947 *A*, 1948 *F*, *W*, *I*, *E*, 1949 *F*, *W*, *I*, *E*

Heron, G., Glasgow Academicals – 1874 *E*, 1875 *E*

Hill, C.C.P., St Andrews University – 1912 *F*, *I*

Hinshelwood, A.J.W., London Scottish – 1966 *F*, *W*, *I*, *E*, *A*, 1967 *F*, *W*, *I*, *E*, *NZ*, 1968 *F*, *W*, *I*, *E*, *A*, 1969 *F*, *W*, *I*, *SA*, 1970 *F*, *W*

Hodgson, C.G., London Scottish – 1968 *I*, *E*

Hogg, C.D., Melrose – 1992 *A* (1, 2), 1993 *NZ* (r)

Hogg, C.G., Boroughmuir – 1978 *F* (r), *W* (r)

Holms, W.F., RIE College – 1886 *W*, *E*, 1887 *I*, *E*, 1889 *W*, *I*

Horsburgh, G.B., London Scottish – 1937 *W*, *I*, *E*, 1938 *W*, *I*, *E*, 1939 *W*, *I*, *E*

Howie, D.D., Kirkcaldy – 1912 *F*, *W*, *I*, *E*, *SA*, 1913 *F*, *W*

Howie, R.A., Kirkcaldy – 1924 *F*, *W*, *I*, *E*, 1925 *W*, *I*, *E*

Hoyer-Millar, G.C., Oxford University – 1953 *I*

Huggan, J.L., London Scottish – 1914 *E*

Hume, J., Royal High School FP – 1912 *F*, 1920 *F*, 1921 *F*, *W*, *I*, *E*, 1922 *F*

Hume, J.W.G., Oxford University, Edinburgh Wanderers – 1928 *I*, 1930 *F*

Hunter, F., Edinburgh University 1882 *I*

Hunter, I.G., Selkirk – 1984 *I* (r), 1985 *F* (r), *W*, *E*

Hunter, J.M., Cambridge University – 1947 *F*

Hunter, M.D., Glasgow High – 1974 *F*

Hunter, W.J., Hawick – 1964 *F*, *NZ*, *W*, 1967 *F*, *W*, *I*, *E*

Hutchison, W.R., Glasgow HS FP – 1911 *E*

Hutton, A.H.M., Dunfermline – 1932 *I*

Hutton, J.E., Harlequins – 1930 *E*, 1931 *F*

Inglis, H.M., Edinburgh Academicals – 1951 *F*, *W*, *I*, *E*, *SA*, 1952 *W*, *I*

Inglis, J.M., Selkirk – 1952 *E*

Inglis, W.M., Cambridge University, Royal Engineers – 1937 *W*, *I*, *E*, 1938 *W*, *I*, *E*

Innes, J.R.S., Aberdeen GS FP – 1939 *W*, *I*, *E*, 1947 *A*, 1948 *F*, *W*, *I*, *E*

Ireland, J.C.H., Glasgow HS FP – 1925 *W*, *I*, *E*, 1926 *F*, *W*, *I*, *E*, 1927 *F*, *W*, *I*, *E*

Irvine, A.R., Heriot's FP – 1972 *NZ*, 1973 *F*, *W*, *I*, *E*, *P*, 1974 *W*, *E*, *I*, *F*, 1975 *I*, *F*, *W*, *E*, *NZ*, *A*, 1976 *F*, *W*, *E*, *I*, 1977 *E*, *I*, *F*, *W*, 1978, *I*, *F*, *E*, *NZ*, 1979 *W*, *E*, *I*, *F*, *NZ*, 1980 *I*, *F*, *W*, *E*, 1981 *F*, *W*, *E*, *I*, *NZ* (1, 2), *R*, *A*, 1982 *E*, *I*, *F*, *W*, *A* (1, 2)

Irvine, D.R., Edinburgh Academicals – 1878 *E*, 1879 *I*, *E*

Irvine, R.W., Edinburgh Academicals – 1871 *E*, 1872 *E*, 1873 *E*, 1884 *E*, 1875 *E*, 1876 *E*, 1877 *I*, *E*, 1878 *E*, 1879 *I*, *E*, 1880 *I*, *E*

Irvine, T.W., Edinburgh Academicals – 1885 *I* (1, 2), 1886 *W*, *I*, *E*, 1887 *I*, *W*, *E*, 1888 *W*, *I*, 1891 *I*

Jackson, K.L.T., Oxford University – 1933 *W*, *E*, *I*, 1934 *W*

Jackson, T.G.H., Army, London Scottish – 1947 *F*, *W*, *E*, *A*, 1948 *F*, *W*, *I*, *E*, 1949 *F*, *W*, *I*, *E*

Jackson, W.D., Hawick – 1964 *I*, 1965 *E*, *SA* 1968 *A*, 1969 *F*, *W*, *I*, *E*

Jamieson, J., West of Scotland – 1883 *W*, *I*, *E*, 1884 *W*, *I*, *E*, 1885 *W*, *I*, (1, 2).

Jardine, I.C., Stirling County – 1993 *NZ*, 1994 *W*, *E* (r)

Jeffrey, J., Kelso – 1984 *A*, 1985 *I*, *E*, 1986 *F*, *W*, *E*, *I*, *R*, 1987 *I*, *F*, *W*, *E*, *WC* (*F*, *Z*, *R*), 1988 *I*, *W*, *A*, 1989 *W*, *E*, *I*, *F*, *Fj*, *R*, 1990 *I*, *F*, *W*, *E*, *NZ* (1, 2), *Arg*, 1991 *F*, *W*, *E*, *I*, *WC* (*J*, *I*, *WS*, *E*, *NZ*)

Johnston, D.I., Watsonians – 1979 *NZ*, 1980 *I*, *F*, *W*, *E*, 1981 *R*, *A*, 1982 *E*, *I*, *F*, *W*, *A* (1, 2), 1983 *I*, *F*, *W*, *NZ*, 1984 *W*, *E*, *I*, *F*, *R*, 1986 *F*, *W*, *E*, *I*, *R*

Johnston, H.H., Edinburgh Collegians – 1877 *I*, *E*

Johnston, J., Melrose – 1951 *SA*, 1952 *F*, *W*, *I*, *E*

Johnston, W.G.S., Cambridge University, Richmond – 1935 *W*, *I*, 1937 *W*, *I*, *E*

Johnston, W.C., Glasgow HS FP – 1922 *F*

Jones, P.M., Gloucester – 1992 *W* (r)

Junor, J.E., Glasgow Academicals – 1876 *E*, 1877 *I, E*, 1878 *E*, 1879 *E*, 1881 *I*

Keddie, R.R., Watsonians – 1967 *NZ*

Keith, G.J., Wasps – 1968 *F, W*

Keller, D.H., London Scottish, Sheffield – 1949 *F, W, I, E*, 1950 *F, W, I*

Kelly, R.F., Watsonians – 1927 *NSW*, 1928 *F, W, E*

Kemp, J.W.Y., Glasgow GS FP – 1954 *W*, 1955 *F, W, I, E*, 1956 *F, W, I, E*, 1957 *F, W, I, E*, 1958 *F, W, A, I, E*, 1959 *F, W, I, E*, 1960 *F, W, I, E, SA*

Kennedy, A.E., Watsonians – 1983 *NZ*, 1984 *W, E, A*

Kennedy, F., Stewart's College FP – 1920 *F, W, I, E*, 1921 *E*

Kennedy, N., West of Scotland – 1903 *W, I, E*

Ker, A.B.M., Kelso – 1988 *W, E*

Ker, H.T., Glasgow Academicals – 1887 *I, W, E*, 1888 *I*, 1889 *W*, 1890 *I, E*

Kerr, D.S., Heriot's FP – 1923 *F, W*, 1924 *F*, 1926 *I, E*, 1927 *W, I, E*, 1928 *I, E*

Kerr, G.C., Durham, Old Dunelmians, Edinburgh Wanderers – 1898 *I, E*, 1899 *I, W, E*, 1900 *W, I, E*

Kerr, J.M., Heriot's FP – 1935 *NZ*, 1936 *I, E*, 1937 *W, I*

Kerr, J.R., Greenock Wanderers – 1905 *E*

Kerr, W., London Scottish – 1953 *E*

Kidston, D.W., Glasgow Academicals – 1883 *W, E*

Kidston, W.H., West of Scotland – 1874 *E*

Kilgour, I.J., RMC Sandhurst – 1921 *F*

King, J.H.F., Selkirk – 1953 *F, W, E*, 1954 *E*

Kininmonth, P.W., Oxford University, Richmond – 1949 *F, W, I, E*, 1950 *F, W, I, E*, 1951 *F, W, I, E, SA* 1952 *F, W, I*, 1954 *F, NZ, I, E, W*

Kinnear, R.M., Heriot's FP – 1926 *F, W, I*

Knox, J., Kelvinside Academicals – 1903 *W, I, E*

Kyle, W.E., Hawick – 1902 *W, I, E*, 1903 *W, I, E*, 1904 *W, I, E*, 1905 *W, I, E, NZ*, 1906 *W, I, E*, 1908 *E*, 1909 *W, I, E*, 1910 *W*

Laidlaw, A.S., Hawick – 1897 *I*

Laidlaw, F.A.L., Melrose – 1965 *F, W, I, E, SA*, 1966 *F, W, I, E, A*, 1967 *F, W, I, E, NZ*, 1968 *F, W, I, A*, 1969 *F, W, I, E, SA*, 1970 *F, W, I, E, A*, 1971 *F, W, I*

Laidlaw, R.J., Jed-Forest – 1980 *I, F, W, E*, 1981 *F, W, E, I, NZ* (1, 2), *R, A*, 1982 *E, I, F, W, A* (1, 2), 1983 *I, F, W, E, NZ*, 1984 *W, E, I, F, R, A*, 1985 *I, F*, 1986 *F, W, E, I, R*, 1987 *I, F, W, E, WC* (F, R, NZ), 1988 *I, F, W, E*

Laing, A.D., Royal High School FP – 1914 *W, I, E*, 1920 *F, W, I*, 1921 *F*

Lambie, I.K., Watsonians – 1978 *NZ* (r), 1979 *W, E, NZ*

Lambie, L.B., Glasgow HS FP – 1934 *W, I, E*, 1935 *W, I, E, NZ*

Lamond, G.A.W., Kelvinside Academicals, Bristol – 1899 *W, E*, 1905 *E*

Lang, D., Paisley – 1876 *E*, 1877 *I*

Langrish, R.W., London Scottish – 1930 *F*, 1931 *F, W, I*

Lauder, W., Neath – 1969 *I, E, SA*, 1970 *F, W, I, A*, 1973 *F*, 1974 *W, E, I, F*, 1975 *I, F, NZ, A*, 1976 *F*, 1977 *E*

Laughland, I.H.P., London Scottish – 1959 *F*, 1960 *W, I, E*, 1961 *SA, W, I, E*, 1962 *F, W, I, E*, 1963 *F, W, I*, 1964 *F, NZ, W, I, E*, 1965 *F, W, I, E, SA*, 1966 *F, W, I, E*, 1967 *E*

Lawrie, J.R., Melrose, Leicester – 1922 *F, W, I, E*, 1923 *F, W, I, E*, 1924 *W, I, E*

Lawrie, K.G., Gala – 1980 *F* (r), *W, E*

Lawson, A.J.M., Edinburgh Wanderers, London Scottish, Heriot's FP – 1972 *F* (r), *E*, 1973 *F*, 1974 *W, E*, 1976 *E, I*, 1977 *E*, 1978 *NZ*, 1979 *W, E, I, F, NZ*, 1980 *W* (r)

Lawther, T.H.B., Old Millhillians – 1932 *SA, W*

Ledingham, G.A., Aberdeen GS FP – 1913 *F*

Lees, J.B., Gala – 1947 *I, A*, 1948 *F, W, E*

Leggatt, H.T.O., Watsonians – 1891 *W, I, E*, 1892 *W, I*, 1893 *W, E*, 1894 *I, E*

Lely, W.G., Cambridge University, London Scottish – 1909 *I*

Leslie, D.G., Dundee HS FP, West of Scotland, Gala – 1975 *I, F, W, E, NZ, A*, 1976 *F, W, E, I*, 1978 *NZ*, 1980 *E*, 1981 *W, E, I, NZ* (1, 2), *R, A*, 1982 *E*, 1983 *I, F, W, E*, 1984 *W, E, I, F, R*, 1985 *F, W, E*

Liddell, E.H., Edinburgh University – 1922 *F, W, I*, 1923 *F, W, I, E*

Lind, H., Dunfermline, London Scottish – 1928 *I*, 1931 *F, W, I, E*, 1932 *SA, W, E*, 1933 *W, E, I*, 1934 *W, I, E*, 1935 *I*, 1936 *E*

Lindsay, A.B., London Hospital – 1910 *I*, 1911 *I*

Lindsay, G.C., London Scottish – 1884 *W*, 1885 *I* (1), 1887 *W, E*

Lindsay-Watson, R.H., Hawick – 1909 *I*

Lineen, S.R.P., Boroughmuir – 1989 *W, E, I, F, Fj, R*, 1990 *I, F, W, E, NZ* (1, 2), *Arg*, 1991 *F, W, E, I, R, WC* (J, Z, I, E, NZ), 1992 *E, I, F, W, A* (1, 2)

Little, A.W., Hawick – 1905 *W*

Logan, K.M., Stirling County – 1992 *A* (2), 1993 *E* (r), *NZ* (t), 1994 *W, E, I, F*

Logan, W.R., Edinburgh University, Edinburgh Wanderers – 1931 *E, SA, W, I*, 1933 *W, E, I*, 1934, *W, I, E*, 1935 *W, I*,

E, NZ, 1936 *W, I, E*, 1937 *W, I, E*

Lorraine, H.D.B., Oxford University – 1933 *W, E, I*

Loudoun-Shand, E.G., Oxford University – 1913 *E*

Lowe, J.D., Heriot's FP – 1934 *W*

Lumsden, I.J., Bath, Watsonians – 1947 *F, W, A*, 1949 *F, W, I, E*

Lyall, G.G., Gala – 1947 *A*, 1948 *F, W, I, E*

Lyall, W.J.C., Edinburgh Academicals – 1871 *E*

Mabon, J.T., Jed-Forest – 1898 *I, E*, 1899 *I*, 1900 *I*

Macarthur, J.P., Waterloo – 1932 *E*

MacCallum, J.C., Watsonians – 1905 *E, NZ*, 1906 *W, I, E, SA*, 1907 *W, I, E*, 1908 *W, I, E*, 1909 *W, I, E*, 1910 *F, W, I, E*, 1911 *F, I, E*, 1912 *F, W, I, E*

McClung, T. Edinburgh Academicals – 1956 *I, E*, 1957 *W, I, E*, 1959 *F, W, I*, 1960 *W*

McClure, G.B., West of Scotland – 1873 *E*

McClure, J.H., West of Scotland – 1872 *E*

McCowan, D., West of Scotland – 1880 *I, E*, 1881 *I, E*, 1882 *I, E*, 1883 *I, E*, 1884 *I, E*

McCowat, R.H., Glasgow Academicals – 1905 *I*

McCrae, I.G., Gordonians – 1967 *E*, 1968 *I*, 1969 *F* (r) *W*, 1972 *F, NZ*

McCrow, J.W.S., Edinburgh Academicals – 1921 *I*.

Macdonald, A.E.D., Heriot's FP – 1993 *NZ*

McDonald, C., Jed-Forest – 1947 *A*

Macdonald, D.C., Edinburgh University – 1953 *F, W*, 1959 *I, E*

Macdonald, D.S.M., Oxford University, London Scottish, West of Scotland – 1977 *E, I, F, W*, 1978 *I, W, E*

Macdonald, J.D., London Scottish, Army – 1966 *F, W, I, E*, 1967 *F, W, I, E*

Macdonald, J.M., Edinburgh Wanderers – 1911 *W*

Macdonald, J.S., Edinburgh University – 1903 *E*, 1904 *W, I, E*, 1905 *W*

Macdonald, K.R., Stewart's College FP – 1956 *F, W, I*, 1957 *W, I, E*

Macdonald, R., Edinburgh University – 1950 *F, W, I, E*

Mcdonald, W.A., Glasgow University – 1889 *W*, 1892 *I, E*

Macdonald, W.G., London Scottish – 1969 *I*(r)

Macdougall, J.B., Greenock Wanderers, Wakefield – 1913 *F*, 1914 *I*, 1921 *F, I, E*

McEwan, M.C., Edinburgh Academicals – 1886 *E*, 1887 *I, W, E*, 1888 *W, I*, 1889 *W, I*, 1890 *W, I, E*, 1891 *W, I, E*, 1892 *E*

MacEwan, N.A., Gala, Highland – 1971 *F, W, I, E, EC*, 1972 *F, W, E, NZ*, 1973 *F, W, I, E, P*, 1974 *W, E, I, F*, 1975 *W, E*

McEwan, W.M.C., Edinburgh Academicals – 1894 *W, E*, 1895 *W, E*, 1896 *W, I, E*, 1897 *I, E*, 1898 *I, E*, 1899 *I, W, E*, 1900 *W, E*

MacEwen, R.K.G., Cambridge University, London Scottish, Lansdowne – 1954 *F, NZ, I, W*, 1956 *F, W, I, E*, 1957 *F, W, I, E*, 1958 *W*

Macfarlan, D.J., London Scottish – 1883 *W*, 1884 *W, I, E*, 1886 *W, I*, 1887 *I*, 1888 *I*

McFarlane, J.L.H., Edinburgh University – 1871 *E*, 1872 *E*, 1873 *E*

McGaughey, S.K., Hawick – 1984 *R*

McGeechan, I.R., Headingley – 1972 *NZ*, 1973 *F, W, I, E, P*, 1974 *W, E, I, F*, 1975 *I, F, W, E, NZ, A*, 1976 *F, W, E, I*, 1977 *E, I, F, W*, 1978 *I, F, W, NZ*, 1979 *W, E, I, F*

McGlashan, T.P.L., Royal High School FP – 1947 *F, I, E*, 1954 *F, NZ, I, E, W.*

MacGregor, D.G., Watsonians, Pontypridd – 1907 *W, I, E*

MacGregor, G., Cambridge University – 1890 *W, I, E*, 1891 *W, I, E*, 1893 *W, I, E*, 1894 *W, I, E*, 1896 *E*

MacGregor, I.A.A., Hillhead HS FP, Llanelli – 1955 *I, E*, 1956 *F, W, I, E*, 1957 *F, W, I*

MacGregor, J.R., Edinburgh University – 1909 *I*

McGuinness, G.M., West of Scotland – 1982 *A* (1, 2), 1983 *I*, 1985 *I, F, W, E*

McHarg, A.F., West of Scotland, London Scottish – 1968 *I, E, A*, 1969 *F, W, I, E*, 1971 *F, W, I, E, EC*, 1972 *F, E, NZ*, 1973 *F, W, I, E, P*, 1974 *W, E, I, F*, 1975 *I, F, W, E, NZ, A*, 1976 *W, E, I*, 1977 *E, I, F, W*, 1978 *I, F, W, NZ*, 1979 *W, E*

McIndoe, F., Glasgow Academicals – 1886 *W, I*

MacIntyre, I., Edinburgh Wanderers – 1890 *W, I, E*, 1891 *W, I, E*

McIvor, D.J., Edinburgh Academicals – 1992 *E, I, F, W*, 1993 *NZ*

Mackay, E.B., Glasgow Academicals – 1920 *W*, 1922 *E*

McKeating, E., Heriot's FP – 1957 *F, W*, 1961 *SA, W, I, E*

McKendrick, J.G., West of Scotland – 1889 *I*

Mackenzie, A.D.G., Selkirk – 1984 *A*

Mackenzie, C.J.G., United Services – 1921 *E*

Mackenzie, D.D., Edinburgh University – 1947 *W, I, E*, 1948 *F, W, I*

Mackenzie, D.K.A. Edinburgh Wanderers – 1939 *I, E*

Mackenzie, J.M., Edinburgh University – 1905 *NZ*, 1909, *W, I, E*, 1910 *W, I, E*, 1911 *W, I*

Mackenzie, R.C., Glasgow Academicals – 1877 *I, E*, 1881 *I, E*

Mackie, G.Y., Highland – 1975 *A*, 1976 *F, W*, 1978 *F*

MacKinnon, A., London Scottish – 1898 *I, E*, 1899 *I, W, E*, 1900 *E*

Mackintosh, C.E.W.C., London Scottish – 1924 *F*

Mackintosh, H.S., Glasgow University, · West of Scotland – 1929 *F, W, I, E*, 1930 *F, W, I, E*, 1931 *F, W, I, E*, 1932 *SA, W, I, E*

MacLachlan, L.P., Oxford University, London Scottish – 1954 *NZ, I, E, W*

Maclagan, W.E., Edinburgh Academicals 1878 *E*, 1879 *I, E*, 1880 *I, E*, 1881 *I, E*, 1882 *I, E*, 1883 *W, I, E*, 1884 *W, I, E*, 1885 *W, I* (1, 2), 1887 *I, W, E*, 1888 *W, I*, 1890 *W, I, E*

McLaren, A., Durham County – 1931 *F*

McLaren, E., London Scottish, Royal High School FP – 1923 *F, W, I, E*, 1924 *F*

McLauchlan, J., Jordanhill – 1969 *E, SA*, 1970 *F, W*, 1971 *F, W, I, E, EC*, 1972 *F, W, E, NZ*, 1973 *F, W, I, E, P*, 1974 *W, E, I, F*, 1975 *I, F, W, E, NZ, A*, 1976 *F, W, E, I*, 1977 *W*, 1978 *I, F, W, E, NZ*, 1979 *W, E, I, F, NZ*

McLean, D.I., Royal High School FP – 1947 *I, E*

Maclennan, W.D., Watsonians – 1947 *F, I*

MacLeod, D.A., Glasgow University – 1886 *I, E*

MacLeod, G., Edinburgh Academicals – 1878 *E*, 1882 *I*

McLeod, H.F., Hawick – 1954 *F, NZ, I, E, W*, 1955 *F, W, I, E*, 1956 *F, W, I, E*, 1957 *F, W, I, E*, 1958 *F, W, A, I, E*, 1959 *F, W, I, E*, 1960 *F, W, I, E, SA*, 1961 *F, SA, W, I, E*, 1962 *F, W, I, E*

MacLeod, K.G., Cambridge University – 1905 *NZ*, 1906 *W, I, E, SA*, 1907 *W, I, E*, 1908 *I, E*

MacLeod, W.M., Fettesian- Lorettonians, Edinburgh Wanderers – 1886 *W, I*

McMillan, K.H.D., Sale – 1953 *F, W, I, E*

MacMillan, R.G., London Scottish, West of Scotland – 1887 *W, I, E*, 1890, *W, I, E*, 1891 *W, E*, 1892 *W, I, E*, 1893 *W, E*, 1894 *W, I, E*, 1895 *W, I, E*, 1897 *I, E*

MacMyn, D.J., Cambridge University, London Scottish – 1925 *F, W, I, E*, 1926 *F, W, I, E*, 1927 *E, NSW*, 1928 *F*

McNeil, A.S.B., Watsonians – 1935 *I*

McPartlin, J.J., Harlequins, Oxford University – 1960 *F, W*, 1962, *F, W, I, E*

Macphail, J.A.R., Edinburgh Academicals – 1949 *E*, 1951 *SA*

Macpherson, D.G., London Hospital – 1910 *I, E*

Macpherson, G.P.S., Oxford University, Edinburgh Academicals – 1922 *F, W, I, E*, 1924 *W, E*, 1925 *F, W, E*, 1927 *F, W, I, E*, 1928 *F, W, E*, 1929 *I, E*, 1930 *F, W, I, E*, 1931 *W, E*, 1932 *SA, E*

Macpherson, N.C., Newport, Mon – 1920 *W, I, E*, 1921 *F, E*, 1923 *I, E*

McQueen, S.B., Waterloo – 1923, *F, W, I, E*

Macrae, D.J. St. Andrews University – 1937 *W, I, E*, 1938 *W, I, E*, 1939 *W, I, E*

Madsen, D.F., Gosforth – 1974 *W, E, I, F*, 1975 *I, F, W, E*, 1976 *F*, 1977 *E, I, F, W*, 1978 *I*

Mair, N.G.R., Edinburgh University – 1951 *F, W, I, E*

Maitland, G., Edinburgh Institution FP – 1885 *W, I* (2)

Maitland, R., Edinburgh Institution FP – 1881 *E*, 1882 *I, E*, 1884 *W*, 1885 *W.*

Maitland, R.P., Royal Artillary – 1872 *E*

Malcolm, A.G., Glasgow University – 1888 *I*

Marsh, J., Edinburgh Academicals – 1875 *W, I*

Marshall, A., Edinburgh Academicals – 1875 *E*

Marshall, G.R., Selkirk – 1988 *A* (r), 1989, *Fj*, 1990 *Arg*, 1991 *WC* (*Z*)

Marshall, J.C., London Scottish – 1954 *F, NZ, I, E, W*

Marshall, K.W., Edinburgh Academicals – 1934 *W, I, E*, 1935 *W, I, E*, 1936 *W*, 1937 *E*

Marshall, T.R., Edinburgh Academicals – 1871 *E*, 1872 *E*, 1873 *E*, 1874 *E*

Marshall, W., Edinburgh Academicals – 1872 *E*

Martin, H. Edinburgh Academicals, Oxford University – 1908 *W, I, E*, 1909 *W, E*

Masters, W.H., Edinburgh Institution FP – 1879 *I*, 1880 *I, E*

Maxwell, F.T., Royal Engineers – 1872 *E*

Maxwell, G.H.H.P., Edinburgh Academicals, RAF, London Scottish – 1913 *I, E*, 1914 *W, I, E*, 1920 *W, E*, 1921 *F, W, I, E*, 1922 *F, E*

Maxwell, J.M., Langholm – 1957 *I*

Mein, J., Edinburgh Academicals – 1871 *E*, 1872 *E*, 1873 *E*, 1874 *E*, 1875 *E*

Melville, C.L., Army – 1937 *W, I, E*

Menzies, H.F., West of Scotland – 1893 *W, I*, 1894 *W, E*

Methuen, A., London Scottish – 1889 *W, I*

Michie, E.J.S., Aberdeen University, London Scottish – 1954 *F, NZ, I, E*, 1955 *W, I, E*, 1956 *F, W, I, E*, 1957 *F, W, I, E*

Millar, J.N., West of Scotland – 1892 *W, I, E*, 1893 *W*, 1895 *I, E*

Millar, R.K., London Scottish – 1924 *I*

Millican, J.G., Edinburgh University – 1973
W, I, E

Milne, C.J.B., Fettesian- Lorettonians, West
of Scotland – 1886 W, I, E

Milne, D.F., Heriot's FP – 1991 WC (J (r))

Milne, I.G., Heriot's FP, Harlequins – 1979
I, F, NZ, 1980 I, F, 1981 NZ (1, 2), R,
A, 1982, E, I, F, W, A (1, 2), 1983 I, F,
W, E, NZ, 1984 W, E, I, F, A, 1985 F,
W, E, 1986 F, W, E, I, R, 1987 I, F, W,
E, WC (F, Z, NZ), 1988 A, 1989 W,
1990 NZ (1, 2)

Milne, K.S., Heriot's FP – 1989 W, E, I, F,
Fj, R, 1990, I, F, W, E, NZ (2), Arg,
1991 F, W (r), E, WC (Z) 1992 E, I, F,
W, A (1), 1993 I, F, W, E, NZ, 1994 W,
E, I, F

Milne, W.N., Glasgow Academicals – 1904
I, E, 1905 W, I

Milroy, E., Watsonians – 1910 W, 1911 E,
1912 W, I, E, SA, 1913 F, W, I, E, 1914
I, E

Mitchell, G.W.E., Edinburgh Wanderers –
1967 NZ, 1968 F, W

Mitchell, J.G., West of Scotland – 1885 W, I
(1, 2)

Moncrieff, F.J., Edinburgh Academicals –
1871 E, 1872 E, 1873 E

Monteith, H.G., Cambridge University,
London Scottish – 1905 E, 1906 W, I, E,
SA, 1907 W, I, 1908 E

Monypenny, D.B., London Scottish – 1899
I, W, E

Moodie, A.R., St Andrews University –
1909 E, 1910 F, 1911 F

Moore, A., Edinburgh Academicals – 1990
NZ (2), Arg, 1991 F, W, E

Morgan, D.W., Stewart's-Melville FP –
1973 W, I, E, P, 1974 I, F, 1975 I, F, W,
E, NZ, A, 1976 F, W, 1977 I, F, W, 1978
I, F, W, E

Morrison, I.R., London Scottish – 1993 I, F,
W, E, 1994 W

Morrison, M.C., Royal High School FP –
1896 W, I, E, 1897 I, E, 1898 I, E, 1899
I, W, E, 1900 W, E, 1901 W, I, E, 1902
W, I, E, 1903 W, I, 1904 W, I, E

Morrison, R.H., Edinburgh University –
1886 W, I, E

Morrison, W.H., Edinburgh Academicals –
1900 W

Morton, D.S., West of Scotland – 1887 I,
W, E, 1888 W, I, 1889 W, I, 1890 I, E

Mowat, J.G., Glasgow Academicals – 1883
W, E

Muir, D.E., Heriot's FP – 1950 F, W, I, E,
1952 W, I, E

Munnoch, N.M., Watsonians – 1952 F, W, I

Munro, D.S., Glasgow High/ Kelvinside –
1994 W, E, I, F

Munro, P., Oxford University, London
Scottish – 1905 W, I, E, NZ, 1906 W, I,
E, SA, 1907 E, 1911 F, W, I

Munro, R., St Andrews University – 1871 E

Munro, S., Ayr, West of Scotland – 1980 I,
F, 1981 F, W, E, I, NZ (1, 2), R, 1984 W

Munro, W.H., Glasgow HS FP – 1947 I, E

Murdoch, W.C.W., Hillhead HS FP – 1935
E, NZ, 1936 W, I, 1939 E, 1948 F, W, I,
E

Murray, G.M., Glasgow Academicals –
1921 I, 1926 W

Murray, H.M., Glasgow University – 1936
W, I

Murray, K.T., Hawick – 1985 I, F, W

Murray, R.O., Cambridge University –
1935 W, E

Murray, W.A.K., London Scottish – 1920
F, I, 1921 F

Napier, H.M., West of Scotland – 1877 I, E,
1878 E, 1879 I, E

Neill, J.B., Edinburgh Academicals – 1963
E, 1964 F, NZ, W, I, E, 1965 F

Neill, R.M., Edinburgh Academicals – 1901
E, 1902 I

Neilson, G.T., West of Scotland – 1891 W,
I, E, 1892 W, E, 1893 W, 1894 W, I, 1895
W, I, E, 1896 W, I, E

Neilson, J.A., Glasgow Academicals – 1879
E, 1879 E

Neilson, R.T., West of Scotland – 1898 I, E,
1899 I, W, 1900 I, E

Neilson, T., West of Scotland – 1874 E

Neilson, W., Merchiston, Cambridge University, London Scottish – 1891 W, E,
1892 W, I, E, 1893 I, E, 1894 E, 1895 W,
I, E, 1896 I, 1897 I, E

Neilson, W.G., Merchistonians – 1894 E

Nelson, J.B., Glasgow Academicals – 1925
F, W, I, E, 1926 F, W, I, E, 1927 F, W, I,
E, 1928 I, E, 1929 F, W, I, E, 1930 F, W,
I, E, 1931 F, W, I

Nelson, T.A., Oxford University – 1898 E

Nichol, J.A., Royal High School FP – 1955
W, I, E

Nicol, A.D., Dundee HS FP – 1992 E, I, F,
W, A (1, 2), 1993 NZ, 1994 W

Nimmo, C.S., Watsonians – 1920 E

Ogilvy, C., Hawick – 1911 I, E, 1912 I

Oliver, G.H., Hawick – 1987 WC (Z), 1990
NZ (2(r)), 1991 WC (Z)

Oliver, G.K., Gala – 1970 A

Orr, C.E., West of Scotland – 1887 I, E, W,
1888 W, I, 1889 W, I, 1890 W, I, E, 1891
W, I, E, 1892 W, I, E

Orr, H.J., London Scottish – 1903 W, I, E,
1904 W, I

Orr, J.E., West of Scotland – 1889 I, 1890 W,
I, E, 1891 W, I, E, 1892 W, I, E, 1893 I,
E

Orr, J.H., Edinburgh City Police – 1947 *F, W*

Osler, F.L., Edinburgh University – 1911 *F, W*

Park, J., Royal High School FP – 1934 *W*

Paterson, D.S., Gala – 1969 *SA*, 1970 *I, E, A*, 1971 *F, W, I, E, EC*, 1972 *W*

Paterson, G.Q., Edinburgh Academicals – 1876 *E*

Paterson, J.R., Birkenhead Park – 1925 *F, W, I, E*, 1926 *F, W, I, E*, 1927 *F, W, I, E, NSW*, 1928 *F, W, I, E*, 1929 *F, W, I, E*

Patterson, D., Hawick – 1896 *W*

Pattullo, G.L., Panmure – 1920 *F, W, I, E*

Paxton, I.A.M., Selkirk – 1981 *NZ* (1, 2), *R, A*, 1982 *E, I, F, W, A* (1, 2), 1983 *I, E, NZ*, 1984 *W, E, I, F*, 1985 *I* (r), *F, W, E*, 1986 *W, E, I, R*, 1987 *I, F, W E, WC* (*F, Z, R, NZ*), 1988 *I, E, A*

Paxton, R.E., Kelso – 1982 *I, A* (2(r))

Pearson, J., Watsonians – 1909 *I, E*, 1910 *F, W, I, E*, 1911 *F*, 1912 *F, W, SA*, 1913 *I, E*

Pender, I.M., London Scottish – 1914 *E*

Pender, N.E.K., Hawick – 1977 *I*, 1978 *F, W, E*

Penman, W.M., RAF – 1939 *I*

Peterkin, W.A., Edinburgh University – 1881 *E*, 1883 *I*, 1884 *W, I, E*, 1885 *I* (1, 2), *W*

Petrie, A.G., Royal High School FP – 1873 *E*, 1874 *E*, 1875 *E*, 1876 *E*, 1877 *E*, 1878 *E*, 1879 *I, E*, 1880 *I, E*

Philp, A., Edinburgh Institution FP – 1882 *E*

Pocock, E.I., Edinburgh Wanderers – 1877 *I, E*

Pollock, J.A., Gosforth – 1982 *W*, 1983 *E, NZ* 1984 *E* (r), *I, F, R*, 1985 *F*

Polson, A.H., Gala – 1930 *E*

Purdie, W., Jed-Forest – 1939 *W, I, E*

Purves, A.B.H.L., London Scottish – 1906 *W, I, E, SA*, 1907 *W, I, E*, 1908 *W, I, E*

Purves, W.D.C.L., London Scottish – 1912 *F, W, I, SA*, 1913 *I, E*

Rea, C.W.W., West of Scotland, Headingley – 1968 *A*, 1969 *F, W, I, SA*, 1970 *F, W, I, A*, 1971 *F, W, E, EC*

Redpath, B.W., Melrose – 1993 *NZ* (t) 1994 *E* (t), *F*

Reed, A.I., Bath – 1993 *I, F, W, E*, 1994 *E, I, F*

Reid, C., Edinburgh Academicals – 1881 *I*, 1882 *I, E*, 1883 *W, I, E*, 1884 *W, I, E*, 1885 *W, I* (1, 2), 1886 *W, I, E*, 1887 *I, W, E*, 1888 *W, I*

Reid, J., Edinburgh Wanderers – 1874 *E*, 1875 *E*, 1876 *E*, 1877 *I, E*

Reid, J.M., Edinburgh Academicals – 1898 *I, E*, 1899 *I*

Reid, M.F., Loretto – 1883 *I, E*

Ralph, W.K.L., Stewart's College FP – 1955 *F, W, I, E*

Renny-Tailyour, H.W., Royal Engineers – 1872 *E*

Renwick, J.M., Hawick – 1972 *F, W, E, NZ*, 1973 *F*, 1974 *W, E, I, F*, 1975 *I, F, W, E, NZ, A*, 1976 *F, W, E* (r), 1977 *I, F, W*, 1978 *I, F, W, E, NZ*, 1979 *W, E, I, F, NZ*, 1980 *I, F, W, E*, 1981 *F, W, E, I, NZ* (1, 2), *R, A*, 1982 *E, I, F, W*, 1983 *I, F, W, E*, 1984 *R*

Renwick, W.L., London Scottish – 1989 *R*

Renwick W.N., London Scottish, Edinburgh Wanderers – 1938 *E*, 1939 *W*

Ritchie, G., Merchistonians – 1871 *E*

Ritchie, G.F., Dundee HS FP – 1932 *E*

Ritchie, J.M., Watsonians – 1933 *W, E, I*, 1934 *W, I, E*

Ritchie, W.T., Cambridge University – 1905 *I, E*

Robb, G.H. Glasgow University – 1881 *I*, 1885 *W*

Roberts, G., Watsonians – 1939 *W, I, E*, 1939 *W, E*

Robertson, A.H., West of Scotland – 1871 *E*

Robertson, A.W., Edinburgh Academicals – 1897 *E*

Robertson, D., Edinburgh Academicals – 1875 *E*

Robertson, D.D., Cambridge University – 1893 *W*

Robertson, I., London Scottish, Watsonians – 1968 *E*, 1969 *E, SA*, 1970 *F, W, I, E, A*

Robertson, I.P.M. Watsonians – 1910 *F*

Robertson, J., Clydesdale – 1908 *E*

Robertson, K.W., Melrose – 1978 *NZ*, 1979 *W, E, I, F, NZ*, 1980 *W, E*, 1981 *F, W, E, I, R, A*, 1982 *E, I, F, A*, (1, 2), 1983 *I, F, W, E*, 1984 *E, I, F, R, A*, 1985 *I, F, W, E*, 1986 *I*, 1987 *F* (r), *W, E, WC* (*F, Z, NZ*), 1988 *E, A*, 1989 *E, I, F*

Robertson, L., London Scottish, United Services – 1908 *E*, 1911 *W*, 1912 *W, I, E, SA*, 1913 *W, I, E*

Robertson, M.A., Gala – 1958 *F*

Robertson, R.D., London Scottish – 1912 *F*

Robson, A., Hawick – 1954 *F*, 1955 *F, W, I, E*, 1956 *F, W, I, E*, 1957 *F, W, I, E*, 1958 *W, A, I, E*, 1959 *F, W, I, E*, 1960 *F*

Rodd, J.A.T., United Services, RN, London Scottish – 1958 *F, W, A, I, E*, 1960 *F, W*, 1962 *F*, 1964 *F, NZ, W*, 1965 *F, W, I*

Rogerson, J., Kelvinside Academicals, – 1894 *W*

Roland, E.T., Edinburgh Academicals – 1884 *I, E*

Rollo, D.M.D., Howe of Fife – 1959 *E*, 1960 *F, W, I, E, SA*, 1961 *F, SA, W, I, E*, 1962 *F, W, E*, 1963 *F, W, I, E*, 1964

F, NZ, W, I, E, 1965 F, W, I, E, SA,
1966 F, W, I, E, A, 1967 F, W, E, NZ,
1968 F, W, I

Rose, D.M., Jed-Forest – 1951 F, W, I, E,
SA, 1953 F, W

Ross, A., Kilmarnock – 1924 F, W

Ross, A., Royal High School FP – 1905 W, I,
E, 1909 W, I

Ross, A.R., Edinburgh University – 1911
W, 1914 W, I, E

Ross, E.J., London Scottish – 1904 E

Ross, G.T., Watsonians – 1954 NZ, I, E, W

Ross, I.A., Hillhead HS FP – 1951 F, W, I, E

Ross, J., London Scottish – 1901 W, I, E,
1902 W, 1903 E

Ross, K.I., Boroughmuir – 1961 SA, W, I,
E, 1962 F, W, I, E, 1963 F, W, E

Ross, W.A., Hillhead HS FP – 1937 W, E

Rottenburg, H., Cambridge University,
London Scottish – 1899 W, E, 1900 W, I,
E

Roughead, W.N., Edinburgh Academicals,
London Scottish – 1927 NSW, 1928 F,
W, I, E, 1930 I, E, 1931 F, W, I, E, 1932
W

Rowan, N.A., Boroughmuir – 1980 W, E,
1981 F, W, E, I, 1984 R, 1985 I, 1987
WC (R), 1988 I, F, W, E

Rowand, R., Glasgow HS FP – 1930 F, W,
1932 E, 1933 W, E, I, 1934 W

Roy, A., Waterloo – 1938 W, I, E, 1939 W,
I, E

Russell, W.L., Glasgow University, Glasgow
Academicals – 1905 NZ, 1906 W, I, E

Rutherford, J.Y., Selkirk – 1979 W, E, I, F,
NZ, 1980 I, F, E, 1981 F, W, E, I, NZ
(1, 2), A, 1982 E, I, F, W, A (1, 2), 1983
E, NZ, 1984 W, E, I, F, R, 1985 I, F, W,
E, 1986 F, W, E, I, R, 1987 I, F, W, E,
WC (F)

Sampson, R.W.F., London Scottish – 1939
W, 1947 W

Sanderson, G.A., Royal High School FP –
1907 W, I, E, 1908 I

Sanderson, J.L.P., Edinburgh Academicals
– 1873 E

Schulze, D.G., London Scottish, Dart-
mouth RNC, Northampton – 1905 E,
1907 I, E, 1908 W, I, E, 1909 W, I, E,
1910 W, I, E, 1911 W

Scobie, R.M., Royal Military College –
1914 W, I, E

Scotland, K.J.F., Royal Signals, Heriot's
FP, Cambridge University, London
Scottish, Leicester, Aberdeenshire – 1957
F, W, I, E, 1958 E, 1959 F, W, I, E, 1960
F, W, I, E, 1961 F, SA, W, I, E, 1962 F,
W, I, E, 1963 F, W, I, E, 1965 F

Scott, D.M., Langholm, Watsonians – 1950
I, E, 1951 W, I, E, SA, 1952 F, W, I,
1953 F

Scott, H., St Andrews University – 1950 E

Scott, J.M.B., Edinburgh Academicals –
1907 E, 1908 W, I, E, 1909 W, I, E, 1910
F, W, I, E, 1911 F, W, I, 1912 W, I, E,
SA, 1913 W, I, E

Scott, J.W., Stewart's College FP, Bradford,
Waterloo – 1925 F, W, I, E, 1926 F, W,
I, E, 1927 F, W, I, E, NSW, 1928 F, W,
E, 1929 E, 1930 F

Scott, M.W., Dunfermline – 1992 A (2)

Scott, R., Hawick – 1898 I, 1900 I, E

Scott, T., Langholm, Hawick – 1896 W,
1897 I, E, 1898 I, E, 1899 I, W, E, 1900
W, I, E

Scott, T.M., Hawick, Melrose – 1893 E,
1895 W, I, E, 1896 W, E, 1897 I, E, 1898
I, E, 1900 W, I

Scott, W.P., West of Scotland – 1900 I, E,
1902 I, E, 1903 W, I, E, 1904 W, I, E,
1905 W, I, E, NZ, 1906 W, I, E, SA,
1907 W, I, E

Scoular, J.G., Cambridge University – 1905
NZ, 1906 W, I, E, SA

Selby, J.A.R., Watsonians – 1920 W, I

Shackleton, J.A.P., London Scottish – 1959
E, 1963 F, W, 1964 NZ, W, 1965 I, SA

Sharp, A.V., Bristol – 1994 E, I, F

Sharp, G., Stewart's FP, Army – 1960 F,
1964 F, NZ, W

Shaw, G.D., Gala, Sale – 1935 NZ, 1936 W,
1937 W, I, E, 1939 I

Shaw, I., Glasgow HS FP – 1937 I

Shaw, J.N., Edinburgh Academicals – 1921,
W, I

Shaw, R.W., Glasgow HS FP – 1934 W, I,
E, 1935 W, I, E, NZ, 1936 W, I, E, 1937
W, I, E, 1938 W, I, E, 1939 W, I, E

Shedden, D., West of Scotland – 1972 NZ,
1973 F, W, I, E, P, 1976 W, E, I, 1977 I,
F, W, 1978 I, F, W

Shiel, A.G., Melrose – 1991 WC (I(r), WS),
1993 I, F, W, E, NZ

Shillinglaw, R.B., Gala, Army – 1960 I, E,
SA, 1961 F, SA

Simmers, B.M., Glasgow Academicals –
1965 F, W, 1966 A, 1967 F, W, I, 1971 F
(r)

Simmers, W.M., Glasgow Academicals –
1926 W, I, E, 1927 F, W, I, E, NSW,
1928 F, W, I, E, 1929 F, W, I, E, 1930 F,
W, I, E, 1931 F, W, I, E, 1932 SA, W, I,
E

Simpson, J.W., Royal High School FP –
1893 I, E, 1894 W, I, E, 1895 W, I, E,
1896 W, I, 1897 E, 1898 W, E

Simpson, R.S., Glasgow Academicals –
1923

Simson, E.D., Edinburgh University, London Scottish – 1902 E, 1903 W, I, E,
1904 W, I, E, 1906 W, I, E, NZ, 1906 W,
I, E, 1907 W, I, E

Simson, J.T., Watsonians – 1905 *NZ*, 1909 *W, I, E*, 1910 *F, W*, 1911 *I*

Simson, R.F., London Scottish – 1911 *E*

Sloan, A.T., Edinburgh Academicals – 1914 *W*, 1920 *F, W, I, E*, 1921 *F, W, I, E*

Sloan, D.A., Edinburgh Academicals, London Scottish – 1950 *F, W, E*, 1951 *W, I, E*, 1953 *F*

Sloan, T., Glasgow Academicals, London Scottish – 1905 *NZ*, 1906 *W, SA*, 1907 *W, E*, 1908 *W*, 1909 *I*

Smeaton, P.W., Edinburgh Academicals – 1881 *I*, 1883 *I, E*

Smith, A.R., Oxford University, 1895 *W, I, E*, 1896 *W, I*, 1897 *I, E*, 1898 *I, E*, 1900 *I, E*

Smith, A.R., Cambridge University, Gosforth, Ebbw Vale, Edinburgh Wands. – 1955 *W, I, E*, 1956 *F, W, I, E*, 1957 *F, W, I, E*, 1958 *F, W, A, I*, 1959 *F, W, I, E*, 1960 *F, W, I, E, SA*, 1961 *F, SA, W, I, E*, 1962 *F, W, I, E*

Smith, D.W.C., Army, London Scottish – 1949 *F, W, I, E*, 1950 *F, W, I*, 1953 *I*

Smith, E.R., Edinburgh Academicals – 1879 *I*

Smith, G.K., Kelso – 1957 *I, E*, 1958 *F, W, A*, 1959 *F, W, I, E*, 1960 *F, W, I, E*, 1961 *F, SA, W, I, E*

Smith, H.O., Watsonians – 1894 *W*, 1896 *W, I, E*, 1898 *I, E*, 1899 *W, I, E*, 1900 *E*, 1902 *E*

Smith, I.R., Gloucester – 1992 *E, I, W, A* (1, 2), 1994 *E* (r), *I, F*

Smith, I.S., Oxford University, Edinburgh University, London Scottish – 1924 *W, I, E*, 1925 *F, W, I, E*, 1926 *F, W, I, E*, 1927 *F, I, E*, 1929 *F, W, I, E*, 1930 *F, W, I*, 1931 *F, W, I, E*, 1932 *SA, W, I, E*, 1933 *W, E, I*

Smith, I.S.G., London Scottish – 1969 *SA*, 1970 *F, W, I, E*, 1971 *F, W, I*

Smith, M.A., London Scottish – 1970 *W, I, E, A*

Smith, R.T., Kelso – 1929 *F, W, I, E*, 1930 *F, W, I*

Smith, S.H., Glasgow Academicals – 1877 *I*, 1878 *E*

Smith, T.J., Gala – 1983 *E, NZ*, 1985 *I, F*

Sole, D.M.B., Bath, Edinburgh Academicals – 1986 *F, W*, 1987 *I, F, W, E, WC (F, Z, R, NZ)*, 1988 *I, F, W, E, A*, 1989 *W, E, I, F, Fj, R*, 1990 *I, F, W, E, NZ* (1, 2), *Arg*, 1991 *F, W, E, I, R, WC (J, I, WS, E, NZ)*, 1992 *E, I, F, W, A* (1, 2)

Somerville, D., Edinburgh Institution FP – 1879 *I*, 1882 *I*, 1883, *W, I, E*, 1884 *E*

Spiers, L.M., Watsonians – 1906 *SA*, 1907 *W, I, E*, 1908 *W, I, E*, 1910 *F, W, E*,

Spence, K.M., Oxford University – 1953 *I*

Spencer, E., Clydesdale – 1898 *I*

Stagg, P.K., Sale – 1965 *F, W, E, SA*, 1966 *F, W, I, E, A*, 1967 *F, W, I, E, NZ*, 1968 *F, W, I, E, A*, 1969 *F, W, I* (r), *SA*, 1970 *F, W, I, E, A*

Stanger, A.G., Hawick – 1989 *Fj, R*, 1990 *I, F, W, E, NZ* (1, 2), *Arg*, 1991 *F, W, E, I, R, WC (J, Z, I, WS, E, NZ)*, 1992 *E, I, F, W, A* (1, 2), 1993 *I, F, W, E, NZ*, 1994 *W, E, I, F*

Stark, D.A., Boroughmuir – 1993 *I, F, W, E*

Steele, W.C.C., Bedford, RAF, London Scottish – 1969 *E*, 1971, *F, W, I, E, EC*, 1972 *F, W, E, NZ*, 1973 *F, W, I, E*, 1975 *I, F, E, NZ* (r), 1976 *W, E, I*, 1977 *E*

Stephen, A.E., West of Scotland – 1885 *W*, 1886 *I*

Steven, P.D., Heriot's FP – 1984 *A*, 1985 *F, W, E*

Steven, R., Edinburgh Wanderers – 1962 *I*

Stevenson, A.K., Glasgow Academicals – 1922 *F, I*, 1923 *F, W, E*

Stevenson, A.M., Glasgow – 1911 *F*

Stevenson, G.D., Hawick – 1956 *E*, 1957 *F*, 1958 *F, W, A, I, E*, 1959 *W, I, E*, 1960 *W, I, E, SA*, 1961 *F, SA, W, I, E*, 1963 *F, W, I*, 1964 *E*, 1965 *F*

Stevenson, H.J., Edinburgh Academicals – 1888 *W, I*, 1889, *W, I*, 1890 *W, I, E*, 1891, *W, I, E*, 1892 *W, I, E*, 1893 *I, E*

Stevenson, L.E., Edinburgh University – 1888 *W*

Stevenson, R.C., London Scottish – 1897 *I, E*, 1898 *E*, 1899 *I, W, E*

Stevenson, R.C., St Andrews University – 1910 *F, I, E*, 1911 *F, W, I*

Stevenson, W.H., Glasgow Academicals – 1925 *F*

Stewart, A.K., Edinburgh University – 1874 *E*, 1876 *E*

Stewart, A.M., Edinburgh Academicals – 1914 *W*

Stewart, C.A.R., West of Scotland – 1880 *I, E*

Stewart, C.E.B., Kelso – 1960 *W*, 1961 *F*

Stewart, J., Glasgow HS FP – 1930 *F*

Stewart, J.L., Edinburgh Academicals – 1921 *I*

Stewart, M.S., Stewart's College FP – 1932 *SA, W, I*, 1933 *W, E, I*, 1934 *W, I, E*

Stewart, W.A., London Hospital – 1913 *F, W, I*, 1914 *W*

Steyn, S.S.L., Oxford University – 1911 *E*, 1912 *I*

Strachan, G.M., Jordanhill – 1971 *E* (r), 1973 *W, I, E, P*

Stronach, R.S., Glasgow Academicals – 1901 *W, E*, 1905 *W, I, E*

Stuart, C.D., West of Scotland – 1909 *I*, 1910 *F, W, I, E*, 1911 *I, E*

Stuart, L.M., Glasgow HS FP – 1923 *F, W, I, E,* 1924 *F,* 1928 *E,* 1930 *I, E*

Suddon, N., Hawick – 1965 *W, I, E, SA,* 1966 *A,* 1968 *E, A,* 1969 *F, W, I,* 1970 *I, E, A*

Sutherland, W.R., Hawick – 1910 *W, E,* 1911 *F, E,* 1912 *F, W, E, SA,* 1913 *F, W, I, E,* 1914 *W*

Swan, J.S., Army, London Scottish, Leicester, Coventry – 1953 *E,* 1954 *F, NZ, I, E, W,* 1955 *F, W, I, E,* 1956 *F, W, I, E,* 1957 *F, W,* 1958 *F*

Swan, M.W., Oxford University, London Scottish – 1958 *F, W, A, I, E,* 1959 *F, W, I*

Sweet, J.B., Glasgow HS FP – 1913 *E,* 1914 *I*

Symington, A.W., Cambridge University – 1914 *W, E*

Tait, A.V., Kelso – 1987 *WC (F (r), Z, R, NZ),* 1988 *I, F, W, E*

Tait, J.G., Edinburgh Academicals, Cambridge University – 1880 *I,* 1885 *I (2)*

Tait, P.W., Royal High School FP – 1935 *E*

Taylor, E.G., Oxford University – 1927 *W, NSW*

Taylor, R.C., Kelvinside-West – 1951 *W, I, E, SA*

Telfer, C.M., Hawick – 1968 *A,* 1969 *F, W, I, E,* 1972 *F, W, E,* 1973 *W, I, E, P,* 1974 *W, E, I,* 1975 *A,* 1976 *F*

Telfer, J.W., Melrose – 1964 *F, NZ, W, I, E,* 1965 *F, W, I,* 1966 *F, W, I, E,* 1967 *W, I, E,* 1968 *E, A,* 1969 *F, W, I, E, SA,* 1970 *F, W, I*

Tennent, J.M., West of Scotland – 1909 *W, I, E,* 1910 *F, W, E*

Thom, D.A., London Scottish – 1934 *W,* 1935 *W, I, E, NZ*

Thom, G., Kirkcaldy – 1920 *F, W, I, E*

Thom, J.R., Watsonians – 1933 *W, E, I*

Thomson, A.E., United Services – 1921 *F, W, E*

Thomson, A.M., St Andrews University – 1949 *I*

Thomson, B.E., Oxford University – 1953 *F, W, I*

Thomson, I.H.M., Heriot's FP, Army – 1951 *W, I,* 1952 *F, W, I,* 1953 *I, E*

Thomson, J.S., Glasgow Academicals – 1871 *E*

Thomson R.H., London Scottish – 1960 *I, E, SA,* 1961 *F, SA, W, I, E,* 1963 *F, W, I, E,* 1964 *F, NZ, W*

Thomson, W.H., West of Scotland – 1906 *SA*

Thomson, W.J., West of Scotland – 1899 *W, E,* 1900 *W*

Timms, A.B., Edinburgh University, Edinburgh Wanderers, Cardiff – 1896 *W,*

1900 *W, I,* 1901 *W, I, E,* 1902 *W, E,* 1903 *W, E,* 1904 *I, E,* 1905 *I, E*

Tod, H.B., Gala – 1911 *F*

Tod, J. Watsonians – 1884 *W, I, E,* 1885 *W, I (1, 2),* 1886 *W, I, E*

Todd, J.K., Glasgow Academicals – 1874 *E,* 1875 *E*

Tolmie, J.M., Glasgow HS FP – 1992 *E*

Tomes, A.J., Hawick – 1976 *E, I,* 1977 *E,* 1978 *I, F, W, E, NZ,* 1979 *W, E, I, F, NZ,* 1980 *F, W, E,* 1981 *F, W, E, I, NZ (1, 2), R, A,* 1982 *E, I, F, W, A (1, 2),* 1983 *I, F, W,* 1984 *W, E, I, F, R, A,* 1985 *W, E,* 1987 *I, F, E (r), WC (F, Z, R, NZ)*

Torrie, T.J. Edinburgh Academicals – 1877 *E*

Townsend, G.P.J., Gala – 1993 *E (r),* 1994 *W, E, I, F*

Tukalo, I., Selkirk – 1985 *I,* 1987 *I, F, W, E, WC (F, Z, R, NZ),* 1988 *F, W, E, A,* 1989 *W, E, I, F, Fj,* 1990 *I, F, W, E, NZ (1),* 1991, *I, (r), WC (J, Z, I, WS, E, NZ)* 1992 *E, I, F, W, A, (1, 2)*

Turk, A.S., Langholm – 1971 *E (r)*

Turnbull, F.O., Kelso – 1951 *F, SA*

Turnbull, D.J., Hawick – 1987 *WC (NZ),* 1988 *F, E,* 1990 *E (r),* 1991 *F, W, E, I, R, WC (Z),* 1993 *I, F, W, E,* 1994 *W*

Turnbull, G.O., West of Scotland, London Scottish, Edinburgh Wanderers – 1896 *I, E,* 1897 *I, E,* 1904 *W*

Turnbull, P., Edinburgh Academicals – 1901 *W, I, E,* 1902 *W, I, E*

Turner, F.H., Oxford University, Liverpool – 1911 *F, W, I, E,* 1912 *F, W, I, E, SA,* 1913 *F, W, I, E,* 1914 *I, E*

Turner, J.W.C., Gala – 1966 *W, A,* 1967 *F, W, I, E, NZ,* 1968 *F, W, I, E, A,* 1969 *F,* 1970 *E, A,* 1971 *F, W, I, E, EC*

Usher, C.M., London Scottish, United Services, Edinburgh Wanderers – 1912 *E,* 1913 *F, W, I, E,* 1914 *E,* 1920 *F, W, I, E,* 1921 *W, E,* 1922 *F, W, I, E*

Valentine, A.R., RNAS, Anthorn – 1953 *F, W, I*

Valentine, D.D., Hawick – 1947 *I, E*

Veitch, J.P., Royal High School FP – 1882 *E,* 1883 *I,* 1884 *W, I, E,* 1885 *I (1, 2),* 1886 *E*

Villar, C., Edinburgh Wanderers – 1876 *E,* 1877 *I, E*

Waddell, G.H., London Scottish, Devonport Services, Cambridge University – 1957 *E,* 1958 *F, W, A, I, E,* 1959 *F, W, I, E,* 1960 *I, E, SA,* 1961 *F,* 1962 *F, W, I, E*

Waddell, H., Glasgow Academicals – 1924 *F, W, I, E,* 1925 *I, E,* 1926 *F, W, I, E,* 1927 *F, W, I, E,* 1930 *W*

Wade, A.L., London Scottish – 1908 *E*

Wainwright, R.I., Edinburgh Academicals

– 1992 *I* (r), *F, A (*1, 2) 1993 *NZ,* 1994 *W, E*

Walker, A., West of Scotland – 1881 *I,* 1882 *E,* 1883 *W, I, E*

Walker A.W., Cambridge University, Birkenhead Park – 1931 *F, W, I, E,* 1932 *I*

Walker, J.G., Fettesian- Lorettonians, West of Scotland – 1882 *E,* 1883 *W*

Walker, M., Oxford University 1952 *F*

Wallace, A.C., Oxford University – 1923 *F,* 1924 *F, W, E,* 1925 *F, W, I, E,* 1926 *F*

Wallace, W.M., Cambridge University – 1913 *E,* 1914 *W, I, E*

Walls, W.A., Glasgow Academicals – 1882 *E,* 1883 *W, I, E,* 1884 *W, I, E,* 1886 *W, I, E*

Walter, M.W., London Scottish – 1906 *I, E, SA,* 1907 *W, I,* 1908 *W, I,* 1910 *I*

Walton, P., Northampton – 1994 *E, I, F*

Warren, J.R., Glasgow Academicals – 1914 *I*

Warren, R.C., Glasgow Academicals – 1922 *W, I,* 1930 *W, I, E*

Waters, F.H., Cambridge University, London Scottish – 1930 *F, W, I, E,* 1932 *SA, W, I*

Waters, J.A., Selkirk – 1933 *W, E, I,* 1934 *W, I, E,* 1935 *W, I, E, NZ,* 1936 *W, I, E,* 1937 *W, I, E*

Waters, J.B., Cambridge University – 1904 *I, E*

Watherston, J.G., Edinburgh Wanderers – 1934 *I, E*

Watherston, W.R.A., London Scottish – 1963 *F, W, I*

Watson, D.H., Glasgow Academicals – 1876 *E,* 1877 *I, E*

Watson, W.S., Boroughmuir – 1974 *W, E, I, F,* 1975 *NZ,* 1977 *I, F, W,* 1979, *I, F*

Watt, A.G.J., Glasgow High/Kelvinside – 1991 *WC (Z),* 1993 *I, NZ*

Watt, A.G.M., Edinburgh Academicals, Army – 1947 *F, W, I, A,* 1948 *F, W*

Weatherstone, T.G., Stewart's College FP – 1952 *E,* 1953, *I, E,* 1954 *F, NZ, I, E, W,* 1955 *F,* 1958 *W, A, I, E,* 1959 *W, I, E*

Weir, G.W., Melrose – 1990 *Arg,* 1991 *R, WC, (J, Z, I, WS, E, NZ),* 1992 *E, I, F, W, A (*1, 2), 1993 *I, F, W, E, NZ,* 1994 *W* (r), *E, I, F*

Welsh, R., Watsonians – 1895 *W, E, I,* 1896 *W*

Welsh, R.B, Hawick – 1967 *I, E*

Welsh W.B., Hawick – 1927 *NSW,* 1928 *F, W, I,* 1929 *I, E,* 1930 *F, W, I, E,* 1931 *F, W, I, E,* 1932 *SA, W, I, E,* 1933 *W, E, I*

Welsh, W.H., Edinburgh University – 1900 *I, E,* 1901 *W, I, E,* 1902 *W, I, E*

Weymss, A., Gala, Edinburgh Wanderers – 1914 *W, I,* 1920 *F, E,* 1922 *F, W, I*

West, L., Edinburgh University, Carlisle, London Scottish, West Hartlepool – 1903 *W, I, E,* 1905 *I, E, NZ,* 1906 *W, I, E*

Weston, V.G., Kelvinside Academicals – 1936 *I, E*

White, D.B., Gala, London Scottish – 1982 *F, W, A (*1, 2), 1987 *W, E, WC (F, R, NZ),* 1988 *I, F, W, E, A,* 1989 *W, E, I, F, Fj, R,* 1990 *I, F, W, E, NZ (*1, 2), 1991 *F, W, E, I, R, WC (J, Z, I, WS, E, NZ),* 1992 *E, I, F, W*

White, D.M., Kelvinside Academicals – 1963 *F, W, I, E*

White, T.B., Edinburgh Academicals – 1886 *W, I,* 1889 *W*

Whittington, T.P., Merchistonians – 1873 *E*

Whitworth, R.J.E., London Scottish – 1936 *I*

Whyte, D.J., Edinburgh Wanderers – 1965 *W, I, E, SA,* 1966 *F, W, I, E, A,* 1967 *F, W, I, E*

Will, J.G., Cambridge University – 1912 *F, W, I, E,* 1914 *W, I, E*

Wilson, A.W., Dunfermline – 1931 *F, I, E*

Wilson, G.A., Oxford University – 1949 *F, W, E*

Wilson, G.R., Royal High School FP – 1886 *E,* 1890 *W, I, E,* 1891 *I*

Wilson, J.H. Watsonians – 1953 *I*

Wilson, J.S., St Andrews University – 1931 *F, W, I, E,* 1932 *E*

Wilson, J.S., United Services, London Scottish – 1908 *I,* 1909 *W*

Wilson, R., London Scottish – 1976 *E, I,* 1977 *E, I, F,* 1978 *I, F,* 1981 *R,* 1983 *L*

Wilson, R.L., Gala – 1951 *F, W, I, E, SA,* 1953 *F, W, E*

Wilson, R.W., West of Scotland – 1873 *E,* 1874 *E*

Wilson, S., Oxford University, London Scottish – 1964 *F, NZ, W, I, E,* 1965 *W, I, E, SA,* 1966 *F, W, I, A,* 1967 *F, W, I, E, NZ,* 1968 *W, I, E*

Wood, A., Royal High School FP – 1873 *E,* 1874 *E,* 1875 *E*

Wood, G., Gala – 1931 *W, I,* 1932 *W, I, E*

Woodburn, J.C., Kelvinside Academicals – 1892 *I*

Woodrow, A.N., Glasgow Academicals – 1887 *I, W, E*

Wotherspoon, W., West of Scotland – 1891 *I,* 1892 *I,* 1893 *W, E* 1894 *W, I, E*

Wright, F.A., Edinburgh Academicals – 1932 *E*

Wright, H.B., Watsonians – 1894 *W*

Wright, K.M., London Scottish – 1929 *F, W, I, E*

Wright, P.H., Boroughmuir – 1992 *A (*1, 2),

1993 *F, W, E,* 1994 *W*
Wright, R.W.J., Edinburgh Wanderers –
1973 *F*
Wright, S.T.H., Stewart's College FP –
1949 *E*
Wright, T., Hawick – 1947 *A*
Wyllie, D.S., Stewart's-Melville FP – 1984
A, 1985 *W* (r), *E,* 1987 *I, F, WC (F, Z,
R, NZ),* 1989 *R,* 1991 *R, WC (J(r), Z),*
1993 *NZ* (r), 1994 *W* (r), *E, I, F*

Young, A.H., Edinburgh Academicals –
1874 *E*
Young, E.T., Glasgow Academicals – 1914
E
Young, R.G., Watsonians – 1970 *W*
Young, T.E.B., Durham – 1911 *F*
Young, W.B., Cambridge University, King's
College Hospital, London Scottish –
1937 *W, I, E,* 1938 *W, I, E,* 1939 *W, I, E,*
1948 *E*

FULL LIST OF SCOTLAND A TEAM PLAYERS

(Matches are listed by the second half of the season in which the games were played, i.e. 1991
indicates season 1990–91 even though the match may have been played in December 1990)

Allan, J., Edinburgh Academicals – 1991 *S*
Appleson, M.E., London Scottish – 1993 *It,
I*
Armstrong, G., Jed-Forest – 1993 *It*
Burnell, A.P., London Scottish – 1992 *S,*
1993 *S, It*
Campbell, S.J., Dundee HS FP – 1994 *F*
Caskie, D.W., Gloucester – 1991 *S,* 1992 *S*
Chalmers, C.M., Melrose – 1993 *It,* 1994 *F*
Corcoran, I., Gala – 1993 *S, It*
Cronin, D.F., Bath, London Scottish – 1991
S, 1992 *S,* 1993 *It*
Dods, M., Gala – 1994 *NZ, It, F*
Dods, P.W., Gala – 1991 *S,* 1992 *S*
Donaldson, A., Currie – 1993 *F*
Edwards, N.G.B., Northampton – 1994 *F*
Ferguson, S.W., Peebles – 1993 *F*
Gray, C.A., Nottingham – 1993 *S★ F★*
Hastings, A.G., Watsonians – 1993 *It★*
Hastings, S., Watsonians – 1993 *It*
Herrington, D.W., Dundee HS FP – 1994
NZ, F
Hogg, C.D., Melrose – 1993 *It, I,* 1994 *NZ,
It, F*
Isaac, G.R., Gala – 1991 *S*
Jardine, I.C., Stirling County – 1993 *S, I, F,*
1994 *NZ, It, I, F*
Jones, P.M., Gloucester – 1992 *S,* 1993 *It*
Kerr, J.A., Haddington – 1993 *F*
Logan, K.M., Stirling County – 1993 *S, I,
F,* 1994 *NZ, It, I*
Macdonald, A.E.D., Heriot's FP – 1992 *S,*
1993 *S, I* (r), 1994 *NZ, F*
McIntosh, D.L.M., Pontypridd – 1993 *I,*
1994 *It*
McIvor, D.J., Edinburgh Academicals –
1993 *F,* 1994 *NZ, F*
McKenzie, K.D., Stirling County – 1994
NZ, It, I★, F★
Maclean, R.R.W., Moseley – 1991 *S*
Marshall, G.R., Selkirk – 1991 *S,* 1992 *S*

Millard, D.B., London Scottish – 1993 *F*
Milligan, K.R., Stewart's-Melville FP –
1993 *F,* 1994 *It, I, F*
Milne, K.S., Heriot's FP – 1992 *S,* 1993 *I*
Moncrieff, M., Gala – 1991 *S,* 1993 *S*
Moore, A., Edinburgh Academicals – 1992 *S*
Morrison, I.R., London Scottish – 1993 *I,*
1994 *I*
Munro, D.S., Glasgow High/ Kelvinside –
1993 *I, F,* 1994 *NZ, It, I*
Nichol, S.A., Selkirk – 1994 *NZ, It, I*
Nicol, A.D., Dundee HS FP – 1993 *I★,* 1994
I
Oliver, G.H., Hawick – 1991 *S,* 1992 *S,*
1993 *S*
Parker, G.A., Melrose – 1994 *NZ*
Redpath, B.W., Melrose – 1994 *NZ, It, F*
Reed, A. I., Bath – 1993 *I*
Reid, S.J., Boroughmuir – 1992 *S,* 1993 *It,*
1994 *F*
Roxburgh, A.J., Kelso – 1993 *S*
Scott, M.W., Edinburgh Academicals – 1993
F
Sharp, A.V., Bristol – 1994 *It, I*
Shepherd, R.J.S., Edinburgh Academicals –
1994 *F*
Shiel, A.G., Melrose – 1992 *S,* 1993 *I*
Smith, G.B., Moseley – 1991 *S*
Smith, I.R., Gloucester – 1993 *It, F*
Stanger, A.G., Hawick – 1992 *S,* 1993 *I*(r)
Stark, D.A., Boroughmuir – 1993 *S, It,*
1994 *I, F*
Townsend, G.P.J., Gala – 1993 *S, It, I,* 1994
I
Tukalo, I., Selkirk – 1991 *S*
Turnbull, D.J., Hawick – 1991 *S,* 1993 *S*
Wainwright, R.I., Edinburgh Academicals
– 1994 *NZ, I*
Walton, P., Northampton – 1994 *It, I*
Watt, A.G.J., Glasgow High/Kelvinside –
1993 *S, I,* 1994 *NZ*

Weir, G.W., Melrose – 1991 *S*, 1992 *S*, 1993 *S*, *It*, 1994 *I*

White, D.B., London Scottish – 1991 *S*

Wilson, G.D., Boroughmuir – 1993 *I* (r), *F*

Wright, P.H., Boroughmuir – 1993 *I*, 1994 *It*, *I*, *F*

Wyllie, D.S., Stewart's-Melville FP – 1991 *S*, 1992 *S*, 1993 *S*, *F*, 1994 *NZ*★, *It*★

FULL LIST OF SCOTLAND B TEAM PLAYERS

(B appearances are listed by the second half of the season in which the games were played, i.e. 1974 indicates season 1973–74 even if the match was played in December 1973)

Aitchison, W.D., Highland – 74 *F*, 75 *F*, 77 *F*, 78 *I* (r)

Aitken, J., Gala – 75 *F*, 76 *F* (capped v *E*, 77)

Allingham, M.J. de G., Heriot's FP – 92 *I* (r)

Appleson, M., London Scottish – 92 *I*, *F*

Armstrong, A.D., Jordanhill – 81 *F*, 82 *F*

Armstrong, G., Jed-Forest – 88 *It*, *F* (capped v *A*, 88)

Ashton, D.M., Ayr – 77 *F*

Baird, G.R.T., Kelso – 80 *I*, *F*, 81 *F* (capped v *A*, 82)

Balfour, R.F.A., Glasgow HS FP – 74 *F*, 75 *F*

Barnes, I.A., Hawick – 72 *F* (capped v *W*, 72)

Barrett, D.N., West of Scotland – 90 *I*, *F*, 91 *I*

Beattie, J.R., Glasgow Academicals – 80 *I*, *F* (capped v *I*, 80)

Bell, D.L., Watsonians – 74 *F*, 75 *F* (capped v *I*, 75)

Berthinussen, J.M., Gala – 81 *F*

Biggar, M.A., London Scottish – 75 *F*★ (capped v *I*, 75)

Black, A.A., Boroughmuir – 72 *F*

Blackwood, A.W., Stewart's- Melville FP – 78 *I*

Breakey, R.W., Gosforth – 76 *F*, 78 *I* (capped v *E*, 78)

Breckenridge, G.M., Glasgow High/Kelvinside) – 90 *F*

Brown, J.F., Ayr – 78 *F*

Bruce Lockhart, D.R.M., London Scottish – 84 *I*, *F*

Bryce, R.D.H., London Scottish – 72 *F*★, 73 *F*★ (capped v *I*, 73)

Bryson, D., Gala – 82 *F*, 90 *I*, *F*

Buchanan-Smith, G.A.E., London Scottish – 89 *F* (capped v *Fj*, 90)

Burnell, A.P., London Scottish – 89 *It* (capped v *E*, 89)

Burnett, H.M., Heriot's FP – 77 *F*★, 78 *I*★, 81 *F*

Burnett, J.N., Heriot's FP – 78 *I*, 80 *I*, *F* (capped v *I*, 80)

Busby, J.D., Glasgow High/ Kelvinside – 90 *I*, *F*

Butcher, D.J.D., Harlequins – 88 *It*, *F*

Calder, F., Stewart's-Melville FP – 84 *I*, *F* (capped v *F*, 86)

Calder, J.H. Stewart's-Melville FP – 80 *I*, *F* (capped v *I*, 81)

Calder, John, Stewart's-Melville FP – 83 *F*

Callander, G.J., Kelso – 82 *F* (capped v *R*, 84)

Campbell, A.J., Hawick – 83 *F*, 84 *I*, *F* (capped v *I*, 84)

Campbell, H., Jordanhill – 78 *I*, 82 *F*

Campbell-Lamerton, J.R.E., London Scottish – 85 *F*, 86 *It* (capped v *F*, 86)

Caskie, D.W., Gloucester – 92 *F*

Chalmers, C.M., Melrose – 88 *F*, 89 *It* (capped v *W*, 89)

Clark, R.L., Edinburgh Wanderers – 72 *F* (capped v *F*, 72)

Cockburn, D.G., Boroughmuir – 83 *F*

Corcoran, I., Gala – 90 *F* (capped v *A*, 92)

Cramb, R.I., Harlequins – 86 *It*, *F* (capped v *R*, 87 *WC*)

Cranston, A.G., Hawick – 73 *F*, 74 *F* (capped v *W*, 76)

Cronin, D.F., Bath – 88 *It* (capped v *I*, 88)

Cunningham, R., Gosforth, Bath – 81 *F*, 83 *F*, 84 *I*★, *F*★, 85 *I*★, *F*★

Cuthbertson, W., Kilmarnock – 80 *I*, *F* (capped v *I*, 80)

Dall, F.N.F., Heriot's FP – 73 *F*

Davies, W.S. Hawick – 76 *F*

Deans, C.T., Hawick – 76 *F*, 77 *F*, 78 *I* (capped v *F*, 78)

Dick, L.G., Loughborough Colleges – 72 *F* (capped v *W*, 72)

Dickson, G., Gala – 77 *F*, 78 *I*, *F* (capped v *NZ*, 79)

Dixon, J.R., Jordanhill – 78 *F*★, 80 *I*★, *F*★

Dods, P.W., Gala – 80 *I*, *F*, 81 *F*, 82 *F* (capped v *I*, 83)

Dougall, A.G., Jordanhill – 78 *F*

Dunlop, A.L., Highland – 80 *I*, *F*

Dunlop, T.D., West of Scotland – 75 *F*, 78 *I*

Duncan, M.D.F., West of Scotland – 85 *F*, 86 *It* (capped v *F*, 86)

Edwards, B., Boroughmuir – 89 *It*, *F*, 90 *I*, *F*

Edwards, N.G.B., Harlequins – 92 *I* (capped v *E*, 92)

Exeter, T.J., Moseley – 88 *It*
Flannigan, C.F., Melrose – 86 *F*, 87 *F*
Flockhart, D.M., Highland – 83 *F*
Fowler, S.G., Dunfermline – 72 *F*, 73 *F*
Fraser, A.S., Madras College FP – 73 *F*
Fraser, J.A., London Scottish – 81 *F*, 83 *F*, 84 *I*, *F*, 85 *I*
Friell, A.P., London Scottish – 75 *F*, 76 *F*, 77 *F*, 78 *F*, 80 *I*, *F*
Gammell, W.B.B., Edinburgh Wanderers – 76 *F*, 77 *F* (capped v *I*, 77)
Gass, C.W., Hawick – 83 *F*, 85 *F*
Glasgow, I.C., Heriot's FP – 91 *F*
Gill, A.D., Gala – 73 *F* (capped v *P*, 73)
Gordon, R.J., London Scottish – 82 *F* (capped v *A*, 82)
Gossman, B.M., West of Scotland – 80 *I*, *F* (capped v *W*, 80)
Gossman, J.S., West of Scotland – 80 *I*, *F* (capped v *E*, 80)
Graham, G., Stirling County – 88 *It*, 89 *It*, 90 *I*, *F*
Grant, A.R., London Scottish – 76 *F*
Gray, C.A., Nottingham – 87 *It*, 88 *It*, *F*, 89 *It* (capped v *W*, 89)
Gray, D., West of Scotland – 78 *I* (capped v *E*, 78)
Gray, I.A., West of Scotland – 75 *F*
Grecian, N.J., London Scottish – 91 *I*
Haldane, R., West of Scotland – 73 *F*, 74 *F*
Hall, R., Watsonians – 77 *F*
Halliday, B.G., Boroughmuir – 78 *F*
Hamilton, J.S., Heriot's FP – 86 *F*, 87 *F*
Hardie, J.A., Aberdeen GS FP – 73 *F*
Harrold, F.J., London Scottish – 92 *I*
Hastings, A.G., Watsonians – 83 *F*, 84 *I*, *F*, 85 *I*, *F* (capped v *F*, 86)
Hastings, S., Watsonians – 86 *It* (capped v *F* 86)
Hay, J.A., Hawick – 89 *F*, 91 *F*
Hegarty, C.B., Hawick – 77 *F* (capped v *I*, 78)
Hewitt, P.J., Heriot's FP – 83 *F*
Hogarth, P.J., Hawick – 85 *I*, *F*, 86 *It*, *F★*, 87 *It★*, *F★*
Hogg, C.D., Melrose – 91 *F* (capped v *A*, 92)
Howie, W.H., Glasgow HS FP – 72 *F*
Hume, J.H., London Scottish – 82 *F*, 83 *F*
Hunter, I.G., Selkirk – 81 *F*, 83 *F★*, 84 *I*, *F* (capped v *I*, 84)
Hunter, M.D., Glasgow HS FP – 72 *F*, 73 *F* (capped v *F*, 74)
Irvine, A.R., Heriot's FP – 73 *F* (capped v *NZ*, 73)
Jardine, I.C., Stirling County – 90 *I*, 92 *I*, *F* (capped v *NZ*, 93)
Jardine, S., Glamorgan Wanderers – 91 *I*
Jeffrey, J., Kelso – 83 *F*, 84 *I*, *F* (capped v *A*, 85)

Johnston, S.G., Watsonians – 85 *I*, *F*, 86 *It*, *F*
Jones, P.M., Gloucester – 91 *I*, 92 *F* (capped v *W*, 92)
Kennedy, A.E., Watsonians – 76 *F*, 81 *F★* (capped v *NZ*, 84)
Ker, A.B.M., Kelso – 87 *It*, *F*, 88 *It★* (capped v *W*, 88)
Laidlaw, R.J., Jed-Forest – 75 *F*, 76 *F*, 77 *F*, 78 *I*, *F*, 80 *I*, *F* (capped v *I*, 80)
Lambie, I.K., Watsonians – 76 *F★*, 78 *F* (capped v *NZ*, 79)
Lawrie, K.G., Gala – 78 *F*, 80 *I*, *F* (capped v *F*, 80)
Leckie, D.E.W., Edinburgh Academicals – 87 *F* (r), 90 *I*
Leslie, D.G., Dundee HS FP – 74 *F*, 75 *F* (capped v *I*, 75)
Lillington, P.M., Durham University – 81 *F*, 82 *F*
Livingstone, E.J., Jordanhill – 76 *F*
McAslan, S.W., Heriot's FP – 84 *F*, 86 *It*, *F*, 87 *It*, *F*
McCallum, D.S.D., Jordanhill – 73 *F*, 74 *F★*
Macdonald, A.E.D., Cambridge University, Heriot's FP – 90 *F*, 91 *I*, *F*, 92 (capped v *NZ* 93)
Macdonald, D.S.M., London Scottish – 76 *F* (capped v *E*, 77)
McGauchie, S., Pontypool – 91 *I*
McGaughey, S.K., Hawick – 84 *F* (capped v *R*, 84)
MacGregor, G.T., Glasgow Academicals – 89 *It*
McGuffie, A.C., Ayr – 89 *It*
McGuinness, G.M., West of Scotland – 77 *F*, 78 *F*, 81 *F*, 82 *F★* (capped v *A*, 82)
McHardy, H.R., Kilmarnock – 74 *F*, 75 *F* (r)
McIntosh, D.L.M., Pontypridd – 92 *I*, *F*
McIvor, D.J., Edinburgh Academicals – 91 *F*, 92 *I* (capped v *E*, 92)
McKenzie, K.D., Stirling County – 90 *I*
Mackenzie, R.S., London Scottish – 74 *F*, 75 *F*
Mackie, G.Y., Highland – 74 *F* (capped v *A*, 76)
McKie, I.D., Sale – 81 *F*, 84 *I*, *F*, 85 *I*
Maclean, R.R.W., Gloucester, Moseley – 88 *It*, *F*, 89 *F*, 91 *F★*
McLeod, D.J., Hawick – 78 *I*, *F*
Macklin, A.J., London Scottish – 85 *F*, 86 *It*, *F*, 87 *It*, *F*, 90 *I★*, *F★*
Mair, C.D.R., West of Scotland – 78 *I*
Marshall, G.R., Wakefield – 88 *It*, *F* (capped v *A*, 88)
Millar, G.P., Heriot's FP – 83 *F*
Milne, D.F., Heriot's FP – 86 *F*, 87 *It*, *F*, 88 *F*, 89 *F*, 91 *F* (capped v Japan, 91 *WC*)
Milne, K.S., Heriot's FP – 86 *It*, 87 *It*, *F*, 88 *It*, *F*, 89 *It* (capped v *W*, 89)

Moncrieff, M., Gala – 91 *F*, 92 *I*, *F*

Moore. A., Gala, Edinburgh Academicals – 87 *It*, 90 *I*, *F* (capped v *NZ*, 90)

Morgan, D.W., Melville College FP – 72 *F*, 73 *F* (capped v *W*, 73)

Morrison, K., Glasgow HS FP – 74 *F*

Munro, D.S., Glasgow High/ Kelvinside – 88 *F*, 89 *F*, 90 *F* (capped v *W*, 94)

Munro, S. Ayr – 80 *I*, *F* (capped v *I*, 80)

Murray, H.A., Dunfermline – 87 *It*

Murray, K.T., Hawick – 85 *I*, *F* (capped v *I*, 85)

Murray, R.W., Hawick – 84 *I*, *F*★, 85 *I*

Nichol, R.A., Hawick – 85 *F*

Nichol, S.A., Selkirk – 91 *I*, *F*

Nicol, A.D., Dundee HS FP – 91 *F*, 92 *I* (capped v *E*, 92)

Oliver, G.H., Hawick – 87 *It*, *F* (capped v *Z*, 87 *WC*)

Parker, H.M., Kilmarnock – 85 *F*, 86 *It*, *F*, 87 *It*, 88 *It*, *F*

Paterson-Brown, T., London Scottish – 87 *F*, 88 *It*, *F*

Patterson, D.W., Edinburgh Academicals – 92 *F*

Paxton, R.E., Kelso – 81 *F*, 82 *F* (capped v *I*, 82)

Pender, N.E.K., Hawick – 75 *F*, 76 *F*, 77 *F* (capped v *I*, 77)

Porter, S.T.G., Malone – 90 *I*, *F*, 91 *I*, *F*

Preston, A.J., Gosforth – 76 *F*

Rafferty, K.P., Heriot's FP – 88 *It*, *F*, 89 *It*, *F*

Ramsey, I.J., Melrose – 88 *It*, *F*

Redpath, A.C., Melrose – 91 *I*, *F*

Reid, S.J., Boroughmuir – 91 *I*, *F*, 92 *F*

Renwick, J.M., Hawick – 72 *F* (capped v *F*, 72)

Renwick, W.L., London Scottish – 88 *It*, *F*★, 89 *It*★ *F* (capped v *R*, 90)

Richardson, C.B.S., Edinburgh Academicals – 85 *I*, 86 *It*★, 89 *It*, *F*★

Richardson, J.F., Edinburgh Academicals – 87 *F*, 89 *It*, *F*, 90 *I*, *F*, 91 *I*★

Roberts, H., London Scottish – 91 *I*

Robertson, G.B., Stirling County – 91 *I*, 92 *I*, *F*

Robertson, K.W., Melrose – 78 *F* (capped v *NZ*, 79)

Rouse, P.R., Dundee HS FP – 90 *F*

Rose, W.B.N., Kilmarnock – 72 *F*

Rowan, N.A., Boroughmuir – 78 *I*, 80 *I*, *F* (capped v *W*, 80)

Runciman, J.G., Melrose – 86 *F*

Rutherford, J.Y., Selkirk – 78 *I*, *F* (capped v *W*, 79)

Scott, J.M., Stewart's-Melville FP – 89 *F*

Scott, M.W., Dunfermline – 92 *I*, *F* (capped v *A*, 92)

Scott, R., London Scottish – 92 *I*, *F*

Scott, S.H., Stewart's-Melville FP – 86 *It*, *F*, 87 *It*, *F*

Shedden, D., West of Scotland – 72 *F*, 73 *F* (capped v *NZ*, 73)

Shiel, D.K., Jed-Forest – 89 *F*, 90 *I*

Smith, D.J.M., Glasgow High – 77 *F*, 78 *I*

Smith, I.R., Gloucester – 91 *I*, *F*, 92 *I*★ (capped v *E*, 92)

Smith, T.J., Gala – 81 *F*, 82 *F* (capped v *E*, 83)

Sole, D.M.B., Exeter University – 84 *I*, *F*, 85 *I*, *F*, 86 *It* (capped v *F*, 86)

Stark, D.A., Kilmarnock, Ayr – 88 *F*, 89 *It*, *F*, 92 *I*, *F* (capped v *I*, 93)

Steven, J., Edinburgh Wanderers – 72 *F*

Steven, P.D., Heriot's FP – 83 *F*, 84 *I*, *F*, 85 *I* (capped v *A*, 85)

Stewart, A.A., London Scottish – 78 *I*

Tait, A.V., Kelso – 85 *I*, *F*, 86 *It*, *F*, 87 *It*, *F* (capped v *F*, 87 *WC*)

Thomson, A.M., Kelso – 86 *F*

Tolbert, R.S., Watsonians – 73 *F*

Tomes, A.J., Hawick – 75 *F* (capped v *F*, 76)

Townsend, G.P.J., Gala – 92 *I*, *F* (capped v *E*, 93)

Tukalo, I., Royal High School FP, Selkirk – 82 *F*, 84 *I*, *F*, 85 *I*, *F* (capped v *I*, 85)

Turnbull, D.J., Hawick – 82 *F*, 85 *I*, *F*, 86 *F*, 87 *It*, *F* (capped v *R*, 87 *WC*)

Turnbull, G.W., Jed-Forest – 74 *F*

Wainwright, R.I., Cambridge University, Edinburgh Academicals – 89 *It*, 91 *I*, 92 *F*★ (capped v *I*, 92)

Waite, T.G., Kelso – 86 *It*, *F*, 87 *It*, *F*

Walker, M., Boroughmuir – 89 *F* (r)

Watson, G.M., Boroughmuir – 72 *F* (capped v *W*, 72)

Watt, A.G.J., Glasgow High/ Kelvinside – 91 *F* (capped v Zimbabwe, 91 *WC*)

Weir, G.W., Melrose – 90 *I* (capped v Argentina, 91)

White, A.B., Hawick – 74 *F*, 75 *F*

White, D.B., Gala – 82 *F* (capped v *F*, 82)

Wilkinson, J.S., Gala – 72 *F*

Williamson, C.J., West of Scotland – 83 *F*, 84 *I*

Wilson, A.C., West of Scotland – 74 *F*

Wilson, G.D., Boroughmuir – 90 *I*, *F*, 92 *I*

Wilson, K.D.M., Boroughmuir – 77 *F*, 81 *F*, 82 *F*

Wilson, R., London Scottish – 75 *F* (capped v *E*, 76)

Wright, M., Kelso 89 *It*, *F*

Wright, P.H., Boroughmuir – 89 *F* (capped v *A*, 92)

Wright, R.W.J., Edinburgh University – 73 *F* (capped v *F*, 73)

Wyllie, D.S., Stewart's-Melville FP – 84 *I*, *F*, 85 *I* (capped v *A*, 85)

Wyroslawski, W., Jordanhill – 74 *F*, 77 *F*

The Royal Bank of Scotland

Statistics & Fixtures

SCOTTISH RUGBY UNION

IV – INTERNATIONAL RESULTS

Scoring Values	Try	Conversion	Penalty goal	Drop goal
1890–91	1	2	2	3
1891–92 to 1892–93	2	3	3	4
1893–94 to 1947–48	3	2	3	4
1948–49 to 1970–71	3	2	3	3
1971–72 to 1991–92	4	2	3	3
1992–93 onwards	5	2	3	3

FULL-CAP HOME INTERNATIONALS

Scotland v England

Played 111 – Scotland 39, England 55, Drawn 17

1871 – Raeburn Place – Scotland 1G 1T to 1T
1872 – Kennington Oval – England 1G 1 DG 2T to 1DG
1873 – Hamilton Crescent – Draw, no scoring
1874 – Kennington Oval – England 1DG to 1T
1875 – Raeburn Place – Draw, no scoring
1876 – Kennington Oval – England 1G 1T to 0
1877 – Raeburn Place – Scotland 1 DG to 0

1878 – Kennington Oval – Draw, no scoring
1879 – Raeburn Place – Draw, Scotland 1DG England 1G
1880 – Whalley Range (Manchester) – England 2G 3T to 1G
1881 – Raeburn Place – Draw, Scotland 1G 1T England 1DG 1T
1882 – Whalley Range (Manchester) – Scotland 2T to 0
1883 – Raeburn Place – England 2T to 1T
1884 – Blackheath – England 1G to 1T
1885 – No Match
1886 – Raeburn Place – Draw, no scoring
1887 – Whalley Range (Manchester) – Draw, 1T each
1888 – No Match
1889 – No Match
1890 – Raeburn Place – England 1G 1T (6) to 0
1891 – Richmond – Scotland 2G 1DG (11) to 1G (4)
1892 – Raeburn Place – England 1G (5) to 0
1893 – Headingley – Scotland 2DG (8) to 0
1894 – Raeburn Place – Scotland 2T (6) to 0
1895 – Richmond – Scotland 1PG 1T (6) to 1PG (3)
1896 – Hampden Park – Scotland 1G 2T (11) to 0
1897 – Fallowfield (Manchester) – England 1G 1DG (12) to 1T (3)
1898 – Powderhall (Edinburgh) – Draw, 1T (3) each
1899 – Blackheath – Scotland 1G (5) to 0
1900 – Inverleith – Draw, no scoring
1901 – Blackheath – Scotland 3G 1T (18) to 1T (3)
1902 – Inverleith – England 2T (6) to 1T (3)
1903 – Richmond – Scotland 1DG 2T (10) to 2T (6)
1904 – Inverleith – Scotland 2T (6) to 1T (3)
1905 – Richmond – Scotland 1G 1T (8) to 0
1906 – Inverleith – England 3T (9) to 1T (3)
1907 – Blackheath – Scotland 1G 1T (8) to 1T (3)
1908 – Inverleith – Scotland 1G 2DG 1T (16) to 26 (10)
1909 – Richmond – Scotland 3G 1T (18) to 1G 1T (8)
1910 – Inverleith – England 1G 3T (14) to 1G (5)
1911 – Twickenham – England 2G 1T (13) to 1G 1T (8)
1912 – Inverleith – Scotland 1G 1T (8) to 1T (3)
1913 – Twickenham – England 1T (3) to 0
1914 – Inverleith – England 2G 2T (16) to 1G 1DG 2T (15)
1920 – Twickenham – England 2G 1T (13) to 1DG (4)
1921 – Inverleith – England 3G 1T (10) to 0
1922 – Twickenham – England 1G 2T (11) to 1G (5)
1923 – Inverleith – England 1G 1T (8) to 2T (6)
1924 – Twickenham – England 3G 1DG (19) to 0
1925 – Murrayfield – Scotland 2G 1DG (14) to 1G 1PG 1T (11)
1926 – Twickenham – Scotland 2G 1DG 1T (17) to 3T (9)
1927 – Murrayfield – Scotland 1G 1DG 4T (21) to 2G 1PG (13)
1928 – Twickenham – England 2T (6) to 0
1929 – Murrayfield – Scotland 4T (12) to 2T (6)
1930 – Twickenham – Draw, no scoring
1931 – Murrayfield – Scotland 5G 1T (28) to 2G 1PG 2T (19)
1932 – Twickenham – England 2G 2T (16) to 1T (3)
1933 – Murrayfield – Scotland 1T (3) to 0
1934 – Twickenham – England 2T (6) to 1T (3)
1935 – Murrayfield – Scotland 2G (10) to 1DG 1T (7)
1936 – Twickenham – England 3T (9) to 1G 1PG (8)

1937 – Murrayfield – England 2T (6) to 1PG (3)
1938 – Twickenham – Scotland 2PG 5T (21) to 1DG 3PG 1T (16)
1939 – Murrayfield – England 3PG (9) to 2T (6)
1947 – Twickenham – England 4G 1DG (24) to 1G (5)
1948 – Murrayfield – Scotland 2T (6) to 1PG (3)
1949 – Twickenham – England 2G 3T (19) to IPG (3)
1950 – Murrayfield – Scotland 2G 1T (13) to 1G 1PG 1T (11)
1951 – Twickenham – England 1G (5) to 1T (3)
1952 – Murrayfield – England 2G 1DG 2T (19) to 1T (3)
1953 – Twickenham – England 4G 2T (26) to 1G 1T (8)
1954 – Murrayfield – England 2G 1T (13) to 1T (3)
1955 – Twickenham – England 1PG 2T (9) to 1PG 1T (6)
1956 – Murrayfield – England 1G 2PG (11) to 1PG 1T (6)
1957 – Twickenham – England 2G 1PG 1T (16) to 1PG (3)
1958 – Murrayfield – Draw, 1PG (3) each
1959 – Twickenham – Draw, 1PG (3) each
1960 – Murrayfield – England 3G 1DG 1PG (21) to 3PG 1T (12)
1961 – Twickenham – England 1PG 1T (6) to 0
1962 – Murrayfield – Draw, 1PG (3) each
1963 – Twickenham – England 2G (10) to 1G 1DG (8)
1964 – Murrayfield – Scotland 3G (15) to 1PG 1T (6)
1965 – Twickenham – Draw, England 1T (3) Scotland 1DG (3)
1966 – Murrayfield – Scotland 1PG 1T (6) to 1DG (3)
1967 – Twickenham – England 3G 2PG 1DG 1T (27) to 1G 2PG 1T (14)
1968 – Murrayfield – England 1G 1PG (8) to 1PG 1DG (6)
1969 – Twickenham – England 1G 1T (8) to 1PG (3)
1970 – Murrayfield – Scotland 1G 2PG 1T (14) to 1G (5)
1971 – Twickenham – Scotland 2G 1DG 1T (16) to 3PG 2T (15)
1971 – Murrayfield – (Centenary Match – non-championship)
        Scotland 4G 1PG 1T (26) to 1PG 1DG (6)
1972 – Murrayfield – Scotland 4PG 1DG 2T (23) to 3PG (9)
1973 – Twickenham – England 2G 2T (20) to 1G 1PG 1T (13)
1974 – Murrayfield – Scotland 1G 2PG 1T (16) to 1DG 1PG 2T (14)
1975 – Twickenham – England 1PG 1T (7) to 2PG (6)
1976 – Murrayfield – Scotland 2G 2PG 1T (22) to 1G 2PG (12)
1977 – Twickenham – England 2G 2PG 2T (26) to 2PG (6)
1978 – Murrayfield – England 2G 1PG (15) to 0
1979 – Twickenham – Draw, 1PG 1T (7) each
1980 – Murrayfield – England 2G 2PG 3T (30) to 2G 2PG (18)
1981 – Twickenham – England 1G 3PG 2T (23) to 1G 1PG 2T (17)
1982 – Murrayfield – Draw, Scotland 2PG 1DG (9) to England 3PG (9)
1983 – Twickenham – Scotland 1G 3PG 1DG 1T (22) to 3PG 1DG (12)
1984 – Murrayfield – Scotland 2G 2PG (18) to 2PG (6)
1985 – Twickenham – England 2PG 1T (10) to 1PG 1T (7)
1986 – Murrayfield – Scotland 3G 5PG (33) to 2PG (6)
1987 – Twickenham – England 2G 3PG (21) to 1G 2PG (12)
1988 – Murrayfield – England 2PG 1DG (9) to 2PG (6)
1989 – Twickenham – Draw, England 4PG (12) to Scotland 1G 3PG (12)
1990 – Murrayfield – Scotland 3PG 1T (13) to 1PG 1T (7)
1991 – Twickenham – England 1G 5PG (21) to 4PG (12)
1991 – Murrayfield (World Cup) – England 2PG 1DG (9) to 2PG (6)
1992 – Murrayfield – England 1G 4PG 1DG 1T (25) to 1PG 1T (7)
1993 – Twickenham – England 1G 3PG 2T (26) to 3PG 1DG (12)
1994 – Murrayfield – England 5 PG (15) to 2PG 1DG 1T (14)

Scotland v France
Played 65 – Scotland 30, France 32, Drawn 3

1910 – Inverleith – Scotland 3G 4T (27) to 0
1911 – Colombes – France 2G 2T (16) to 1G 1DG 2T (15)
1912 – Inverleith – Scotland 5G 1PG 1T (31) to 1T (3)
1913 – Parc des Princes – Scotland 3G 2T (21) to 1T (3)
1920 – Parc des Princes – Scotland 1G (5) to 0
1921 – Inverleith – France 1T (3) to 0
1922 – Colombes – Draw, 1T (3) each
1923 – Inverleith – Scotland 2G 2T (16) to 1GM (3)
1924 – Stade Pershing – France 4T (12) to 1DG 1PG 1T (10)
1925 – Inverleith – Scotland 2G 5T (25) to 1DG (4)
1926 – Colombes – Scotland 1G 1PG 4T (20) to 1PG 1T (6)
1927 – Murrayfield – Scotland 4G 1PG (23) to 2T (6)
1928 – Colombes – Scotland 5T (15) to 2T (6)
1929 – Murrayfield – Scotland 1PG 1T (6) to 1T (3)
1930 – Colombes – France 1DG 1T (7) to 1T (3)
1931 – Murrayfield – Scotland 2PG (6) to 1DG (4)
1947 – Colombes – France 1G 1T (8) to 1PG (3)
1948 – Murrayfield – Scotland 2PG 1T (9) to 1G 1PG (8)
1949 – Colombes – Scotland 1G 1T (8) to 0
1950 – Murrayfield – Scotland 1G 1T (8) to 1G (5)
1951 – Colombes – France 1G 2PG 1T (14) to 2PG 2T (12)
1952 – Murrayfield – France 2G 1PG (13) to 1G 2PG (11)
1953 – Colombes – France 1G 1DG 1PG (11) to 1G (5)
1954 – Murrayfield – France 1T (3) to 0
1955 – Colombes – France 1PG 4T (15) to 0
1956 – Murrayfield – Scotland 2PG 2T (12) to 0
1957 – Colombes – Scotland 1DG 1PG (6) to 0
1958 – Murrayfield – Scotland 1G 1PG 1T (11) to 2PG 1T (9)
1959 – Colombes – France 2DG 1T (9) to 0
1960 – Murrayfield – France 2G 1T (13) to 1G 1PG 1T (11)
1961 – Colombes – France 1G 1DG 1PG (11) to 0
1962 – Murrayfield – France 1G 2PG (11) to 1PG (3)
1963 – Colombes – Scotland 1G 1DG 1PG (11) to 1DG 1PG (6)
1964 – Murrayfield – Scotland 2G (10) to 0
1965 – Colombes – France 2G 2T (16) to 1G 1T (8)
1966 – Murrayfield – Draw, Scotland 1T (3) France 1PG (3)
1967 – Colombes – Scotland 2PG 1DG (9) to 1G 1T (8)
1968 – Murrayfield – France 1G 1T (8) to 1PG 1T (6)
1969 – Colombes – Scotland 1PG 1T (6) to 1PG (3)
1970 – Murrayfield – France 1G 1DG 1T (11) to 2PG 1T (9)
1971 – Colombes – France 2G 1PG (13) to 1G 1PG (8)
1972 – Murrayfield – Scotland 1G 1PG 1DG 2T (20) to 1G 1PG (9)
1973 – Parc des Princes – France 3PG 1DG 1T (16) to 2PG 1DG 1T (13)
1974 – Murrayfield – Scotland 1G 3PG 1T (19) to 1PG 1DG (6)
1975 – Parc des Princes – France 1PG 1DG 1T (10) to 3PG (9)
1976 – Murrayfield – France 3PG 1T (13) to 1PG 1DG (6)
1977 – Parc des Princes – France 2G 1PG 2T (23) to 1PG (3)
1978 – Murrayfield – France 1G 3PG 1T (19) to 1G 1PG 1DG 1T (16)
1979 – Parc des Princes – France 2PG 1DG 3T (21) to 1G 1PG 2T (17)
1980 – Murrayfield – Scotland 2G 2PG 1T (22) to 1PG 1DG 2T (14)
1981 – Parc des Princes – France 1G 2PG 1T (16) to 1G 1PG (9)

1982 – Murrayfield – Scotland 3PG 1DG 1T (16) to 1PG 1T (7)
1983 – Parc des Princes – France 1G 1T 3PG (19) to 1G 2DG 1PG (15)
1984 – Murrayfield – Scotland 1G 5PG (21) to 1G 1DG 1PG (12)
1985 – Parc des Princes – France 1PG 2T (11) to 1PG (3)
1986 – Murrayfield – Scotland 6PG (18) to 1DG 2PG 2T (17)
1987 – Parc des Princes – France 3PG 1DG 4T (28) to 1G 4PG 1T (22)
1987 – Christchurch (World Cup) – Draw, Scotland 2T 4PG (20) France 1G 2T
      2PG (20)
1988 – Murrayfield – Scotland 4PG 1DG 2T (23) to 1G 1PG 1DG (12)
1989 – Parc des Princes – France 2G 1PG 1T (19) to 1PG (3)
1990 – Murrayfield – Scotland 2G 3PG (21) to 0
1991 – Parc des Princes – France 2PG 3DG (15) to 2PG 1DG (9)
1992 – Murrayfield – Scotland 2PG 1T (10) to 2PG (6)
1993 – Parc des Princes – France 3PG 1T (14) to 1PG (3)
1994 – Murrayfield – France 2G 2PG (20) to 4PG (12)

Scotland v Ireland

Played 106 – Scotland 55, Ireland 45, Drawn 5, Abandoned 1

1877 – Ormeau (Belfast) – Scotland 4G 2DG 2T to 0
1878 – No Match
1879 – Ormeau (Belfast) – Scotland 1G 1DG 1T to 0
1880 – Hamilton Crescent – Scotland 1G 2DG 2T to 0
1881 – Ormeau (Belfast) – Ireland 1DG to 1T
1882 – Hamilton Crescent – Ireland 2T to 0
1883 – Ormeau (Belfast) – Scotland 1G 1T to 0
1884 – Raeburn Place – Scotland 2G 2T to 1T
1885 – Ormeau (Belfast) – Abandoned, Scotland 1T Ireland 0
1885 – Raeburn Place – Scotland 1G 2T to 0
1886 – Raeburn Place – Scotland 3G 1DG 2T to 0
1887 – Ormeau (Belfast) – Scotland 1G 1GM 2T to 0
1888 – Raeburn Place – Scotland 1G to 0
1889 – Ormeau (Belfast) – Scotland 1DG to 0
1890 – Raeburn Place – Scotland 1DG 1T (5) to 0
1891 – Ballynafeigh (Belfast) – Scotland 3G 1DG 2T (14) to 0
1892 – Raeburn Place – Scotland 1T (2) to 0
1893 – Ballynafeigh (Belfast) – Draw, no score
1894 – Lansdowne Road – Ireland 1G (5) to 0
1895 – Raeburn Place – Scotland 2T (6) to 0
1896 – Lansdowne Road – Draw, no score
1897 – Powderhall (Edinburgh) – Scotland 1G 1PG (8) to 1T (3)
1898 – Balmoral (Belfast) – Scotland 1G 1T (8) to 0
1899 – Inverleith – Ireland 3T (9) to 1PG (3)
1900 – Lansdowne Road – Draw, no score
1901 – Inverleith – Scotland 3T (9) to 1G (5)
1902 – Balmoral (Belfast) – Ireland 1G (5) to 0
1903 – Inverleith – Scotland 1T (3) to 0
1904 – Lansdowne Road – Scotland 2G 3T (19) to 1T (3)
1905 – Inverleith – Ireland 1G 2T (11) to 1G (5)
1906 – Lansdowne Road – Scotland 2G 1GM (13) to 2T (6)
1907 – Inverleith – Scotland 3G (15) to 1PG (3)
1908 – Lansdowne Road – Ireland 2G 2T (16) to 1G 1PG 1T (11)
1909 – Inverleith – Scotland 3T (9) to 1PG (3)

1910 – Balmoral (Belfast) – Scotland 1G 3T (14) to 0
1911 – Inverleith – Ireland 2G 2T (16) to 1DG 2T (10)
1912 – Lansdowne Road – Ireland 1DG 1PG 1T (10) to 1G 1T (8)
1913 – Inverleith – Scotland 4G 3T (29) to 2G 1DG (14)
1914 – Lansdowne Road – Ireland 2T (6) to 0
1920 – Inverleith – Scotland 2G 1PG 2T (19) to 0
1921 – Lansdowne Road – Ireland 3T (9) to 1G 1T (8)
1922 – Inverleith – Scotland 2T (6) to 1T (3)
1923 – Lansdowne Road – Scotland 2G 1T (13) to 1T (3)
1924 – Inverleith – Scotland 2G 1T (13) to 1G 1T (8)
1925 – Lansdowne Road – Scotland 2G 1DG (14) to 1G 1PG (8)
1926 – Murrayfield – Ireland 1T (3) to 0
1927 – Lansdowne Road – Ireland 2T (6) to 0
1928 – Murrayfield – Ireland 2G 1T (13) to 1G (5)
1929 – Lansdowne Road – Scotland 2G 2T (16) to 1DG 1T (7)
1930 – Murrayfield – Ireland 1G 3T (14) to 1G 2T (11)
1931 – Lansdowne Road – Ireland 1G 1T (8) to 1G (5)
1932 – Murrayfield – Ireland 4G (20) to 1G 1T (8)
1933 – Lansdowne Road – Scotland 2DG (8) to 2T (6)
1934 – Murrayfield – Scotland 2G 1PG 1T (16) to 3T (9)
1935 – Lansdowne Road – Ireland 4T (12) to 1G (5)
1936 – Murrayfield – Irleand 1DG 2T (10) to 1DG (4)
1937 – Lansdowne Road – Irleand 1G 2T (11) to 1DG (4)
1938 – Murrayfield – Scotland 2G 1DG 1PG 2T (23) to 1G 3T (14)
1939 – Lansdowne Road – Ireland 1PG 1GM 2T (12) to 1T (3)
1947 – Murrayfield – Ireland 1T (3) to 0
1948 – Lansdowne Road – Ireland 2T (6) to 0
1949 – Murrayfield – Ireland 2G 1PG (13) to 1PG (3)
1950 – Lansdowne Road – Ireland 3G 2PG (21) to 0
1951 – Murrayfield – Ireland 1DG 1T (6) to 1G (5)
1952 – Lansdowne Road – Ireland 1PG 3T (12) to 1G 1PG (8)
1953 – Murrayfield – Ireland 4G 2T (26) to 1G 1PG (8)
1954 – Ravenhill (Belfast) – Ireland 2T (6) to 0
1955 – Murrayfield – Scotland 2PG 1DG 1T (12) to 1PG (3)
1956 – Lansdowne Road – Ireland 1G 3T (14) to 2G (10)
1957 – Murrayfield – Ireland 1G (5) to 1PG (3)
1958 – Lansdowne Road – Ireland 2PG 2T (12) to 2T (6)
1959 – Murrayfield – Ireland 1G 1PG (8) to 1PG (3)
1960 – Lansdowne Road – Scotland 1DG 1T (6) to 1G (5)
1961 – Murrayfield – Scotland 2G 1PG 1T (16) to 1G 1T (8)
1962 – Lansdowne Road – Scotland 1G 1DG 2PG 2T (20) to 1PG 1T (6)
1963 – Murrayfield – Scotland 1PG (3) to 0
1964 – Lansdowne Road – Scotland 2PG (6) to 1PG (3)
1965 – Murrayfield – Ireland 2G 1DG 1T (16) to 1DG 1PG (3)
1966 – Lansdowne Road – Scotland 1G 2T (11) to 1PG (3)
1967 – Murrayfield – Ireland 1G (5) to IPG (3)
1968 – Lansdowne Road – Ireland 1G 1PG 2T (14) to 2PG (6)
1969 – Murrayfield – Ireland 2G 2T (16) to 0
1970 – Lansdowne Road – Ireland 2G 2T (16) to 1G 1DG 1T (11)
1971 – Murrayfield – Ireland 1G 2PG 2T (17) to 1G (5)
1972 – No Match
1973 – Murrayfield – Scotland 2PG 3DG 1T (19) to 2PG 2T (14)
1974 – Lansdowne Road – Ireland 1G 1PG (9) to 2PG (6)
1975 – Murrayfield – Scotland 2PG 2DG 2T (20) to 1G 1PG 1T (13)

1976 – Lansdowne Road – Scotland 4PG 1DG (15) to 2PG (6)
1977 – Murrayfield – Scotland 2PG 1DG 3T (21) to 1G 3PG 1TG (18)
1978 – Lansdowne Road – Ireland 1G 2PG (12) to 3PG (9)
1979 – Murrayfield – Draw, 1PG 2T (11) each
1980 – Lansdowne Road – Ireland 1G 3PG 1DG 1T (22) to 2G 1PG (15)
1981 – Murrayfield – Scotland 1PG 1DG 1T (10) to 1G 1PG (9)
1982 – Lansdowne Road – Ireland 6PG 1DG (21) to 1G 2PG (12)
1983 – Murrayfield – Ireland 1G 3PG (15) to 2PG 1DG 1T (13)
1984 – Lansdowne Road – Scotland★ 3G 2PG 2T (32) to 1G 1PG (9)
1985 – Murrayfield – Ireland 2G 1DG 1PG (18) to 4PG 1DG (15)
1986 – Lansdowne Road – Scotland 2PG 1T (10) to 1G 1PG (9)
1987 – Murrayfield – Scotland 1G 2DG 1T (16) to 1G 1PG 1DG (12)
1988 – Lansdowne Road – Ireland 2G 1PG 1DG 1T (22) to 2G 2PG (18)
1989 – Murrayfield – Scotland 4G 3PG 1T (37) to 3G 1PG (21)
1990 – Lansdowne Road – Scotland 1G 1PG 1T (13) to 2PG 1T (10)
1991 – Murrayfield – Scotland 2G 4PG 1T (28) to 3G 1DG 1T (25)
1991 – Murrayfield (World Cup) – Scotland 2G 3PG 1DG (24) to 4PG 1TG
    (15)
1992 – Lansdowne Road – Scotland 2G 2PG (18) to 2PG 1T (10)
1993 – Murrayfield – Scotland 1G 1PG 1T (15) to 1PG (3)
1994 – Lansdowne Road – Draw, 2PG (6) each

★ includes one penalty try

Scotland v Wales
Played 98 – Scotland 42, Wales 54, Drawn 2

1883 – Raeburn Place – Scotland 3G to 1G
1884 – Newport – Scotland 1DG 1T to 0
1885 – Hamilton Crescent – Draw, no scoring
1886 – Cardiff – Scotland 2G 1T to 0
1887 – Raeburn Place – Scotland 4G 8T to 0
1888 – Newport – Wales 1T to 0
1889 – Raeburn Place – Scotland 2T to 0
1890 – Cardiff – Scotland 1G 2T (8) to 1T (2)
1891 – Raeburn Place – Scotland 1G 2DG 6T (15) to 0
1892 – Swansea – Scotland 1G 1T (7) to 1T (2)
1893 – Raeburn Place – Wales 1PG 3T (9) to 0
1894 – Newport – Wales 1DG 1T (7) to 0
1895 – Raeburn Place – Scotland 1G (5) to 1GM (4)
1896 – Cardiff – Wales 2T (6) to 0
1897 – No Match
1898 – No Match
1899 – Inverleith – Scotland 1GM 2DG 3T (21) to 2G (10)
1900 – Swansea – Wales 4T (12) to 1T (3)
1901 – Inverleith – Scotland 3G 1T (18) to 1G 1T (8)
1902 – Cardiff – Wales 1G 3T (14) to 1G (5)
1903 – Inverleith – Scotland 1PG 1T (6) to 0
1904 – Swansea – Wales 3G 1PG 1T (21) to 1T (3)
1905 – Inverleith – Wales 2T (6) to 1T (3)
1906 – Cardiff – Wales 3T (9) to 1PG (3)
1907 – Inverleith – Scotland 2T (6) to 1PG (3)
1908 – Swansea – Wales 2T (6) to 1G (5)
1909 – Inverleith – Wales 1G (5) to 1PG (3)

1910 – Cardiff – Wales 1G 3T (14) to 0
1911 – Inverleith – Wales 2G 1DG 6T (32) to 1DG 2T (10)
1912 – Swansea – Wales 2G 2DG 1T (21) to 2T (6)
1913 – Inverleith – Wales 1G 1T (8) to 0
1914 – Cardiff – Wales 2G 2DG 1PG 1T (24) to 1G (5)
1920 – Inverleith – Scotland 2PG 1T (9) to 1G (5)
1921 – Swansea – Scotland 1G 1PG 2T (14) to 2DG (8)
1922 – Inverleith – Draw, Scotland 1PG 2T (9) Wales 1G 1DG (9)
1923 – Cardiff – Scotland 1G 2T (11) to 1G 1PG (8)
1924 – Inverleith – Scotland 4G 1PG 4T (35) to 2G (10)
1925 – Swansea – Scotland 1G 1DG 5T (24) to 1G 1PG 2T (14)
1926 – Murrayfield – Scotland 1G 1PG (8) to 1G (5)
1927 – Cardiff – Scotland 1G (5) to 0
1928 – Murrayfield – Wales 2G 1T (13) to 0
1929 – Swansea – Wales 1G 3T (14) to 1DG 1PG (7)
1930 – Murrayfield – Scotland 1G 1DG 1T (12) to 1G 1DG (9)
1931 – Cardiff – Wales 2G 1T (13) to 1G 1T (8)
1932 – Murrayfield – Wales 1PG 1T (6) to 0
1933 – Swansea – Scotland 1G 1PG 1T (11) to 1T (3)
1934 – Murrayfield – Wales 2G 1T (13) to 1PG 1T (6)
1935 – Cardiff – Wales 1DG 2T (10) to 2T (6)
1936 – Murrayfield – Wales 2G 1T (13) to 1T (3)
1937 – Swansea – Scotland 2G 1T (13) to 2T (6)
1938 – Murrayfield – Scotland 1G 1PG (8) to 2T (6)
1939 – Cardiff – Wales 1G 1PG 1T (11) to 1PG (3)
1947 – Murrayfield – Wales 2G 1PG 3T (22) to 1G 1PG (8)
1948 – Cardiff – Wales 1G 1PG 2T (14) to 0
1949 – Murrayfield – Scotland 2T (6) to 1G (5)
1950 – Swansea – Wales 1DG 1PG 2T (12) to 0
1951 – Murrayfield – Scotland 2G 1DG 1PG 1T (19) to 0
1952 – Cardiff – Wales 1G 2PG (11) to 0
1953 – Murrayfield – Wales 1PG 3T (12) to 0
1954 – Swansea – Wales 1PG 4T (15) to 1T (3)
1955 – Murrayfield – Scotland 1G 1DG 1PG 1T (14) to 1G 1T (8)
1956 – Cardiff – Wales 3T (9) to 1PG (3)
1957 – Murrayfield – Scotland 1DG 1PG 1T (9) to 1PG 1T (6)
1958 – Cardiff – Wales 1G 1T (8) to 1PG (3)
1959 – Murrayfield – Scotland 1PG 1T (6) to 1G (5)
1960 – Cardiff – Wales 1G 1PG (8) to 0
1961 – Murrayfield – Scotland 1T (3) to 0
1962 – Cardiff – Scotland 1G 1T (8) to 1DG (3)
1963 – Murrayfield – Wales 1DG 1PG (6) to 0
1964 – Cardiff – Wales 1G 1PG 1T (11) to 1T (3)
1965 – Murrayfield – Wales 1G 2PG 1T (14) to 2DG 2PG (12)
1966 – Cardiff – Wales 1G 1T (8) to 1PG (3)
1967 – Murrayfield – Scotland 1G 1DG 1T (11) to 1G (5)
1968 – Cardiff – Wales 1G (5) to 0
1969 – Murrayfield – Wales 1G 2PG 2T (17) to 1PG (3)
1970 – Cardiff – Wales 3G 1T (18) to 1DG 1PG 1T (9)
1971 – Murrayfield – Wales 2G 1PG 2T (19) to 4PG 2T (18)
1972 – Cardiff – Wales 3G 3PG 2T (35) to 1G 2PG (12)
1973 – Murrayfield – Scotland 1G 1T (10) to 3PG (9)
1974 – Cardiff – Wales 1G (6) to 0
1975 – Murrayfield – Scotland 3PG 1DG (12) to 2PG 1T (10)

1976 – Cardiff – Wales 2G 3PG 1T (28) to 1G (6)
1977 – Murrayfield – Wales 2G 2PG (18) to 1G 1DG (9)
1978 – Cardiff – Wales 1PG 1DG 4T (22) to 2PG 2T (14)
1979 – Murrayfield – Wales 1G 3PG 1T (19) to 3PG 1T (13)
1980 – Cardiff – Wales 1G 1PG 2T (17) to 1G (6)
1981 – Murrayfield – Scotland ★2G 1PG (15) to 2PG (6)
1982 – Cardiff – Scotland 4G 2DG 1T (34) to 1G 4PG (18)
1983 – Murrayfield – Wales 1G 3PG 1T (19) to 1G 3PG (15)
1984 – Cardiff – Scotland 2G 1PG (15) to 1G 1PG (9)
1985 – Murrayfield – Wales 1G 1DG 4PG 1T (25) to 2G 2DG 1PG (21)
1986 – Cardiff – Wales 5PG 1DG 1T (22) to 1PG 3T (15)
1987 – Murrayfield – Scotland 2G 2PG 1DG (21) to 1G 2PG 1DG (15)
1988 – Cardiff – Wales 2G 2DG 1PG 1T (25) to 2T 4PG (20)
1989 – Murrayfield – Scotland 1G 2PG 1DG 2T (23) to 1PG 1T (7)
1990 – Cardiff – Scotland 3PG 1T (13) to 1G 1PG (9)
1991 – Murrayfield – Scotland 2G 3PG 1DG 2T (32) to 1G 2PG (12)
1992 – Cardiff – Wales 1G 3PG (15) to 2PG 1DG (9)
1993 – Murrayfield – Scotland 5PG 1T (20) to 0
1994 – Cardiff – Wales 1G 4PG 2T (26) to 2PG (6)

★ includes 1 penalty try

FULL-CAP INTERNATIONALS AGAINST OTHER COUNTRIES

Scotland v Argentina

1990 – Murrayfield – Scotland
    5G 1PG 4T (49) to 1PG (3)
1994 – Buenos Aires – Argentina
    1G 3PG (15) to 5PG (15)
1994 – Buenos Aires – Argentina
    1G 3PG 1DG (19) to 3PG 1DG 1DG
    1T (17)
(The countries met twice in 1969 and once in 1973, but Scotland did not award caps.)

Scotland v Australia

Played 13 – Scotland 6, Australia 7

1947 – Murrayfield – Australia
    2G 2T (16) to 1DG 1PG (7)
1958 – Murrayfield – Scotland
    2PG 2T (12) to 1G 1T (8)
1966 – Murrayfield – Scotland
    1G 1PG 1T (11) to 1G (5)
1968 – Murrayfield – Scotland
    2PG 1T (9) to 1PG (3)
1970 – Sydney Cricket Ground – Australia
    1G 1PG 5T (23) to 1PG (3)
1975 – Murrayfield – Scotland
    1G 1T (10) to 1PG (3)

1981 – Murrayfield – Scotland
    1G 5PG 1DG (24) to 1PG 3T (15)
1982 – Ballymore (Brisbane) – Scotland
    1G 1PG 1DG (12) to 1PG 1T (7)
1982 – Sydney Cricket Ground – Australia
    3G 5PG (33) to 3PG (9)
1984 – Murrayfield – Australia
    3G 5PG 1T (37) to 4PG (12)
1988 – Murrayfield – Australia
    3G 2PG 2T (32) to 1G 1PG 1T (13)
1993 – Sydney Football Ground – Australia
    1G 3PG 3T (27) to 1G 2PG (12)
1993 – Ballymore (Brisbane) – Australia
    1G 5PG 4T (37) to 1G 1PG 1T (13)

Scotland v Fiji

1989 – Murrayfield – Scotland
    4G 2PG 2T (38) to 3PG 2T (17)
(The countries met in 1982 and 1993, but Scotland did not award caps.)

Scotland v Japan

1991 – Murrayfield (World Cup) – Scotland
    5G 3PG 2T (47) to 1G 1DG (9)
(The countries have met on four other occasions, but Scotland did not award caps for any of those matches.)

Scotland v New South Wales

1927 – Murrayfield – Scotland
   2G (10) to 1G 1T (8)

Scotland v New Zealand

Played 17 – New Zealand 15, Drawn 2

1905 – Inverleith – New Zealand
   4T (12) to 1DG 1T (7)
1935 – Murrayfield – New Zealand
   3G 1T (18) to 1G 1T (8)
1954 – Murrayfield – New Zealand
   1PG (3) to 0
1964 – Murrayfield – Draw, no scoring
1967 – Murrayfield – New Zealand
   1G 2PG 1T (14) to 1DG (3)
1972 – Murrayfield – New Zealand
   1G 2T (14) to 2PG 1DG (9)
1975 – Auckland – New Zealand
   4G (24) to 0
1976 – Murrayfield – New Zealand
   2G 2PG (18) to 1G 1DG (9)
1979 – Murrayfield – New Zealand
   2G 2T (20) to 2PG (6)
1981 – Dunedin – New Zealand
   1PG 2T (11) to 1T (4)
1981 – Auckland – New Zealand
   6G 1T (40) to 1G 2PG 1DG (15)
1983 – Murrayfield – Draw, Scotland
   5PG 2DG 1T (25) New Zealand 2G
   3PG 1T (25)
1987 – Christchurch (World Cup) –
New Zealand 2G 6PG (30) to 1PG (3)
1990 – Dunedin – New Zealand
   4G 1PG 1T (31) to 2G 1T (16)
1990 – Auckland – New Zealand
   1G 5PG (21) to 2G 2PG (18)
1991 – Cardiff (World Cup) – New Zealand
   3PG 1T (13) to 2PG (6)
1993 – Murrayfield – New Zealand
   5G 2PG 2T (51) to 5PG (15)

Scotland v Romania

Played 6 – Scotland 4, Romania 2

1981 – Murrayfield – Scotland
   4PG (12) to 2PG (6)
1984 – Bucharest – Romania
   2G 3PG 1DG 1T (28) to 1G 3PG 1DG
1T (22)
1986 – Bucharest – Scotland
   3G 5PG (33) to 5PG 1DG (18)
1987 – Dunedin (World Cup) – Scotland
   8G 1PG 1T (55) to 2G 4PG 1T (28)

1989 – Murrayfield – Scotland
   3G 2PG 2T (32) to 0
1991 – Bucharest – Romania
   2G 2PG (18) to 1G 2PG (12)

Scotland v South Africa

Played 8 – Scotland 3, South Africa 5

1906 – Hampden Park – Scotland
   2T (6) to 0
1912 – Inverleith – South Africa
   2G 2T (16) to 0
1932 – Murrayfield – South Africa
   2T (6) to 1T (3)
1951 – Murrayfield – South Africa
   7G 1DG 2T (44) to 0
1960 – Port Elizabeth – South Africa
   3G 1T (18) to 26 (10)
1961 – Murrayfield – South Africa
   2PG 2T (12) to 1G (5)
1965 – Murrayfield – Scotland
   1G 1DG (8) to 1G (5)
1969 – Murrayfield – Scotland
   1PG 1T (6) to 1PG (3)

Scotland v Western Samoa

1991 – Murrayfield (World Cup) – Scotland
   2G 4PG 1T (28) to 1PG 1DG (6)
(The countries also met in 1993, but Scotland
did not award caps.)

Scotland v Zimbabwe

1987 – Wellington (World Cup) – Scotland
   8G 3T (60) to 1G 5PG (21)
1991 – Murrayfield (World Cup) – Scotland
   5G 2PG 1DG 3T (51) to 2G (12)
(The countries met twice in 1988, but
Scotland did not award caps.)

Scotland v SRU President's XV

1973 – Murrayfield – Scotland
   2G 1PG 3T (27) to 2G 2T (16)

Scotland v SRV President's XV

1973 – Murrayfield – Scotland 2G 2PG 2T
(38) to 3PG 2T (17)

1946 'Victory' Internationals

Scotland 11 New Zealand Army 6
   (Murrayfield)
Wales 6 Scotland 25 (Swansea)
Scotland 9 Ireland 0 (Murrayfield)
England 12 Scotland 8 (Twickenham)
Scotland 13 Wales 11 (Murrayfield)
Scotland 27 England 0 (Murrayfield)

Statistics & Fixtures

SCOTLAND XV AND SCOTLAND MATCHES WHERE NO CAPS WERE AWARDED

Scotland XV v Argentina
1969 – Argentina 20–3 (Buenos Aires)
1969 – Scotland XV 6–3 (Buenos Aires)
1973 – Scotland XV 12–11 (Murrayfield)

Scotland v Barbarians
1970 – Barbarians 33–17 (Murrayfield)
1983 – Barbarians 26–13 (Murrayfield)
1991 – Draw 16–16 (Murrayfield)

Scotland v Canada
1991 – Canada 24–19
    (Saint John, New Brunswick)

Scotland and Scotland XV v Fiji
1982 – Scotland XV 32–12 (Murrayfield)
1993 – Scotland 21–10 (Suva)

Scotland XV v France XV
1986 – Draw, 16–16 (Tarbes)
1987 – Scotland XV 15–12 (Netherdale)

Scotland XV v Japan
1976 – Scotland XV 34–9 (Murrayfield)
1977 – Scotland XV 74–9 (Tokyo)
1986 – Scotland XV 33–18 (Murrayfield)
1989 – Japan 28–24 (Tokyo)

Scotland XV v Spain
1986 – Scotland XV 39–17
    (Cornella, Barcelona)
1987 – Scotland XV 25–7 (Murrayfield)
(Spain have also played against Scotland A.)

Scotland XV and Scotland v Tonga
1974 – Scotland XV 44–8 (Murrayfield)
1993 – Scotland 23–5 (Nuku'alofa)

Scotland v United States
1991 – Scotland 41–12
    (Hartford, Connecticut)

Scotland v Western Samoa
1993 – Western Samoa 28–11 (Apia)

Scotland XV v Zimbabwe
1988 – Scotland XV 31–10 (Bulawayo)
1988 – Scotland XV 34–7 (Harare)

A TEAM INTERNATIONALS

Scotland A v France A
1993 – France 29–19 (Rubislaw)
1994 – Scotland 12–9 (Rennes)

Scotland A v Ireland A
1992 – Scotland 22–13 (Lansdowne Road)
1993 – Scotland 24–9 (Millbrae, Ayr)

Scotland A v Italy
1992 – Scotland 22–17 (The Greenyards)
1993 – Italy 18–15 (Rovigo)

Scotland A v New Zealand
1993 – New Zealand 20–9 (Old Anniesland)

Scotland A v Spain
1990 – Scotland 39–7 (Seville)
1991 – Scotland 36–16 (Murrayfield)
1992 – Scotland 35–14 (Madrid)

B TEAM INTERNATIONALS

Scotland B v France B
Played 20 – Scotland 8, France 12

1971 – France 23–9 (Oyonnax)
1972 – France 17–15 (Bught Park, Inverness)
1974 – France 13–9 (Bayonne)
1975 – Scotland 19–6 (Greenyards)
1976 – France 14–6 (Rheims)
1977 – France 19–16 (Hughenden)
1978 – France 11–3 (Le Havre)
1979 – Match at Ayr cancelled because of
    snow
1980 – Scotland 6–0 (Aurillac)
1981 – Scotland 18–4 (Millbrae, Ayr)
1982 – France 44–4 (Bourgoin-Jallieu)
1983 – France 26–12 (Mayfield, Dundee)
1984 – Scotland 13–10 (Albi)
1985 – Scotland 21–12 (Murrayfield)
1986 – Scotland 12–10
    (Villefranche-sur-Saone)
1987 – France 15–9
    (University Park, St Andrews)
1988 – Scotland 18–12 (Chalon-sur-Saone)
1989 – Scotland 14–12 (Greenyards)
1990 – France 31–9 (Oyonnax)
1991 – France 31–10 (Hughenden)
1992 – France 27–18 (Albi)

Scotland B v Ireland B
Played 7 – Scotland 2, Ireland 4, Drawn 1

1977 – Ireland 7–3 (Murrayfield)
1979 – Scotland 20–13 (Lansdowne Road)
1983 – Scotland 22–13 (Greenyards)
1984 – Ireland 23–20 (Galway)
1989 – Draw, 22–22 (Murrayfield)
1990 – Ireland 16–0 (Ravenhill, Belfast)
1991 – Ireland 29–19 (Murrayfield)

Scotland B v Italy B
Played 4 – Scotland 4, Italy 0

1985 – Scotland 9–0 (Old Anniesland)
1986 – Scotland 24–6 (Benevento)
1987 – Scotland 37–0 (Seafield, Aberdeen)
1988 – Scotland 26–3 (L'Aquila)

UNDER-21
INTERNATIONALS

Scotland v France
1993 – France 67–9 (Dijon)
1994 – France 21–12 (Inverleith)

Scotland v Ireland
1993 – Ireland 18–3 (Murrayfield back pitch)
1994 – Ireland 24–6 (Anglesea Road, Dublin)

Scotland v Italy
1986 – Scotland 22–6 (Piacenza)
1987 – Draw 17–17 (New Anniesland)
1992 – Italy 29–18 (Poynder Park)
1994 – Italy 33–30 (San Dona di Piave)

Scotland v Netherlands
1984 – Scotland 24–9 (Hilversum)
1985 – Scotland 18–6 (Hughenden)

Scotland v New Zealand
Rugby News Youth XV
1988 – New Zealand Youth XV 21–15
     (Murrayfield)

Scotland v Wales
1987 – Wales 39–19 (Wrexham)
1988 – Wales 20–13 (Murrayfield)
1989 – Wales 26–18
        (The Gnoll, Neath)
1990 – Wales 24–10 (Millbrae, Ayr)
1991 – Wales 23–15 (Stradey Park, Llanelli)
1992 – Wales 28–19 (Bridgehaugh, Stirling)

1993 – Wales 16–8 (Myreside)
1994 – Wales 36–0 (Ely, Cardiff)

UNDER-19
INTERNATIONALS

Scotland v Australian Schools
1991 – Australian Schools 17–12
     (Murrayfield)

Scotland v England
1990 – England 17–9 (Millbrae, Ayr)
1991 – Scotland 24–7 (Bridgehaugh, Stirling)
1992 – England 20–9
     (Kingston Park, Gosforth)
1993 – England 28–3 (Millbrae, Ayr)
1994 – England 11–6 (Waterloo)

Scotland v Italy
1986 – Scotland 22–6 (Piacenza)
1987 – Italy 22–6 (Meggetland)
1988 – Italy 21–18 (Villorba, Treviso)
1989 – Scotland 29–13 (Millbrae, Ayr)

Scotland v Romania
1991 – Romania 27–3
     (Steaua Stadium, Bucharest)

Scotland v Wales
1991 – Wales 23–20 (Stradey Park, Llanelli)
1992 – Wales 16–12 (Bridgehaugh, Stirling)
1993 – Wales 20–3
     (National Stadium, Cardiff)
1994 – Wales 25–15 (Bridgehaugh, Stirling)

UNDER-18
INTERNATIONALS

Scotland v Belgium
1984 – Scotland 35–10 (Brussels)

Scotland v Ireland
1992 – Scotland 4–0 (Galway)
1993 – Scotland 20–14 (Millbrae, Ayr)
1994 – Ireland 10–5 (Ravenhill, Belfast)

Scotland v Italy
1988 – Draw 25–25 (Villorba, Treviso)
1989 – Scotland 21–12 (Millbrae, Ayr)

Scotland v Japan Schools
1990 – Scotland 28–23 (Murrayfield)

Scotland v Netherlands
1985 – Scotland 36–0 (Hilversum)
1990 – Scotland 32–0 (Hilversum)
1991 – Scotland 21–7 (Greenyards)

Scotland v Spain
1991 – Spain 24–19 (Madrid)
1992 – Spain 13–12 (Burnbrae)
1993 – Spain 31–28 (Madrid)
1994 – Scotland 11–3
       (Beveridge Park, Kirkcaldy)

Scotland v Sweden
1985 – Scotland 32–0 (Malmö)
1986 – Scotland 43–4 (Murrayfield)
1989 – Scotland 85–6 (Trelleborg)

Scotland v West Germany
1982 – West Germany 15–12 (Berlin)
1984 – Scotland 9–7 (Meggetland)
1987 – Scotland 50–9 (Hanover)

INTERNATIONAL AND DISTRICT RESULTS AND TABLES 1993–94

New Zealand in Scotland
South of Scotland 5, New Zealand 84
   (Netherdale)
Scotland A 9, New Zealand 20
   (Old Anniesland)
Scotland Development XV 12, New Zealand 31
   (Myreside)
Scotland 15, New Zealand 51 (Murrayfield)
(Hastings, A.G., 4pg, Chalmers pg)

INTERNATIONAL CHAMPIONSHIP

	P	W	D	L	F	A	Pts
Wales	4	3	0	1	78	51	6
England	4	3	0	1	60	49	6
France	4	2	0	2	84	69	4
Ireland	4	1	1	2	49	70	3
Scotland	4	0	1	3	38	70	1

(Wales won the championship trophy on points difference.)

Wales 29, Scotland 6
   (Cardiff National Stadium)
(Hastings, A.G. 2pg)

France 35, Ireland 15 (Parc des Princes)
Scotland 14, England 15 (Murrayfield)
(Wainwright t, Hastings, A.G., 2pg
Townsend, dg)
Ireland 15, Wales 17 (Lansdowne Road)
Wales 24, France 15
   (Cardiff National Stadium)
England 12, Ireland 13 (Twickenham)
Ireland 6, Scotland 6 (Lansdowne Road)
(Hastings, A.G. 2pg)
France 14, England 18 (Parc des Princes)
Scotland 12, France 20 (Murrayfield)
(Hastings, A.G. 4pg)
England 15, Wales 8 (Twickenham)

Scotland A
Scotland A 9, New Zealand 20
   (Old Anniesland)
(Dods pg, Wyllie 2dg)

Italy 18, Scotland A 15 (Rovigo)
(Dods 5pg)

Scotland A 24, Ireland A 9 (Millbrae)
(Morrison t, Munro t, Wainwright t,
Townsend 3c pg)

France A 9, Scotland A 12 (Rennes)
(Dods 3pg, Chalmers dg)

McEwan's 70/- District Championship
Semi-finals:
Glasgow 21, Edinburgh 6 (Hughenden)
South 37, North and Midlands 13
   (Riverside Park)

Final:
South 28, Glasgow 14 (The Greenyards)

Third-place play-off:
Edinburgh 28, North and Midlands 25
   (The Greenyards)

Scottish Districts v Irish Provinces
Glasgow 22, Munster 17 (New Anniesland)
North and Midlands 19, Connacht 20
   (McKane Park)
Leinster 8, Edinburgh 13
   (Donnybrook, Dublin)
Ulster 44, South 26 (Ravenhill, Belfast)
Edinburgh 39, Ulster 13 (Hawkhill, Leith)

South 16, Leinster 26 (The Greenyards)
Connacht 25, Glasgow 47
    (Galway Sportsground)
Munster 6, North and Midlands 13
    (Musgrave Park, Cork)

Scottish Under-21 District Championship

	P	W	D	L	F	A	Pts
South	3	3	0	0	118	41	6
Edinburgh	3	2	0	1	74	37	4
North and Midlands	3	1	0	2	40	116	2
Glasgow	3	0	0	3	49	87	0

Edinburgh 30, North and Midlands 9
    (Meggetland)
South 30, Glasgow 23 (Mansfield Park)
North and Midlands 22, Glasgow 16
    (Beveridge Park)
Edinburgh 9, South 18 (Hughenden)
Glasgow 10, Edinburgh 35 (Hughenden)
South 70, North and Midlands 9
    (Mansfield Park)

Digital Under-18 District Championship

	P	W	D	L	F	A	Pts
South	3	2	0	1	57	14	4
North and Midlands	3	2	0	1	33	18	4
Edinburgh	3	1	0	2	24	43	2
Glasgow	3	1	0	2	12	51	2

North and Midlands 8, Edinburgh 13
    (Inverness Royal Academy)
North and Midlands 6, South 5 (Ellon)
Edinburgh 3, Glasgow 12 (North Berwick)

Glasgow 0, North and Midlands 19
    (Millbrae)
Edinburgh 8, South 23 (Biggar)
South 29, Glasgow 0 (Netherdale)

1994 WOMEN'S RUGBY WORLD CUP RESULTS

Results
USA 111 Sweden 0
England 66 Russia 0
France 77 Scottish Students 0
Canada 5 Wales 11
USA 121 Japan 0
France 31 Ireland 0
Canada 28 Kazakhstan 0
Sweden 5 Japan 10
Scotland 51 Russia 0
Scottish Universities 5 Ireland 18
Wales 29 Kazakhstan 0

QUARTER FINALS
England 24 Canada 10
USA 76 Ireland 0
France 99 Japan 0
Wales 8 Scotland 0

PLATE COMPETITION
Sweden 20 Russia 13
Scottish Students 0 Kazakhstan 27

SEMI FINALS
USA 56 Wales 15
England 18 France 6

FINAL
USA 23 England 38

V–FIXTURES 1994–95

INTERNATIONAL AND OTHER REPRESENTATIVE FIXTURES

International and Inter-District Matches

1994

22 October	South v Ulster	Poynder Park, Kelso
	Glasgow v Leinster	Burnbrae, Glasgow
	Connacht v North and Midlands	Sportsground, Galway
	Munster v Edinburgh	Thomond Park, Limerick
29 October	Leinster v South	Donnybrook, Dublin
	Ulster v Glasgow	Ravenhill, Belfast
	North and Midlands v Munster	Beveridge Park, Kirkcaldy
	Edinburgh v Connacht	Meggetland, Edinburgh
9 November	Scotland A v South Africa	The Greenyards, Melrose
12 November	Combined Scottish Districts v South Africa	Old Anniesland, Glasgow
15 November	Scottish Select v South Africa	Rubislaw, Aberdeen
19 November	**Scotland v South Africa†**	**Murrayfield**
3 December	South v Scottish Exiles	Murrayfield
	Glasgow v North and Midlands	Hughenden, Glasgow
10 December	North and Midlands v Edinburgh	Duffus Park, Cupar
	Scottish Exiles v Glasgow	Murrayfield
14 December	South v Edinburgh	Riverside Park, Jedburgh
17 December	Edinburgh v Glasgow	Myreside, Edinburgh
	North and Midlands v South	Rubislaw, Aberdeen
21 December	Scottish Exiles v North and Midlands	Murrayfield
24 December	Glasgow v South	Bridgehaugh, Stirling
	Edinburgh v Scottish Exiles	Murrayfield

1995

7 January	Scotland A v Italy	McDiarmid Park, Perth
20 January	Scotland A v France A	Hughenden, Glasgow
21 January	Scotland v Canada	Murrayfield
3 February	Scotland A v Ireland A	Myreside, Edinburgh
	Scotland U21 v Ireland U21	Myreside, Edinburgh

4 February	**Scotland v Ireland†**	**Murrayfield**
17 February	France U21 v Scotland U21	in Paris
18 February	**France v Scotland**	**Parc des Princes**
3 March	Scotland U21 v Wales U21	Inverleith, Edinburgh
4 March	**Scotland v Wales†**	**Murrayfield**
18 March	**England v Scotland**	**Twickenham**
1 April	Spain U18 v Scotland U18	in Spain
8 April	Scotland U19 v England U19	in Scotland
	Scotland U18 v Ireland U18	in Scotland
15 April	Scotland U21 v Italy U21	
22 April	**Scotland v Romania**	**Murrayfield**
28/29 April/7 May	**Scotland visit to Spain**	**Spain**
29 April	Wales U19 v Scotland U19	in Wales
20 May/24 June	**Rugby World Cup**	**South Africa**

† **Royal Bank**

Other Representative Matches
1994

19 October	Edinburgh U21 v Glasgow U21	Murrayfield
	North and Midlands U21 v South U21	Murrayfield
	Scottish Exiles U21 v Scottish Universities	
22 October	Connacht U19 v North and Midlands U19	Galway
26 October	Glasgow U21 v South U21	Murrayfield
	Scottish Exiles U21 v North and Midlands U21	Murrayfield
	Edinburgh U21 v Scottish Universities	Meggetland
	Northumberland Colts v South U18	Tynedale
5/6 November	Scottish Exiles U21 in Combined Exiles U21 Tournament	in London
7 November	North and Midlands v Northumberland	Kirkcaldy
	Northern Division of England U21 v South U21	Carlisle
9 November	Glasgow U21 v North and Midlands U21	Murrayfield
	Edinburgh U21 v Scottish Exiles U21	Murrayfield
16 November	South U21 v Scottish Universities	Jedburgh
19 November	Scottish U18 v Scottish Schools	Murrayfield
26 November	Edinburgh U18 v North and Midlands U18	Musselburgh
	Glasgow U18 v South U18	Bishopbriggs
30 November	Scottish Exiles U21 v Glasgow U21	Murrayfield
	South U21 v Edinburgh U21	Murrayfield
	North and Midlands U21 v Scottish Universities	Cupar
3 December	South U18 v Edinburgh U18	Melrose
	Glasgow U18 v Edinburgh U18	Ayr
7 December	South U21 v Scottish Exiles U21	Murrayfield
	North and Midlands U21 v Edinburgh	Murrayfield
	Glasgow U21 v Scottish Universities	Scotstoun
10 December	North and Midlands U18 v Glasgow U18	Blairgowrie
	South U18 v Edinburgh U18	Langholm
31 December	U21 Trial	Murrayfield

1995

1 February	Glasgow District Union v South District Union	Hughenden
	Midlands Distict Union v Edinburgh District Union	Cupar
15 February	Midlands District Union v Glasgow District Union	Cupar
	Edinburgh District Union v South District Union	in Edinburgh
1 March	Edinburgh District Union v Glasgow District Union	in Edinburgh
	South District Union v Midlands District Union	Hawick
22 March	Scottish U19 v Scottish Union	Murrayfield

SRU Youth Leagues

11 March	Play-off	winners Midlands League v winners North League
11 April	Semi-final	winners Glasgow League v winners South League
13 April	Semi-final	North/Midlands Leagues Play-off v winners Edinburgh League
26 April	Final	Murrayfield

Other International Matches Season 1994–95

1994

26 November   Wales v South Africa

1995

21 January	France v Wales
	Ireland v England
4 February	England v France
10 February	Wales v England
4 March	Ireland v France
18 March	Wales v Ireland

Scottish Schools International Matches Season 1994–95

1994

9 November	International Trial	Murrayfield
19 November	Scottish Youth v Scotland	Murrayfield
19 December	France v Scotland	Rouen
28 December	Scotland B v Australia	Glasgow
31 December	Scotland v Australia	Murrayfield

1995

7 January	Scotland v Wales	Goldenacre, Edinburgh
21 January	Scotland v New Zealand	Murrayfield
25 January	Scotland B v New Zealand	Edinburgh
22 March	Schools Cup final	Murrayfield
25 March	England v Scotland	Twickenham
8 April	Scotland v Ireland	Glasgow

International Matches 1995–96

1995

October/November   Western Samoa tour to Scotland and England

1996

20 January	Scotland v France + U21
3 February	Wales v Scotland + U21
17 February	Scotland v England + Italy v A
3 March	France A v Scotland A
16 March	Ireland v Scotland + A + U21
6 April	Italy U21 v Scotland U21
	Scotland U18 v Spain U18
13 April	England U19 v Scotland U19
	Ireland U18 v Scotland U18
20 April	Scotland U19 v Wales U19
May/June	Scotland Tour to New Zealand

1995 RUGBY WORLD CUP

Pool A	Pool B
Australia	Western Samoa
South Africa	England
Canada	Argentina
Europe 3	Europe 2

Pool C	Pool D
Europe 1	Scotland
Asia	Ivory Coast
New Zealand	France
Ireland	Tonga

Date	Venue	Pool	Teams
Thurs 25 May	Cape Town	A	Australia v SA
Fri 26 May	Rustenburg	D	Scotland v Ivory Coast
	Pretoria	D	France v Tonga
	Port Elizabeth	A	Canada v Europe 3
Sat 27 May	East London	B	W Samoa v Europe 2
	Bloemfontein	C	Europe 1 v Asia
	Durban	B	England v Argentina
	Johannesburg	C	NZ v Ireland
Tues 30 May	East London	B	W Samoa v Argentina
	Cape Town	A	S Africa v Europe 3
	Rustenburg	D	France v Ivory Coast
	Pretoria	D	Scotland v Tonga
Wed 31 May	Port Elizabeth	A	Australia v Canada
	Bloemfontein	C	Ireland v Asia
	Durban	B	England v Europe 2
	Johannesburg	C	NZ v Europe 1
Sat 3 June	Rustenburg	D	Tonga v Ivory Coast
	Stellenbosch	A	Australia v Europe 3
	Pretoria	D	Scotland v France
	Port Elizabeth	A	Canada v S Africa
Sun 4 June	East London	B	Argentina v Europe 2
	Bloemfontein	C	New Zealand v Asia
	Johannesburg	C	Ireland v Europe 1
	Durban	B	England v W Samoa
Sat 10 June	Durban	(E)	Winners D v R-Up C
	Johannesburg	(F)	Winners A v R-Up B
Sun 11 June	Cape Town	(H)	Winners B v R-Up A
	Pretoria	(G)	Winners C v R-Up D
Sat 17 June	Durban	Winners E v Winners F	
Sun 18 June	Cape Town	Winners G v Winners H	
Thurs 22 June	Pretoria	Play-off	
Sat 24 June	Johannesburg	Final	

McEWAN'S 70/- LEAGUE 1994–95

The following kick-off times for Saturday games in Season 1994–95 are recommended by the Committee:

All September and 1, 8, 15, and 22 October 1994	3.00 p.m.
29 October and 5 November 1994	2.30 p.m.
Remainder of November, all of December and 7 and 14 January 1995	2.00 p.m.
21 and 28 January 1995	2.30 p.m.
Remainder of Season	

Any club which, because of local or exceptional circumstances, is intending to deviate from the recommended kick-off times for a National League match, should advise the Administrative Secretary so that the Union has knowledge of the change and is able to advise the media, the referee observer, and any other interested parties.

© Scottish Rugby Union, 1994

1994

10 September

Division 1
Edinburgh Acads v Dundee High School FP
Glasgow High/Kelvinside v Boroughmuir
Hawick v Heriot's FP
Melrose v Currie
Stewart's Melville FP v Gala
Stirling County v West of Scotland
Watsonians v Jed-Forest

Division 2
Biggar v Kelso
Edinburgh Wanderers v Wigtownshire
Glasgow Acads v Corstorphine
Gordonians v Haddington
Grangemouth v Peebles
Musselburgh v Kirkcaldy
Selkirk v Preston Lodge FP

Division 3
Ayr v Dunfermline
East Kilbride v Clarkston
Edinburgh Univ v Trinity Acads
Hillhead/Jordanhill v Stewartry
Kilmarnock v Hutchesons/Aloysians
Langholm v Dumfries
Portobello FP v Royal High

Division 4
Aberdeen Grammar School FP v Howe of Fife
Alloa v Cambuslang
Ardrossan Acads v Dalziel High School FP
Duns v Morgan Academy FP
Glenrothes v Highland
Livingston v Perthshire
North Berwick v St Boswells

Division 5
Allan Glen's v Penicuik
Cartha Queen's Park v Berwick
Clydebank v Lismore
Cumbernauld v Paisley
Falkirk v Madras College FP
Irvine v Linlithgow
Leith Acads v Hillfoots

Division 6
Annan v Aberdeenshire
Dunbar v Greenock Wanderers
Forrester FP v Waysiders/Drumpellier
Lenzie v Murrayfield
Marr v Earlston
Ross High v Harris Academy FP
St Andrews Univ v Aberdeen Univ

Division 7
Cumnock v Lasswade
Edinburgh Northern v Walkerburn
Garnock v Broughton FP
Holy Cross v Whitecraigs
Hyndland FP v Moray
Lochaber v Waid Academy FP
RAF Kinloss v Panmure

17 September

Division 1
Boroughmuir v Stewart's Melville FP
Currie v Watsonians
Dundee High School FP v Stirling County
Gala v Melrose
Heriot's FP v Glasgow High/Kelvinside
Jed-Forest v Edinburgh Acads
West of Scotland v Hawick

Division 2
Corstorphine v Gordonians
Haddington v Musselburgh
Kelso v Grangemouth
Kirkcaldy v Selkirk
Peebles v Glasgow Acads
Preston Lodge FP v Edinburgh Wanderers
Wigtownshire v Biggar

Division 3
Clarkston v Langholm
Dumfries v Edinburgh Univ
Dunfermline v Kilmarnock
Hutchesons/Aloysians v Hillhead/Jordanhill
Royal High v East Kilbride
Stewartry v Portobello
Trinity Acads v Ayr

Division 4
Cambuslang v Glenrothes
Dalziel High School FP v North Berwick
Highland v Livingston
Howe of Fife v Duns
Morgan Academy FP v Alloa
Perthshire v Ardrossan Acads
St Boswells v Aberdeen Grammar School FP

Division 5
Berwick v Irvine
Hillfoots v Clydebank
Linlithgow v Allan Glen's
Lismore v Cumbernauld
Madras College FP v Cartha Queen's Park
Paisley v Falkirk
Penicuik v Leith Acads

Division 6
Aberdeenshire v Forrester FP
Aberdeen Univ v Ross High
Earlston v Lenzie
Greenock Wanderers v St Andrews Univ
Harris Academy FP v Marr
Murrayfield v Annan
Waysiders/Drumpellier v Dunbar

Division 7
Broughton FP v Edinburgh Northern
Lasswade v Garnock
Moray v RAF Kinloss
Panmure v Holy Cross
Waid Academy FP v Cumnock
Walkerburn v Hyndland FP
Whitecraigs v Lochaber

24 September

Division 1
Edinburgh Acads v Currie
Gala v Boroughmuir
Glasgow High/Kelvinside v West of Scotland
Hawick v Dundee High School FP
Stewart's Melville FP v Heriot's FP
Stirling County v Jed-Forest
Watsonians v Melrose

Division 2
Biggar v Preston Lodge FP
Edinburgh Wanderers v Selkirk
Glasgow Acads v Kelso
Gordonians v Peebles
Grangemouth v Wigtownshire
Kirkcaldy v Haddington
Musselburgh v Corstorphine

Division 3
Ayr v Dumfries
East Kilbride v Stewartry
Edinburgh Univ v Clarkston
Hutchesons/Aloysians v Dunfermline
Kilmarnock v Trinity Acads
Langholm v Royal High
Portobello v Hillhead/Jordanhill

Division 4
Aberdeen GS FP v Dalziel HS FP
Ardrossan Acads v Highland
Duns v St Boswells
Glenrothes v Alloa
Livingston v Cambuslang
Morgan Academy FP v Howe of Fife
North Berwick v Perthshire

Division 5
Allan Glen's v Berwick
Cartha Queen's Park v Paisley
Clydebank v Penicuik
Falkirk v Cumbernauld
Irvine v Madras College FP
Leith Acads v Linlithgow
Lismore v Hillfoots

Division 6
Aberdeen Univ v Greenock Wanderers
Annan v Earlston
Dunbar v Aberdeenshire
Forrester FP v Murrayfield
Lenzie v Harris Academy FP
Marr v Ross High
St Andrews Univ v Waysiders/Drumpellier

Division 7
Edinburgh Northern v Lasswade
Garnock v Cumnock
Holy Cross v Moray
Hyndland FP v Broughton FP
Lochaber v Panmure
RAF Kinloss v Walkerburn
Waid Academy FP v Whitecraigs

1 October

Division 1
Currie v Stirling County
Dundee HS FP v Glasgow High/Kelvinside
Heriot's FP v Boroughmuir
Jed-Forest v Hawick
Melrose v Edinburgh Acads
Watsonians v Gala
West of Scotland v Stewart's Melville FP

Division 2
Corstorphine v Haddington
Edinburgh Wanderers v Kirkcaldy
Kelso v Gordonians
Peebles v Musselburgh
Preston Lodge FP v Grangemouth
Selkirk v Biggar
Wigtownshire v Glasgow Acads

Division 3
Clarkston v Ayr
Dumfries v Kilmarnock
Hillhead/Jordanhill v East Kilbride
Portobello v Hutchesons/Aloysians
Royal High v Edinburgh Univ
Stewartry v Langholm
Trinity Acads v Dunfermline

Division 4
Alloa v Livingston
Cambuslang v Ardrossan Acads
Dalziel High School FP v Duns
Glenrothes v Morgan Academy FP
Highland v North Berwick
Perthshire v Aberdeen Grammar School FP
St Boswells v Howe of Fife

Division 5
Berwick v Leith Acads
Cumbernauld v Cartha Queen's Park
Falkirk v Lismore
Linlithgow v Clydebank
Madras College FP v Allan Glen's
Paisley v Irvine
Penicuik v Hillfoots

Division 6
Aberdeenshire v St Andrews Univ
Earlston v Forrester FP
Harris Academy FP v Annan
Marr v Aberdeen University
Murrayfield v Dunbar
Ross High v Lenzie
Waysiders/Drumpellier v Greenock Wanderers

Division 7
Broughton FP v RAF Kinloss
Cumnock v Edinburgh Northern
Garnock v Waid Academy FP
Lasswade v Hyndland FP
Moray v Lochaber
Panmure v Whitecraigs
Walkerburn v Holy Cross

8 October

Division 1
Boroughmuir v West of Scotland
Edinburgh Acads v Watsonians
Gala v Heriot's FP
Glasgow High/Kelvinside v Jed-Forest
Hawick v Currie
Stewart's Melville FP v Dundee HS FP
Stirling County v Melrose

Division 2
Biggar v Edinburgh Wanderers
Glasgow Acads v Preston Lodge FP
Gordonians v Wigtownshire
Grangemouth v Selkirk
Haddington v Peebles
Kirkcaldy v Corstorphine
Musselburgh v Kelso

Division 3
Ayr v Royal High
Dunfermline v Dumfries
East Kilbride v Portobello
Edinburgh Univ v Stewartry
Hutchesons/Aloysians v Trinity Acads
Kilmarnock v Clarkston
Langholm v Hillhead/Jordanhill

Division 4
Aberdeen Grammar School FP v Highland
Ardrossan Acads v Alloa
Duns v Perthshire
Howe of Fife v Dalziel High School FP
Livingston v Glenrothes
Morgan Academy FP v St Boswells
North Berwick v Cambuslang

Division 5
Allan Glen's v Paisley
Cartha Queen's Park v Falkirk
Clydebank v Berwick
Hillfoots v Linlithgow
Irvine v Cumbernauld
Leith Acads v Madras College FP
Lismore v Penicuik

Division 6
Aberdeen Univ v Waysiders/Drumpellier
Annan v Ross High
Dunbar v Earlston
Forrester FP v Harris Academy FP
Greenock Wanderers v Aberdeenshire
Lenzie v Marr
St Andrews Univ v Murrayfield

Division 7
Edinburgh Northern v Garnock
Holy Cross v Broughton FP
Hyndland FP v Cumnock
Lochaber v Walkerburn
RAF Kinloss v Lasswade
Waid Academy FP v Panmure
Whitecraigs v Moray

15 October

Division 1
Currie v Glasgow High/Kelvinside
Dundee High School FP v Boroughmuir
Edinburgh Acads v Gala
Jed-Forest v Stewart's Melville FP
Melrose v Hawick
Watsonians v Stirling County
West of Scotland v Heriot's FP

Division 2
Biggar v Kirkcaldy
Edinburgh Wanderers v Grangemouth
Kelso v Haddington
Peebles v Corstorphine
Preston Lodge FP v Gordonians
Selkirk v Glasgow Acads
Wigtownshire v Musselburgh

Division 3
Clarkston v Dunfermline
Dumfries v Trinity Acads
East Kilbride v Hutchesons/Aloysians
Hillhead/Jordanhill v Edinburgh Univ
Portobello v Langholm
Royal High v Kilmarnock
Stewartry v Ayr

Division 4
Alloa v North Berwick
Cambuslang v Aberdeen Grammar School FP
Dalziel High School FP v St Boswells
Glenrothes v Ardrossan Acads
Highland v Duns
Livingston v Morgan Academy FP
Perthshire v Howe of Fife

Division 5
Berwick v Hillfoots
Cartha Queen's Park v Lismore
Cumbernauld v Allan Glen's
Falkirk v Irvine
Linlithgow v Penicuik
Madras College FP v Clydebank
Paisley v Leith Acads

Division 6
Aberdeenshire v Waysiders/Drumpellier
Earlston v St Andrews Univ
Harris Academy FP v Dunbar
Lenzie v Aberdeen Univ
Marr v Annan
Murrayfield v Greenock Wanderers
Ross High v Forrester FP

Division 7
Broughton FP v Lochaber
Cumnock v RAF Kinloss
Edinburgh Northern v Waid Academy FP
Garnock v Hyndland FP
Lasswade v Holy Cross
Moray v Panmure
Walkerburn v Whitecraigs

5 November

Division 1
Boroughmuir v Jed-Forest
Gala v West of Scotland
Glasgow High/Kelvinside v Melrose
Hawick v Watonians
Heriot's FP v Dundee High School FP
Stewart's Melville FP v Currie
Stirling County v Edinburgh Acads

Division 2
Corstorphine v Kelso
Glasgow Acads v Edinburgh Wanderers
Gordonians v Selkirk
Grangemouth v Biggar
Haddington v Wigtownshire
Kirkcaldy v Peebles
Musselburgh v Preston Lodge FP

Division 3
Ayr v Hillhead/Jordanhill
Dunfermline v Royal High
Edinburgh Univ v Portobello
Hutchesons/Aloysians v Dumfries
Kilmarnock v Stewartry
Langholm v East Kilbride
Trinity Acads v Clarkston

Division 4
Aberdeen Grammar School FP v Alloa
Ardrossan Acads v Livingston
Duns v Cambuslang
Howe of Fife v Highland
Morgan Academy FP v Dalziel High School FP
North Berwick v Glenrothes
St Boswells v Perthshire

Division 5
Allan Glen's v Falkirk
Clydebank v Paisley
Hillfoots v Madras College FP
Irvine v Cartha Queen's Park
Leith Acads v Cumbernauld
Lismore v Linlithgow
Penicuik v Berwick

Division 6
Aberdeen Univ v Aberdeenshire
Annan v Lenzie
Dunbar v Ross High
Forrester FP v Marr
Greenock Wanderers v Earlston
St Andrews Univ v Harris Academy FP
Waysiders/Drumpellier v Murrayfield

Division 7
Holy Cross v Cumnock
Hyndland FP v Edinburgh Northern
Lochaber v Lasswade
Panmure v Walkerburn
RAF Kinloss v Garnock
Waid Academy FP v Moray
Whitecraigs v Broughton FP

26 November

Division 1
Currie v Boroughmuir
Dundee High School FP v West of Scotland
Edinburgh Acads v Hawick
Jed-Forest v Heriot's FP
Melrose v Stewart's Melville FP
Stirling County v Gala
Watsonians v Glasgow High/Kelvinside

Division 2
Biggar v Glasgow Acads
Edinburgh Wanderers v Gordonians
Grangemouth v Kirkcaldy
Kelso v Peebles
Preston Lodge FP v Haddington
Selkirk v Musselburgh
Wigtownshire v Corstorphine

Division 3
Clarkston v Dumfries
East Kilbride v Edinburgh Univ
Hillhead/Jordanhill v Kilmarnock
Langholm v Hutchesons/Aloysians
Portobello v Ayr
Royal High v Trinity Acads
Stewartry v Dunfermline

Division 4
Alloa v Duns
Ardrossan Acads v Morgan Academy FP
Cambuslang v Howe of Fife
Glenrothes v Aberdeen Grammar School FP
Highland v St Boswells
Livingston v North Berwick
Perthshire v Dalziel High School FP

Division 5
Berwick v Linlithgow
Cartha Queen's Park v Allan Glen's
Cumbernauld v Clydebank
Falkirk v Leith Acads
Irvine v Lismore
Madras College FP v Penicuik
Paisley v Hillfoots

Division 6
Annan v Aberdeen Univ
Earlston v Waysiders/Drumpellier
Harris Academy FP v Greenock Wanderers
Lenzie v Forrester FP
Marr v Dunbar
Murrayfield v Aberdeenshire
Ross High v St Andrews Univ

Division 7
Broughton FP v Panmure
Cumnock v Lochaber
Edinburgh Northern v RAF Kinloss
Garnock v Holy Cross
Hyndland FP v Waid Academy FP
Lasswade v Whitecraigs
Walkerburn v Moray

1995
14 January

Division 1
Boroughmuir v Melrose
Gala v Dundee High School FP
Glasgow High/Kelvinside v Edinburgh Acads
Hawick v Stirling County
Heriot's FP v Currie
Stewart's Melville FP v Watsonians
West of Scotland v Jed-Forest

Division 2
Corstorphine v Preston Lodge FP
Glasgow Acads v Grangemouth
Gordonians v Biggar
Haddington v Selkirk
Kirkcaldy v Kelso
Musselburgh v Edinburgh Wanderers
Peebles v Wigtownshire

Division 3
Ayr v East Kilbride
Dumfries v Royal High
Dunfermline v Hillhead/Jordanhill
Edinburgh Univ v Langholm
Hutchesons/Aloysians v Clarkston
Kilmarnock v Portobello

Division 4
Aberdeen Grammar School FP v Livingston
Duns v Glenrothes
Dalziel High School FP v Highland
Howe of Fife v Alloa
Morgan Academy FP v Perthshire
North Berwick v Ardrossan Acads
St Boswells v Cambuslang

Division 5
Allan Glen's v Irvine
Clydebank v Falkirk
Hillfoots v Cumbernauld
Leith Acads v Cartha Queen's Park
Linlithgow v Madras College FP
Lismore v Berwick
Penicuik v Paisley

Division 6
Aberdeenshire v Earlston
Aberdeen Univ v Murrayfield
Dunbar v Lenzie
Forrester FP v Annan
Greenock Wanderers v Ross High
St Andrews Univ v Marr
Waysiders/Drumpellier v Harris Academy FP

Division 7
Holy Cross v Edinburgh Northern
Lochaber v Garnock
Moray v Broughton FP
Panmure v Lasswade
RAF Kinloss v Hyndland FP
Waid Academy FP v Walkerburn
Whitecraigs v Cumnock

The Royal Bank
of Scotland

28 January

Division 1
Currie v West of Scotland
Edinburgh Acads v Stewart's Melville FP
Hawick v Gala
Jed-Forest v Dundee High School FP
Melrose v Heriot's FP
Stirling County v Glasgow High/Kelvinside
Watsonians v Boroughmuir

Division 2
Biggar v Musselburgh
Edinburgh Wanderers v Haddington
Glasgow Acads v Kirkcaldy
Grangemouth v Gordonians
Preston Lodge FP v Peebles
Selkirk v Corstorphine
Wigtownshire v Kelso

Division 3
East Kilbride v Kilmarnock
Edinburgh Univ v Hutchesons/Aloysians
Hillhead/Jordanhill v Trinity Acads
Langholm v Ayr
Portobello v Dunfermline
Royal High v Clarkston
Stewartry v Dumfries

Division 4
Alloa v St Boswells
Ardrossan Acads v Aberdeen Grammar School FP
Cambuslang v Dalziel High School FP
Glenrothes v Howe of Fife
Highland v Perthshire
Livingston v Duns
North Berwick v Morgan Academy FP

Division 5
Allan Glen's v Lismore
Cartha Queen's Park v Clydebank
Cumbernauld v Penicuik
Falkirk v Hillfoots
Irvine v Leith Acads
Madras College FP v Berwick
Paisley v Linlithgow

Division 6
Annan v Dunbar
Earlston v Murrayfield
Forrester FP v Aberdeen Univ
Harris Academy FP v Aberdeenshire
Lenzie v St Andrews Univ
Marr v Greenock Wanderers
Ross High v Waysiders/Drumpellier

Division 7
Broughton FP v Walkerburn
Cumnock v Panmure
Edinburgh Northern v Lochaber
Garnock v Whitecraigs
Hyndland FP v Holy Cross
Lasswade v Moray
RAF Kinloss v Waid Academy FP

11 February

Division 1
Boroughmuir v Edinburgh Acads
Dundee High School FP v Currie
Gala v Jed-Forest
Glasgow High/Kelvinside v Hawick
Heriot's FP v Watsonians
Stewart's Melville FP v Stirling County
West of Scotland v Melrose

Division 2
Corstorphine v Biggar
Gordonians v Glasgow Acads
Haddington v Biggar
Kelso v Preston Lodge FP
Kirkcaldy v Wigtownshire
Musselburgh v Grangemouth
Peebles v Selkirk

Division 3
Ayr v Edinburgh Univ
Clarkston v Stewartry
Dumfries v Hillhead/Jordanhill
Dunfermline v East Kilbride
Hutchesons/Aloysians v Royal High
Kilmarnock v Langholm
Trinity Acads v Portobello

Division 4
Aberdeen Grammar School FP v North Berwick
Dalziel High School v Alloa
Duns v Ardrossan Acads
Howe of Fife v Livingston
Morgan Academy FP v Highland
Perthshire v Cambuslang
St Boswells v Glenrothes

Division 5
Berwick v Paisley
Clydebank v Irvine
Hillfoots v Cartha Queen's Park
Leith Acads v Allan Glen's
Linlithgow v Cumbernauld
Lismore v Madras College FP
Penicuik v Falkirk

Division 6
Aberdeenshire v Ross High
Aberdeen Univ v Earlston
Dunbar v Forrester FP
Greenock Wanderers v Lenzie
Murrayfield v Harris Academy FP
St Andrews Univ v Annan
Waysiders/Drumpellier v Marr

Division 7
Holy Cross v RAF Kinloss
Lochaber v Hyndland
Moray v Cumnock
Panmure v Garnock
Waid Academy FP v Broughton FP
Walkerburn v Lasswade
Whitecraigs v Edinburgh Northern

S
t
a
t
i
s
t
i
c
s
&
F
i
x
t
u
r
e
s

SCOTTISH
RUGBY UNION

25 February

Division 1
Currie v Jed-Forest
Edinburgh Acads v Heriot's FP
Glasgow High/Kelvinside v Gala
Hawick v Stewart's Melville FP
Melrose v Dundee High School FP
Stirling County v Boroughmuir
Watsonians v West of Scotland

Division 2
Biggar v Corstorphine
Edinburgh Wanderers v Peebles
Glasgow Acads v Musselburgh
Gordonians v Kirkcaldy
Grangemouth v Haddington
Preston Lodge FP v Wigtownshire
Selkirk v Kelso

Division 3
Ayr v Hutchesons/Aloysians
East Kilbride v Trinity Acads
Edinburgh Univ v Kilmarnock
Hillhead/Jordanhill v Clarkston
Langholm v Dunfermline
Portobello v Dumfries
Stewartry v Royal High

Division 4
Aberdeen GS FP v Morgan Academy FP
Alloa v Perthshire
Ardrossan Acads v Howe of Fife
Cambuslang v Highland
Glenrothes v Dalziel High School FP
Livingston v St Boswells
North Berwick v Duns

Division 5
Allan Glen's v Clydebank
Cartha Queen's Park v Penicuik
Cumbernauld v Berwick
Falkirk v Linlithgow
Irvine v Hillfoots
Leith Acads v Lismore
Paisley v Madras College FP

Division 6
Annan v Greenock Wanderers
Dunbar v Aberdeen Univ
Forrester FP v St Andrews Univ
Harris Academy FP v Earlston
Lenzie v Waysiders/Drumpellier
Marr v Aberdeenshire
Ross High v Murrayfield

Division 7
Cumnock v Walkerburn
Edinburgh Northern v Panmure
Garnock v Moray
Holy Cross v Waid Academy FP
Hyndland FP v Whitecraigs
Lasswade v Broughton FP
RAF Kinloss v Lochaber

11 March

Division 1
Boroughmuir v Hawick
Dundee High School FP V Watsonians
Gala v Currie
Heriot's FP v Stirling County
Jed-Forest v Melrose
Stewart's Melville FP v Glasgow High/Kelvinside
West of Scotland v Edinburgh Acads

Division 2
Corstorphine v Grangemouth
Haddington v Glasgow Acads
Kelso v Edinburgh Wanderers
Kirkcaldy v Preston Lodge FP
Musselburgh v Gordonians
Peebles v Biggar
Wigtownshire v Selkirk

Division 3
Clarkston v Portobello
Dumfries v East Kilbride
Dunfermline v Edinburgh Univ
Hutchesons/Aloysians v Stewartry
Kilmarnock v Ayr
Royal High v Hillhead/Jordanhill
Trinity Acads v Langholm

Division 4
Dalziel High School FP v Livingston
Duns v Aberdeen Grammar School FP
Highland v Alloa
Howe of Fife v North Berwick
Morgan Academy FP v Cambuslang
Perthshire v Glenrothes
St Boswells v Ardrossan Acads

Division 5
Berwick v Falkirk
Clydebank v Leith Acads
Hillfoots v Allan Glen's
Lismore v Paisley
Linlithgow v Cartha Queens Park
Madras College FP v Cumbernauld
Penicuik v Irvine

Division 6
Aberdeenshire v Lenzie
Aberdeen Univ v Harris Academy FP
Earlston v Ross High
Greenock Wanderers v Forrester FP
Murrayfield v Marr
St Andrews Univ v Dunbar
Waysiders/Drumpellier v Annan

Division 7
Broughton FP v Cumnock
Lochaber v Holy Cross
Moray v Edinburgh Northern
Panmure v Hyndland FP
Waid Academy FP v Lasswade
Walkerburn v Garnock
Whitecraigs v RAF Kinloss